States of Shock

For Dominique Bourgon, Jean-Claude Bourgon,
Hidetaka Ishida and Kuniko Ishida

States of Shock

Stupidity and Knowledge in the Twenty-First Century

———————

Bernard Stiegler

Translated by Daniel Ross

polity

First published in language as *États de Choc. Betise et savoir au XXIè siecle*
© Mille et une nuits, department de la Librairie Arthème Fayard, 2012

This English edition © Polity Press, 2015
Reprinted in 2017

Polity Press
65 Bridge Street
Cambridge CB2 1UR, UK

Polity Press
350 Main Street
Malden, MA 02148, USA

ISBN-13: 978-0-7456-6493-4
ISBN-13: 978-0-7456-6494-1(pb)

A catalogue record for this book is available from the British Library.

Library of Congress Cataloging-in-Publication Data
Stiegler, Bernard.
  [États de choc. English]
  States of shock : stupidity and knowledge in the 21st century / Bernard Stiegler.
      pages cm
  Includes bibliographical references.
  ISBN 978-0-7456-6493-4 (hardback : alk. paper) – ISBN 978-0-7456-6494-1
(pbk. : alk. paper) 1. Poststructuralism. 2. Education and globalization.
3. Knowledge, Sociology of–History–21st century. I. Title.
  B2430.S7523E8313 2014
  194–dc23
                        2014026157

Typeset in 10.5/12 Sabon
by Toppan Best-set Premedia Limited
Printed and bound in the United Kingdom by Clays Ltd, St Ives PLC

For further information on Polity, visit our website: politybooks.com

Contents

Introduction

1 Sovereignty and submission

In 2010 several texts appeared in France and Europe, manifestos, petitions and academic analyses concerning academic and scientific life. Quite a number of newspaper articles about national education and teaching also appeared. And various polls showed that these questions were indeed of major concern to the French people – the number one concern according to one poll, and according to others number two.[1]

At the same time, *Inside Job*, Charles Ferguson's 2010 documentary about financialization – an austere subject, perhaps, but one that did not prevent it from finding a record audience (and receiving a prize at Cannes), prior to the explosion of what is now called the problem of 'sovereign debt'[2] – highlighted the role that American universities, and certain academics, have played in the establishment of a literally suicidal financial system.

Furthermore, in 2011 the private ratings agencies downgraded the 'ratings' of Ireland, Greece, Spain, the United States, Japan and Italy (as well as certain French banks) – radically challenging the very idea of sovereignty, an idea that lies at the base of those historical movements that emerged from the eighteenth century and shaped the modern world, a world in which, until recently, we more or less believed we still lived (however 'postmodern' it may have become).

The movements that arose in the nineteenth century in order to constitute a 'public thing', itself forming a sovereign public power – that is, a *res publica*, and in this sense a republic – led to the widespread introduction of public education, positing in principle and by right that any citizen should have the chance and the duty to receive an education that will grant them access to that autonomy referred to by Kant as *Mündigkeit*, that is, 'maturity' or 'majority', through which the foundation would be laid for a public community and a sovereign politics.

In other words, the questions raised by *Inside Job* in the field of economics were echoed in appeals and articles about the dilapidated state of academic research and public education, and the collapse, and not just in Europe, of the economic and political credibility of the Western world, and of its legacy for the entirety of humanity, all this belonging on the same register. *All* these questions and the calamities accompanying them (and in particular the protean regression they threaten to bring with them) are generated by the very system that is sending us headlong into a world where political and economic sovereignty are eliminated and the forming of maturity via education is abandoned, a maturity that, as the autonomy obtained by frequently engaging with rational knowledge, was for the *Aufklärer* the *sine qua non* of such a sovereignty.

Western universities are in the grip of a deep malaise, and a number of them have found themselves, through some of their faculty, giving consent to – and sometimes considerably compromised by – the implementation of a financial system that, with the establishment of hyper-consumerist, drive-based and 'addictogenic' society,[3] leads to economic and political ruin on a global scale. If this has occurred, it is because their goals, their organizations and their means have been put entirely at the service of the destruction of sovereignty. That is, they have been placed in the service of the destruction of sovereignty as conceived by the philosophers of what we call the Enlightenment, a sovereignty founded on *Mündigkeit*, maturity or majority understood as the exit from *Unmündigkeit*, immaturity or minority, in the Kantian sense of these notions.

Abandoning this obligation – even though we must understand its limits, so that a new political discourse can be elaborated, and a new critique of political economy, capable of projecting an alternative to what has proven to be paving the way for a global political and economic catastrophe – will lead capitalism to be destroyed from the inside, and by itself. Such an outcome does not depend on hateful speech or actions: democracy is being destroyed, not by those who 'hate democracy', but by those who have abandoned critique – given that a genuine democracy will constantly critique what, in it, means that it never stops changing. Public space and public time constitute a democratic public thing, a democratic public good, only to the extent that they are always precarious, and those democrats who are so sure of themselves as to doubt nothing (in their democracy) are always democracy's worst enemies.

In the Western industrial world, however, democracy has given way – and has done for quite some time – to consumerism (which is now taking hold in countries that seem to feel little need for democracy). This consumerism is itself based on the liquidation of maturity through the *systemic generalization of minority and the industrial dilution of responsibility*, or in other words: based on the reign of stupidity [*bêtise*], and of what so often accompanies it, namely cowardice and viciousness. It is this development that has been internalized by the academic world as simply a fact, with no alternative. And it is the possibility that there *is* an alternative to this fact, and as a new law, that we wish to assert here.

2 The war of reason against reason

The *Aufklärung*, writes Kant, is *Mündigkeit*, that is, maturity, that reason that is formed only through 'humanity's emergence from its [...] *Unmündigkeit*, its minority. [That is, from] the inability to use one's own understanding without the guidance of another.'[4] The passage from immaturity to maturity, from minority to majority, is a conquest, according to Kant, and this conquest is referred to as the *Aufklärung*: the *Aufklärung* is an historical movement. What was gained with the Enlightenment, and thanks to it, is, however, what is at present being lost: it is literally being squandered in the course of a war of reason, and in this war, as we shall see, reason stands on both sides of the conflict, as if reason were at war with itself.

Theodor Adorno and Max Horkheimer posited in 1944, in *Dialectic of Enlightenment*, that this historical movement leads to a reversal and eventually to an inversion of the goals of this Enlightenment, and that reason as a political, economic and social stake thereby decomposes into what Weber and Habermas called *rationalization* – where reason comes to serve what the Frankfurt School called *reification*.

These questions – sovereignty, minority, majority, reason and even history – no longer seem to be posed in these terms, as if what is referred to as 'postmodernity'[5] had emptied them of content. For this reason, at the very moment when we are discovering that some of the greatest universities participated in the implementation of a system conceived by the 'conservative revolution' – a system lying at the origin of financialization[6] and installing an economy of carelessness [*économie de l'incurie*] on a global scale, founded on a systemic

extension of stupidity, which is also to say one of submission, infantilization and regression to minority – it also seems that the legacy
of twentieth-century thought is simply to leave the human beings of
the twenty-first century totally defenceless and unarmed in the face
of a situation that appears hopeless.

This is also why I believe we must reopen the question of what
links academic research, public education, politics and economics. It
is a question that must be revisited in a profound way. We must, on
the basis of the questions raised by not only Adorno and Horkheimer
but also Karl Polanyi,[7] re-read both:

- the texts of so-called 'poststructuralist' thought; and
- the corpus that dominated the Parisian intellectual scene prior to
  the appearance of this so-called 'French thought' – that is, the
  dialectical philosophies of Hegel and Marx.

As for the texts or initiatives that have recently emerged from the
academic world, triggered by the crisis of the university and the
school, I refer in particular to five:

- a call to the political responsibility of academics launched in Italy
  with the title *After the End of the University*, confronting the cata-
  strophic policy pursued in that country by Silvio Berlusconi (http://
  th-rough.eu/writers/bifo-eng/after-end-university);
- a legal challenge undertaken in Portugal by three economists at
  the University of Coimbra and an economist at the University of
  Lisbon, against the ratings agencies responsible for downgrading
  Portugal's sovereign debt rating;
- a petition launched in France in favour of 'slow science'
  (slowscience.fr);
- a call for the organization of a civil society seminar on the stakes
  of research (sciencescitoyennes.org);
- a manifesto launched in Paris calling for the development of digital
  humanities in French universities, signed by researchers from the
  EHESS, the laboratories of CNRS, and some thirty French
  universities.

This final text did indeed clear my vision, which was essential in
order to comprehend the crisis of the university, a crisis that stems
from the radical transformation of the modern world brought about
by the appearance of analogue technologies in the twentieth century
and the development of digital technologies in the twenty-first century.

I will attempt to show that the disarming and rearming of thought are essentially tied to the possibility of theorizing and practising these *hypomnēmata* – I will try to show this by offering a commentary on *The Postmodern Condition* (1979), in the context of the advent of public access to the internet via the world wide web, which occurred on 30 April 1993, fourteen years after Jean-François Lyotard published his book.

3 Shocks, therapies, pharmacology

As for the poll that showed (in the context of the then upcoming 2012 French presidential election) that education and teaching are the premier concern of the French public, it echoes an article that appeared in *Le Figaro* on 29 July 2011, on which I will offer a detailed commentary in the next chapter.[8]

The crisis in education – education, which was conceived on the basis of writing in order to form a 'public that reads', as Kant said – is nothing new. In Part II, I argue:

- that the reason this has become of such concern to the French public is that the situation has reached a point of no return, directly related above all to the deployment of analogue technologies during the 1960s (leading to the hegemonic rule of what Adorno and Horkheimer called the culture industry), and then, beginning in the 1990s, of digital technologies;
- that this question involves the entire academic project, and that it amounts to the question of what, with Ars Industrialis, I refer to as 'technologies of the spirit'.[9]

This analysis leads me to propose in the second part of this work that, in all universities and in all disciplines, 'digital studies' programs should be developed (of which so-called 'digital humanities' would be a specific element).

In the course of these inquiries I will relate the crises of education and the university to Naomi Klein's analysis, in *The Shock Doctrine: The Rise of Disaster Capitalism*,[10] of the way in which this shock strategy was applied in the United States to complete the destruction of public education in the wake of the Hurricane Katrina disaster. The current economic catastrophe is no doubt the subject of similar strategies, referred to as 'shock therapies'. And Europe is now massively confronted with just such strategies.

Faced with this situation, universities – that is, academics, lecturers and students – must assume their responsibilities at a time when this strategy, which is a 'market' strategy, is, in Europe, attacking the very structures of political sovereignty.

This work aims to supply conceptual, that is, *peaceful*, weapons, and to open up prospects for action founded on rational, that is, *political*,[11] argument, in order positively to oppose proposals for, or impositions of, 'shock therapies'. These should be opposed in France, in Europe and throughout the industrial world, a world fortunate enough still to possess public education and research systems, but also in those countries that once had such systems but have since lost them – for example, Chile, where 2011 was marked by a battle by students for the right to public higher education, and against the catastrophic degradation of teaching and research that occurred after privatization, a situation orchestrated by Augusto Pinochet, by Milton Friedman and by the latter's so-called 'Chicago School' of economics.

Working here from a pharmacological perspective that I have already put forward elsewhere,[12] I develop an analysis of the question of therapies in general, given that technological shocks, which have constituted the basis of capitalism ever since the implementation of what Joseph Schumpeter called 'Creative Destruction' (the capital letters are his),[13] must *in our time* be rethought.

A 'social therapeutics' for the shocks caused by technological *pharmaka* is what politics must prescribe. For a lengthy period of time this did in fact take place, from the moment politics became, in the industrial ages of the nineteenth and twentieth centuries, a political economy that required an overall industrial policy. But this is no longer the case, specifically since the 'conservative revolution'.[14] I argue here that it is therefore a matter of completely rethinking industrial political economy in the hyper-industrial epoch of the twenty-first century. This is why I propose a re-reading of Hegel in chapter 5 and of Marx in chapter 6.

The shock therapies implemented by neoliberalism – under the guidance of Milton Friedman, whose methods were put to the test in Chile after the assassination of Salvador Allende – may have proven their 'efficacity' in the short term (while nevertheless leading in the medium to long term to the contemporary catastrophe wherein this suicidal doctrine proves to have installed an economy of carelessness and neglect). But if this has been possible, it is only because the university, as a project of modernity fundamentally proceeding from the Enlightenment and the Kantian discourse on *The Conflict of the Faculties* (I will return to this in chapter 8), has been incapable of thinking *shock* in general, and the shock that technics *always* is, insofar as it is irreducibly pharmacological, this being even more true when technics becomes technology.

Universities may not have managed to know or do anything about this, but this is less because they have been prevented from doing so, or because they have been bought off (even if this has also happened), than because their development has been based on something that has remained unthinkable, even repressed:[15] the repression of the role of technics in the constitution of the 'noetic soul' in general,[16] and in the formation[17] of every form of knowledge. And the repression in particular of the role of technics in theoretical knowledge: the mnemotechnics that is writing is the condition of possibility of reason (of *logos* and of its logic) as theorematic faculty. Analogue and digital mnemotechnologies, however, represent a new stage of the process of grammatization, a process through which alphabetic writing led to the foundation of the *polis*.

Digital technology is a new stage of writing (and thus also of reading),[18] an industrial system founded on the production and activation of traces, of 'grammes' and 'graphemes'[19] that discretize, affect, reproduce and transform every flux and flow (well beyond just language). This writing is produced and written in silicon with new codes, tools, instruments and devices of publication, and the story must be told from this perspective, from clay and papyrus to today's micro-electronic structures (and tomorrow's nano-electronic, if not bionic) that encode in silicon the industrial standards we refer to as ASCII, XML, and so on, that 'scan' the algorithms of search engines that automate reading and writing, and that index, 'tag' and categorize the new metalanguages which all of this presupposes – the totality of which results in generalized traceability and trackability.

The massive and brutal eruption of these new kinds of *hypomnēmata* radically changes the very conditions of education and research, as well as the relations between educational institutions and universities on the one hand, and what lies outside them on the other hand. This protean 'outside' is now permanently 'inside', thanks to computers and mobile phones, but also to those 'reforms' intended to dictate to the Academy in its totality the non-academic imperatives to which it is now required to submit. These imperatives arise from a *technological shock strategy*, the result of which is that the conditions of autonomy and heteronomy of academic institutions in a broad sense (in a sense whereby education and research together form the academic world, the matrix for which takes shape in Athens in the fourth century BCE) find themselves radically changed.

With Pierre Macherey, to whom I shall refer later in this work,[20]
I question the validity of a discourse – which I find fantastical – prem-
ised on the necessity and possibility of 'resisting' by maintaining the
illusion of a 'university without condition'. I do indeed support the
need to assert the autonomy of the university, but as a *dependent*
autonomy, and in a way as a conditional freedom[21] – as a pharmacology of autonomy under retentional conditions. Such conditions constitute the condition (always precarious, never assured for anyone)
of *responsibility*, a recurring theme in the writings that Jacques
Derrida devoted to the university. It is clearly Derrida's thinking that
makes possible my own discourse here, which is therefore not an
'anti-Derridian' discourse, but which, if I may put it like this, envis-
ages the possibility of a deconstruction of deconstruction.[22]

4   Responsibilities

Technical traces – the existence of which is the condition of formation
of what Freud called mnesic traces for the human psyche, that is, of
the 'soul' (in Aristotle's sense) constituted by a libidinal economy –
are the milieu of that cerebral plasticity on the basis of which the
psychic apparatus is formed, or what Simondon called the psychic
individual. These technical traces, which constitute 'tertiary retentions',[23] are now being placed under the control of a global industry,
even though the university is yet to understand fully their role in the
noetic activity through which are formed and trained not only the
psychic apparatus, but the social apparatus, and knowledge itself,
under the auspices of what is called 'reason'. This fact, which inscribes
the economy of the *libido sciendi* within the irreducible horizon of
an industrial political economy, demands that we think libidinal
economy in the industrial epoch.

   This book was written after the economic crisis brought about
by the 2008 collapse of Lehman Brothers, as well as the insurance
company AIG.[24] It builds on more general analyses of the consequences of this economic crisis,[25] and strives to deepen the lessons to
be learned in terms of the responsibility of academics in general in
relation to the epistemic, economic, social, psychic, aesthetic and
political aspects of the crisis – and more particularly for philosophy
and for the industrial economy, the crisis of which is that it is a
libidinal diseconomy.

   The thesis of this work is that the question of knowledge, of its
irreducibly instrumental dimension – that is, its ambiguous, *because
pharmacological*, dimension – and, given this condition, of its place

in industrial society, lies at the heart of all these questions. This is why it is also and at the same time a matter of investigating the future role of universities in the re-elaboration of the educational project in the context of the development of new digital technologies,[26] as well as their role in the invention of a new global society, founded on a new industrial model in which knowledge would be fundamentally re-valorized, rather than compromised and discredited, as has been the case in recent decades, as a result of the difficult relationship it has maintained with its economic, social and political environment. It is, then, a matter of struggling against what Paul Valéry long ago described as the lowering of 'spirit value', the lowering of the value of spirit.[27]

This work thus attempts to continue the discussion I began in *Taking Care of Youth and the Generations*: a reading of French thinkers of the second half of the twentieth century. That book concentrated in particular on certain aspects of the work of Michel Foucault. Here, in dialogue with texts by Gilles Deleuze, Jacques Derrida and Jean-François Lyotard, I return to the intergenerational question that I introduced in the first chapter of *Taking Care*.

This earlier debate focused on the question of discipline in Foucault,[28] and the evolution of its meaning, that is, on his relation to discipline understood successively in terms of *epistēmē*, *epimēleia*, *melētē*, *tekhnē*, and so on,[29] and on what seemed to me to be unresolved contradictions in this evolution,[30] that is, ultimately, in the thinking of writing, and the links between the thinking of discipline and the thinking (and non-thinking) of writing. Continuing this debate, this book will in a certain sense be a critical and contextualized introduction to poststructuralist thought, to its legacy, and to the necessity of continuing it, but of doing so in a renewed way.

The question that will arise is indeed that of the role that poststructuralism *could* play, but that it *does not* play, in a situation where, for the first time in human history, the entire world seems threatened by 'impersonal forces' that it has itself unleashed. These forces are both rational, in that they are the outcome of conscious and reflective human activity, and irrational, in that they are removing any control we might have, and not only are they conditioning consciousness 'behind its back',[31] but they are doing the same to the unconscious.

On the basis of these analyses, I try to pose anew the question of responsibility in general, in regard to the past, present and future responsibilities of the university after Fukushima. This nuclear catastrophe of unprecedented global magnitude, with incalculable consequences in a thousand spheres, occurred at a time when financialization has managed to annihilate political legitimacy and every form of sovereignty. It has crystallized, and taken to a new level, the questions thrown up by a set of technological disasters, and by the discovery of toxicities of all kinds, that have marked the first decade of the twenty-first century, after that inaugural shock that took place on 11 September 2001 – from Benfluorex (or Mediator) in France and elsewhere, to attention deficit disorder throughout the world, and passing through the systemic dilution of responsibility in and by the 'financial industry', not to mention all the disruptions of the biosphere.

What we learn from *Inside Job* is that American economics professors played an important role in the so-called 'financial industry', and were sometimes able to amass small fortunes – the financial sector being willing to spend an enormous amount in order to influence the public sphere in general:

> Between 1998 and 2008, the financial industry spent over 5 billion dollars on lobbying and campaign contributions. And since the crisis, they're spending even more money. The financial industry also exerts its influence in a more subtle way; one that most Americans don't know about. It has corrupted the study of economics itself.[32]

George Soros himself confirms this analysis in the clearest possible terms:

> Deregulation had tremendous financial *and intellectual* support. [...] The economics profession was the main source of that *illusion*.[33]

And the narrator adds:

> Since the 1980s, academic economists have been major advocates of deregulation, and played powerful roles in shaping U.S. government policy. Very few of these economic experts warned about the crisis. And even after the crisis, many of them opposed reform.

Interviews then follow with Martin Feldstein, economics professor at Harvard, Glenn Hubbard, dean of the Columbia Business School, and Frederic Mishkin, professor at the same university in New York.[34] The film also mentions the positions of Laura Tyson at Berkeley, Ruth Simmons, president of Brown University, and Larry Summers, former Treasury Secretary under Clinton and president of Harvard University.

It is tempting to conclude that if everything has gone so badly, this must be due, in terms of academic responsibility, to economists. It must be due, that is, to the fact that this discipline has given up its theoretical dimension, its discipline in the sense of its rigour, its rationality. And it has done so in order to become econometrics, that is, a technology of indicators, and a mathematization of anticipation that is ever-more self-fulfilling, that is, as Derrida and Lyotard put it, performative, a technology of models and simulations that is turning into a technology of dissimulation, the eventual result of which is the development of financial software that can only ruin the economy. Many economists themselves have reached such conclusions, those who belong to currents of the discipline that are for this reason known as 'heterodox economics': they attack neoliberalism for basing itself on a concept of rationality that has been corrupted by its abandonment of all criticism of its own status as scientific – the capacity for critique being the basis of all reason – and that therefore leads to the spread of practices whose result is profound economic irrationality.

It is indeed tempting to think this way – it is all the fault, in terms of universities, of economists who are either corrupt or simply inadequately equipped with critical sense, that is, rational sense – and it would be comfortable to be able to leave it at that. But this would be a grave error, in the first place because, especially as concerns philosophy, it has itself, since 1968, very generally abandoned the economic field and the critique of political economy, and this abandonment was even greater after the collapse of the Communist bloc. Having attempted to outline the theoretical stakes of this situation in *For a New Critique of Political Economy*, here I shall continue and deepen this analysis by attempting to show that the abandonment of economic questions and of the critique of political economy rests on much more general theoretical misunderstandings – and is founded on a *repression* lying at the very origin of philosophy.

Before clarifying these points, it is necessary to reiterate here[35] that the fundamental issue in this global crisis is not essentially financial. If the financial industry has become violently toxic since the 'conservative revolution', accelerating and intensifying the destructive effects of contemporary capitalism, the more fundamental question relates to the obsolescence of the consumerist industrial model, a model that arose at the beginning of the twentieth century with Fordism and was consolidated with the American New Deal of 1933, before expanding to Europe with the Marshall Plan and eventually to the entire world with the 'conservative revolution' that began in the late 1970s.

As I have already tried to show, contemporary philosophy, as a general rule, and with the exception of the Frankfurt School, has largely ignored the toxic, addictive and self-destructive becoming of consumerism. Hence philosophy has allowed the arguments of Herbert Marcuse and Guy Debord on this subject to fall into oblivion, but also those of many others (such as Henri Lefebvre) – and contemporary writers who have addressed this subject (such as André Gorz), too, have been neglected.

As Marx understood in 1857,[36] just as Schumpeter made it the new leitmotiv of American capitalism under the name of 'innovation', and just as it is now expressly thematized with the advent of digital networks and the 'information society', knowledge has become the crucial issue in the economic war currently destroying the world. 'Poststructuralist' thought has at times been able to teach us things about this situation, and in some ways to fight against it, as we shall see. But it has done so on the basis of two misconceptions themselves grounded in the original repression of the technical question by nascent philosophy – a repression that, strangely, 'poststructuralist' philosophy has itself in some ways exposed, while nevertheless perpetuating it.[37]

The two misunderstandings that such a repression reinforces concern:

• the meaning of what Marx referred to as the 'proletariat'; and
• the status of the drives in Freudian theory.

These points will be argued at length in chapter 6, which concludes the first part of this work. The second part will attempt to draw some theoretical and practical consequences from these re-readings of the philosophies of the nineteenth and twentieth centuries – re-readings conducted in the aftermath of 2008 – by advancing a series of proposals that together constitute a call to the international academic community to constitute what in 1920 Marcel Mauss called an 'internation'.

The first part was written after the second: it outlines the conceptual underpinnings. Therefore the reader who prefers to begin with the positive proposals I put forth in the second part may do so without much problem. For a thorough understanding of these proposals, however, it is necessary to read the first part. The first part is composed of six chapters, of which the fifth is the most difficult. Readers may also skip this chapter, and turn from the fourth directly to the sixth chapter, returning to the fifth at a later time if possible.[38]

Part I

Pharmacology of Stupidity: Introduction to the Poststructuralist Epoch

1

Unreason

Humanity, instead of entering a truly human state, is sinking into a new kind of barbarism.

Theodor Adorno and Max Horkheimer[1]

5 'A torrent of events is pouring down on mankind': madness and regression

The impression that humanity has fallen under the domination of unreason or madness [*déraison*] overwhelms our spirit, confronted as we are with systemic collapses, major technological accidents, medical or pharmaceutical scandals, shocking revelations, the unleashing of the drives, and acts of madness of every kind and in every social milieu – not to mention the extreme misery and poverty that now afflict citizens and neighbours both near and far.

The notion that the rationalization characteristic of industrial societies leads to a regression into unreason is far from new. In 1944, in *Dialektik der Aufklärung*, translated into French by Éliane Kaufholz under the title *La Dialectique de la Raison*, Theodor Adorno and Max Horkheimer characterized this inversion of reason as a *regression* (*Rückschritt*) 'which is taking place everywhere today'.[2] And they warned their contemporaries that 'if enlightenment does not undertake work that reflects on this regressive moment, it seals its own fate'.[3]

If we then read the analyses of Karl Polanyi, also published in 1944, on the effects of the 'self-regulating market' and the 'de-socialization of the economy'[4] (which begins in the epoch of the *Aufklärung*), we are bound to wonder, almost seventy years later, about the degree to which 'reason-formed-in-the-epoch-of-the-Enlightenment' (I am attempting here to translate what Adorno and Horkheimer called the *Aufklärung*) has or has not undertaken this work of reflection:

> A self-adjusting market [...] could not exist for any length of time without annihilating the human and natural substance of society; it would have physically destroyed man and transformed his surroundings into a wilderness. [...] Nothing could seem more inept than [...] to argue the inevitable self-destruction of civilization on account of some technical quality of its economic organization. [...] Yet it is this we are undertaking. [...] As if the forces of change had been pent up for a century, a torrent of events is pouring down on mankind. A social transformation of planetary range is being topped by wars of an entirely new type in which a score of states have crashed.[5]

6   Still and always acting out: madness, irresponsibility, baseness

The *Aufklärung*, which the French translator of *Dialektik der Aufklärung* chose to translate as '*la Raison*', dressed up with a magisterial capital letter, this *Aufklärung* that will fail to undertake this work of reflection (and that will largely ignore the analyses of Polanyi) is not an impersonal power: it is a noetic possibility within each of us, and as such it constitutes, as a potential shared by everyone but one that must be actualized, a responsibility that is always both individual and collective. We are all reason-able in potential – if not in actuality.

The question is that of the passage to the act – reasonable *or* unreasonable [*déraisonnable*].

The passage to the noetic act, that is, to the reasonable act, is what the *Aufklärung* embodied by Kant conceived as an historical conquest: there is a *history* of reason here firstly in this sense (as passage to the historical act of reason – or of unreason). And this history is a *social history* – translating *Aufklärung* as Reason unfortunately effaces this historical and social dimension. It was on the basis of this Enlightenment legacy – of which Kant is the tutelary figure enjoining the reader to take their responsibility by daring to know (*sapere aude!*) and by passing from minority to majority – that Adorno and Horkheimer authored their *Dialektik der Aufklärung*.

To pass into the act of reason, which Aristotle called *noēsis*, is precisely and above all to struggle against that unreason [*déraison*] that manifests itself in many forms – between stupidity [*bêtise*] and madness [*folie*] and prospering on the terrain of ignorance, fantasy and, nowadays, the industrial exploitation of the drives,[6] that is, as the planetary-wide extension and universalization of what Gilles Deleuze described as *baseness*.[7]

If reason forms itself (in passing through a *Bildung*), this is also and above all because it de-forms itself. It is a state that, both mental and social, is essentially precarious – and it is perhaps this that we, the latecomers of the twenty-first century, are the ones to have discovered: this 'conquest' we make remains always radically to be re-made and defended. What Adorno and Horkheimer added to the Kantian definition of the *Aufklärung* as conquest is that it must always be defended *against itself*, since it constantly tends, in becoming rationalization (that is, reification),[8] to turn against itself as knowledge becomes stupidity – this dialecticization of the *Aufklärung* occurring after Weber's discovery that rationalization is characteristic of capitalist becoming.

Presenting itself in this way in the garb of rationalization, reason cannot avoid engendering the temptation of irrationality.

What perhaps we today have also discovered, and what we experience so painfully and anxiously, is that reason presupposes retentional conditions[9] for its *Bildung* (I have described these elsewhere,[10] and I will return to them in detail in the following). These conditions form and support individual and collective memory, which depend on hypomnesic techniques (on *hypomnēmata*) that have today been industrialized, and which, with the development of rationalization, are no longer in the control of any public or noetic powers: they have passed into the hands of what Polanyi called the 'self-regulating market'.[11]

Hence what is occurring, on a scale and in conditions that were hitherto inconceivable, is the effect of what Gramsci described as a cultural hegemony that de-forms reason[12] – reason understood in Enlightenment terms as that historical and social conquest that now seems to decompose so rapidly into rationalization. Hence the reign of stupidity, baseness (vulgarity) and madness that, disturbing us greatly but preventing us from transforming this inquietude into thinking, instead gives rise to fear, which is a bad counsellor.[13]

We have perhaps failed to reflect on Adorno and Horkheimer's thinking in relation to what they referred to as the *Aufklärung*, conceived in the eighteenth century as the conquest of maturity and the struggle against minority. Perhaps this failure has consisted in continuing to ignore the need for an analysis of the hypomnesic conditions of this conquest that is the formation of reason, in particular at the moment when new mnemotechnics and retentional technologies are appearing. But perhaps it also consists in ignoring the economico-political conditions of appropriation and expropriation of these *hypomnēmata*,[14] which has made possible the 'disembedding of the market', a market that has become self-regulating but at the same time self-destroying,[15] because it transforms its 'environment into a desert'.[16]

In their analysis of the culture industry, Adorno and Horkheimer themselves spoke of a new form of *hypomnēmata*. But this did not lead them to the reflexive leap they called for. On the contrary: as I tried to show in *Technics and Time, 3*, to accomplish this leap we must return to the *Critique of Pure Reason* and inscribe the question of *hypomnēmata*, that is, of image-objects (and object-images),[17] at the very heart of what Kant called the *schematism*. The technical exteriorization of the schematism does not, contrary to what Adorno and Horkheimer argued in their critique of Hollywood, entail its destruction,[18] but is, on the contrary, the condition of both its possibility and its impossibility: the condition of its *pharmacological precariousness*.

In the present work I again take up this analysis but in other terms, in order to draw constitutional and institutional consequences, that is, in order to derive principles, prescriptions, proposals and political and economic prospects. This will lead to an examination of the responsibility of academics and the university – but also, more broadly, of the responsibility of public powers and authorities in general in relation to the passage to the act of being reason-able – especially in an age in which France has enacted a law on the responsibility of universities.[19]

7 Reason and responsibility: what is an academic?

What Adorno and Horkheimer called the *Aufklärung* is first of all a movement of individual and collective responsibility that tends to cause potentially reasonable beings to leave their minority, so that they achieve an individual, psychic, moral and intellectual maturity, which becomes social and political maturity, and so that they then become capable of *actual* reason, and through that, capable of *acting* rationally, both individually and collectively.

We, those who belong to the twenty-first century, have yet to respond to the injunction of Adorno and Horkheimer, or, more generally, to that which might return us to the questions of Polanyi, and do so as that which has been repressed. We would thus have ignored, forgotten and ultimately erased, over the course of the decades from the post-war period until the beginning of the twenty-first century, the properly *tragic* character of the warnings issued by these three Jewish émigrés.

Who, more precisely, is this *we* that would be responsible? Who is it that ought to have become a *we* by gathering together individuals who are really reasonable into action, not just a *we* that would be reasonable in potential (that would be the 'people' of the Enlightenment), in some way a *we* reasonable in action yet still incarnating the *Aufklärung* addressed by Adorno and Horkheimer? Who is this *we*, if not the academic and university world, and especially, among all the disciplines constituting this world, *philosophy*?

Academics can in fact enjoy their qualifications as masters or professors only provided that, in principle, in the disciplinary field in which they are recognized and authorized to teach and conduct research, they have become officially mature. They must be in a way 'officers' of maturity, and in principle and in an exemplary way have left their minority behind, in principle protected from those regressive temptations that are like cobblestones along the path to maturity. And these 'officers' are recognized as such because they have themselves in principle contributed to the 'conquest' of reason ('conquests' that should in principle always contribute to a *good academic thesis*).

If, in a world constituted by beings who are *all* reasonable in potential (and capable as such of creating a world [*faire monde*], and of doing so by struggling against that vileness [*immonde*] that the *Dialectic of Enlightenment* called 'barbarism'), reason is a universally shared law or right, and therefore a universally shared responsibility, then those who succeed in achieving the formation of their noetic potential, and thereby pass into noetic acts – acts that form the current milestones of their discipline, linked to the past milestones of which such a discipline is the legacy – are those who bear a special responsibility.

To what extent is this still true, however, in the age of the French law on the responsibilities of universities? To what extent is it true for universities that, accepting secondary school graduates who have earned a diploma obtained by over 80 per cent of students, have become primarily vocational, and where it is no longer the sciences that dominate but technology, the latter having itself developed into what is sometimes called 'technoscience'? To what extent is the assumption of such a responsibility, that is, such as it has been conceived since the *Aufklärung*, still possible, given that the university thinks according to a Kantian model that completely ignores the technological becoming of knowledge? I will return to these questions in chapter 8, and through a reading of certain passages of Kant's *Conflict of the Faculties*.[20]

8   The impasse – knowledge discredited, school disqualified

In an article published in *Le Figaro*,[21] François Hauter points out that the question of education has become a source of anxiety and conflict not only in France but in Germany and the United Kingdom. He reports that in order to struggle against this situation, which afflicts every large industrialized nation, the United States has set up many 'charter schools', to which the states have delegated their responsibility,[22] and that these schools 'get results':[23] the central issue here is a new division of responsibility.

In his analysis of the causes leading to the need for another way of sharing out responsibility – a sharing that according to Enlightenment tradition constitutes the historical conquest of individual and collective maturity founded on a passage to the act of reason of which we are all bearers, and for which we are all responsible in potential – Hauter nevertheless reaches an impasse. One almost always finds this impasse whenever one delves into the torrent of discourse that addresses and is disturbed by the collapse of education systems in industrial and hyper-industrial societies,[24] and that tries to come up with alternative proposals (as I myself will try to do here).

This impasse consists in ignoring and even in repressing the fact that in contemporary society – dominated by the 'violence of public debate on schooling' and by 'the bitterness of the invective between parents and teachers about their *respective responsibilities*'[25] – the problem with education in general and teaching in particular is the result of the immense discredit with which knowledge has been afflicted – theoretical knowledge as much as *savoir-faire* and *savoir-vivre*.

In contemporary society, all forms of knowledge have been weakened, if not annihilated. Savoir-faire (skills, know-how) has all but disappeared, and savoir-vivre (knowledge of how to live, manners, etiquette, and so on) has been dissolved into the behavioural standardization imposed by consumerism. As for scientific and theoretical knowledge, which has become a primary function for economic and industrial development, it is the subject of deep distrust – including among teachers, who feel overwhelmed or even invalidated by the pace and character of its evolution.

This is why, if '73 per cent of children, according to a recent survey, do not like going to high school', and if 'French schools produce frustration by pitting children against one another from childhood', that is, according to Hauter, by making school above all a place of competition,[26] this is firstly (if not only) because these children radically doubt not only the value of their teachers (who, as mentioned, themselves feel invalidated by the evolution of knowledge), but also the validity of the knowledge they are being taught, and which their teachers are no longer able to embody – either for themselves, or in the eyes of their pupils or the parents of these pupils.

This scepticism on the part of youth, this non-recognition by the 'descendant' generation in relation to its 'ascendance', which thus loses its ascendancy, unfortunately extends past merely the theoretical and scholarly forms of knowledge: it is also and perhaps primarily ways of life (which are in principle transmitted from one generation to another) that have been discredited. As such, it is education in all its forms that is being challenged,[27] given that education in general is this intergenerational transmission, well beyond school teaching, wherein those who are older – teachers, parents, grandparents – are in principle the representatives of the different forms of knowledge through which they find and from which they draw their authority.

Since the *Aufklärung* this authority, which maturity defined as the conquest of reason constitutes, has been founded on the distinction between knowledge and belief, and therefore on the possibility of rationally distinguishing between *knowledge, opinion* and *dogma* (for example, as revelation) – against all 'argument from authority', that is, not founded in reason. This distinction is a critical faculty that is historically conquered – and it is the republic (in the Kantian sense)[28] that organizes the sharing out of this faculty, as condition of shared responsibility, and does so through institutions, notably teaching institutions and academies. This authority itself has a long history, which precedes the *Aufklärung*. Such authority is the outcome of a process of critical transindividuation, that is, of an accumulation of judgements that converge towards a particular developmental stage of knowledge in a given field of reality, and that thereby constitute what we call a *discipline*.

Over the course of the last few decades, however, the technological becoming of knowledge has disrupted the conditions of the transindividuation of that disciplinary knowledge that is reputedly 'rational', that is, the result of critique deriving from logical, public disputation. And this disruption has interfered with the critical faculty itself as the capacity to distinguish between knowledge, opinion and dogma.

This new reality, which is as frightening as it is complex insofar as its consequences are immense, is completely ignored – and perhaps repressed – by François Hauter, as well as by most contemporary discourse on the widespread academic malaise that afflicts our age (schools, colleges and universities of all kinds, academies, institutions of 'auxiliary science' – librarianship, archive science, and so on – editorial and publishing functions, administrative science, academic inspections, and so on and so forth).

9   Knowledge, generations and marketing

At the same time, François Hauter believes the current education crisis in France can be reduced to the effect of a 'devastating centralism' typical of the French republic, that is, of its government, its public authorities and its 'republican elitism' – even though his article begins with the observation that schools in Germany, the United Kingdom and North America have similar problems. In fact, Hauter does not quite say that in France the problems in schools are *due* to centralism: he says rather that France is incapable of adopting solutions to these problems along the lines of charter schools (of which he is an unapologetic and uncritical advocate) because the totally ossified French education system rests on a 'national taste for confrontation' that conjoins with the republican centralism conceived and imposed by Jules Ferry with respect to national education.

The consequence of this reasoning is that France, according to Hauter, would be incapable of adopting the solution that seems to him the best, and the one chosen by the United States: the celebrated 'charter schools'. France would be incapable of following suit because such a solution means abandoning elitism (which completely governs the organization of education in France) and moving to *collaborative* learning:

> [In the] American system [of charter schools], three children are brought together around a table: a strong learner, an average learner and one who is struggling. They must adapt to each other, help each other, and work together. This is what is called, rather stupidly, 'teamwork'.

'Stupidly'.

And why not? The problem is that, in doing so, we propose a solution without having identified the problem – an approach that is hardly rational, if not indeed stupid. For if it is true that the problem is related to changes in knowledge itself, the place of knowledge, its becoming in society, the nature of intergenerational relations that it produces and that it transforms, and where – and this is my thesis – *the authority of knowledge is regressing along with the regression of the generations, and vice versa*, then the purported success of this method, which rests on mutual *intra*-generational adaptation, in all likelihood serves only to encourage younger generations to adapt to educational neglect and carelessness, to fend for themselves, just as the inhabitants of New Orleans were abandoned after Hurricane Katrina, the younger generation being here confronted with a pre-sumed or real (or even maintained) invalidity of its ascendants, and cut off from them.

Hauter's article seems to have been written less in order to analyse a problem than to criticize a model: the so-called 'French model', which he would have us believe is decidedly and definitively obsolete. This argument, so prevalent today, an argument that is no doubt not completely false, usually fails to reflect on what it is that has been surpassed, questions that extend far beyond the 'French model', which is why these are also issues for Germany, the United Kingdom and the United States, as Hauter himself points out – in fact, this intergenerational catastrophe affects most large countries (and notably Japan).

To clarify this 'French problem' that he sees in the 'French model', Hauter maintains that teaching in France consists in a national organ-ization of the 'confrontation' between students, deriving from the centralism instituted by Jules Ferry, 'who, glancing at his watch at 10:15 each Monday morning, would know that every grade four student in France was doing mathematics'. Ferry thus ignored, accord-ing to Hauter, the specificity of each local organization, each of which therefore suffered from a lack of *autonomy*, preventing teachers and school leaders from taking responsibility and thus preventing them from taking initiatives, in particular 'innovative' ones. For Hauter this suggests that egalitarianism is a hidden and perverse way of organizing the confrontation of all against all, and that centralism, under the guise of equal opportunity, is in fact a principle of selection through competition that stifles individual initiative.

A classical critique, then, but a critique that does not for one second question the effects of the mass media, which, as the audio-visual media, synchronizes and in fact short-circuits that public life and public debate founded on the republican school, and does so by capturing and destroying attention, superimposing audiovisual programme schedules on scholastic programmes, and competing against the latter by use of the colossal means at their disposal. The goal is no longer to elevate pupils [*d'élever des élèves*] but to get television 'ratings' by any means possible, especially for the younger generations – given that 43 per cent of purchases are prescribed by children to their parents. And the aim is to impose behavioural models that are the exact opposite of everything that would constitute education, whether that is familial, religious or national.

10 A 'high-voltage line that is best avoided', Madame la Marquise

In relation to the French situation, however, there is something even worse than republican centralism, according to Hauter. For in France:

> This national taste for confrontation reaches insane proportions when it culminates, as is the case today, in a clash between the generations. Everywhere, and I have seen this right across France, young people are frightening to older adults, who are more and more numerous. The discourse of older people against adolescents is imbued with intolerance: young people slide into a downward spiral, they are illiterate, violent, depressed, drug addicts and alcoholics. Public schools are unable to halt this general downward slide.

Hauter totally rejects this notion – which he correctly sees as a series of clichés – and comes to the defence of the 'younger generation'.

In fashioning himself as an advocate of youth, however, he tends to oppose to these clichés other clichés, mirror images of those he is opposing. Hauter argues that it is really the elderly, that is, grandparents,[29] who are 'frightened of youth', but that, apart from a minority of perhaps 10 per cent of young people and their parents, relationships are in general quite good:

> Parent–child relationships are [in 2011] more relaxed than they were previously, parents communicate, they share activities and travel with their children, they are aware that the period from twelve to eighteen is the most sensitive, the most risky. They are *attentive and responsible*. But the grandparents fail to perceive this everyday equilibrium, and reject the Facebook generation.[30]

In other words, while it may be true that 10 per cent of young people and the families in which they grow up are doing badly, the others, that is, 90 per cent, are doing well, and even better than before: they are more educated, more open, more attentive and more responsible, and the parents get along better with their children than they do with their own parents – those children who have grown up and are becoming the 'Facebook generation'. Everything is going fine (at least for 90 per cent), Madame la Marquise.[31]

It would be interesting to know, however, what kind of data underlies these assertions, and who these 'attentive and responsible' parents may be, capable of forging relationships with their children that are 'more relaxed than they were previously'. For if one refers to international studies such as those on which I have commented in *Taking Care of Youth and the Generations*, or those cited by Michel Desmurget,[32] then there is reason seriously to question this discourse, which comes across as a relaxant (if not as a soporific), but is not very nuanced in the way it opposes the generations to one another. Ultimately, it is scarcely responsible, confronted with a situation that the author himself recognizes, at the beginning of the article, as constituting 'a high-voltage line that is best avoided', at least as a subject of discussion within families in general: not just within that 10 per cent who have gone astray (children and parents) and who frighten the elderly (the marginalized, the ghettoized, the 'poorly integrated', or even the immigrants that a minister, falsifying national statistics, recently accused of chronic educational failure, and so on), but *in every segment of the population*.[33]

At the beginning of his article Hauter explicitly suggests – as a preliminary remark intended to characterize the general framework of the propositions to be advanced in what follows and at the end of the article, but which actually states the exact opposite – the following:

If there is a personal subject that, if handled badly, may *create a gulf* between mother and daughter, brother and sister, or best friends, it is the subject of the education of children. [...] *Parents and grandparents tiptoe around on eggshells*: the smallest broach of the topic can *destroy the peace of families and irremediably divide siblings*.[34]

Where, then, do we find these relationships that would be 'more relaxed than they were previously'?

11 Intergenerational conflicts, infantilization of parents and technologies

In reality, these relationships are increasingly anaesthetized and in some sense suspended. This occurs in various ways, all of which aim to bypass and short-circuit the necessary conflicts between mature parental authority and those who, in their minority, want to become mature.

During the period when a child, who recognizes this authority of majority, and who constructs himself or herself through identifying with it, becomes an adult, parental authority becomes unsustainable to this adult-in-becoming, who can develop – become adult, that is, mature – only by learning to break with this parental authority, that is, to critique it. This authority then becomes, in the eyes of the adolescent, an 'argument from authority', that is, an arbitrary authority ruling over them, precisely as though they were a minor being prevented from achieving their majority. Those 'parent–child relationships' that Hauter claims are 'more relaxed' may in reality often be *the very obstacle to becoming adult*, being on the contrary part of an infantilization of parents themselves[35] – who thus become 'friends' with their children.

Intergenerational conflict, which is structurally necessary in order to become an adult, is founded on what I have elsewhere referred to as an Antigone complex,[36] which may lead to a process of negative sublimation when the work of mourning that is the rupture of becoming adult (which we call adolescence) fails to lead to a recognition and acceptance of intergenerational difference and its necessity.

For if becoming-adult goes well, and in particular since the *Aufklärung*, then when it passes through this necessary rupture that is the passage from minority to majority, the young adult places themselves under the authority of a knowledge that exceeds and sublimates the confrontational familial framework. It does so by introducing them into knowledge as the fields of rational transindividuation, forged and traced through the logical disputations that encompass familial intergenerational conflict, while displacing it towards another field of intergenerational relations. All knowledge, of any kind, is always an authorized case of this other field of relations, precisely because, in this passage to adulthood, it constitutes a 'third' area (and always by building upon what Freud, after Groddeck, called the Id: this is at least what I tried to show in *Taking Care of Youth and the Generations*).[37]

This normal, necessary scene, however, in which the familial relationship becomes tense and then confrontational so that minors will be able to achieve their majority, has been short-circuited by the capture and diversion of individual, familial and collective attention towards the objects and subjects of the mass media and, through them, towards objects of consumption. And it is indeed the goal of this capture of attention to channel the desire of individuals towards commodities. This destroys the very thing that could found the desire of the social group as the circulation of desire between members of this group.

These social groups and their institutions are being short-circuited in terms of the *forming and training of attention*. This is particularly true for those tasks given to this function since the *Aufklärung*: to form that attentional form based specifically on the potential for reason, a potential that can pass into actuality – to majority in actuality – only on the condition of being formed via passage through the logical disputations lying at the origin of those disciplines called rational. Teaching recreates the pathways to these disciplines within those who are taught.

What the international studies previously mentioned show is that today there is a vast diversion and deformation of this attention, occurring in *all* social categories, far beyond any 10 per cent of the population (and from where exactly did Hauter pluck this figure?). If the United States and Japan are in some way 'ahead' of Europe, for example, in terms of the deficit of conversation within the family (which has decreased by an average of 60 per cent in fifteen US states – adolescent muteness is now a serious problem), nevertheless the tendency is global, and occurs throughout Europe, notably in France, Germany and Great Britain.[38] It is because this catastrophe makes intergenerational education impossible that charter schools are being established to ratify this disaster – and we shall see how this is related to what Naomi Klein calls the 'shock doctrine'.[39]

In general terms, what Hauter completely ignores or denies is the destructive role that marketing plays in intergenerational relations. Marketing has, since the 1960s, *based itself in an essential way on generational distinctions*, but in doing so it has purely and simply liquidated the formation of these relations, substituting itself for everything involved in the transmission of those symbolic statements through which the generations are bonded to one another.

To this must be added another factor, one that Hauter himself introduces at the end of his analysis: 'It is as if the acceleration of technological change and the increase in life expectancy have thrown the French generations brutally against each other.'[40] Although this is obviously not simply wrong – and I will myself develop this question of the relationship between technology and the generations in the final chapter[41] – it nevertheless ignores two fundamental points:

- on the one hand, these changes mostly concern retentional (and relational) technologies that themselves profoundly modify both knowledge and intergenerational relations;
- on the other hand, marketing now very precisely substitutes itself for the public powers that would in the past have ensured the socialization of retentional technologies,[42] insofar as they constituted the techno-logical condition of the formation and transmission of knowledge – which marketing now 'socializes', as it does all technologies from the 1960s on, and does so essentially in the direction of the younger generations, so as to make these generations vectors of these technologies; hence these generations have become prime targets, to be exploited in terms of the power of prescription, by inverting the relations between minority and majority and by inciting an intergenerational rupture that fails to lead to any introduction into the circuits of knowledge, but that does lead, on the contrary, to the reinforcement of the discredit that now afflicts all forms of knowledge.

12   Knowledge and 'creative destruction'

In Western society, the knowledge taught in schools derives from the university, as it has existed since the founding of the University of Bologna in 1088.

In the context of consumerism – that is, the 'Creative Destruction' that lies behind production, which depends on corporations setting up 'research and development' departments via which they can conduct a war of technological innovation and destruction – the place of universities, and also the nature and status of the knowledge and science through which they consist, and that school is charged with transmitting to the greatest possible number, has, in the course of the twentieth century, undergone radical upheaval.

Jacques Derrida alluded to this in a text to which we shall return, when he analysed the way in which the university has been affected by this transformation of its 'outside':

> In Kant's day, this 'outside' could be confined to a margin of the university. This is no longer so certain or simple. Today, in any case, it is the university that has become its margin. Certain departments of the university at least have been reduced to this condition. The State no longer entrusts certain research to the university.[43]

Nevertheless, it does not seem that this historic upheaval – which radically contests (as we shall see in detail) what, since the *Constitutio habita* of the University of Bologna (1158), has been posited as the necessity of the principle of university autonomy – has been genuinely thought *as such*, at least in France. This historic upheaval has not been thought by the university, either explicitly or collectively (through the cooperation of academic disciplines), nor has it been thought by those in charge of 'reforming' it: political representatives. The fact that this transformational upheaval has been enacted and accomplished through political acts, through actions, passages to action, or that it has been made the subject of analyses and studies that are often extensive – none of this means that it has been thought or reflected upon *as such*. It has, rather, been *internalized*, either as a fact to be observed as such, but not debated, or without even being aware of this fact and its historical genesis – but in either case, it would thus be a fact to which we would need to submit.[44]

It is, then, a situation that remains unthought, and the risk is thus that it will lead only to unreflective and ill-considered actions, to action that is stupid, and to stupidity in relation to the struggle against that stupidity that is the regression of reason. In this unthought situation the university, and especially philosophy departments, have far more responsibility than politicians, whatever side of politics the latter are on: if there is any 'autonomy' of the university, which has something to do with the question of 'sovereignty', then it lies precisely in this responsibility.

It is the university that, after the establishment of this autonomy (which confers, since the *Aufklärung*, the passage to the act of majority in the Kantian sense: by struggling against minority), must *nourish* society – and in particular the political sphere, that is, the citizenry – by supplying the concepts through which the representatives of this sphere must present to citizens the proposals via which they claim to represent them.

The *responsibility of the university* is the subject of this book, which thus tries to follow up the reflections of Adorno and Horkheimer, but by going back over the paths traced after them by 'French thought' – if it is true that, ultimately, the university and the school of tomorrow will be the institutions through which reason-in-potential, always accompanied by its shadow, unreason-in-potential, can and must become reason-in-actuality, that is, must struggle *with this shadow* against the passage to the act of stupidity or madness. But *with* this shadow means not only against it, but by reckoning with it, and by relying on it, and even on the *basis* of this shadow.

The shadow is on both sides – and its reason (the reason of and for this shadow, that is, its necessity) must *deal with this shadow itself*,[45] in thinking *from* its shadow, if not *faster than* its shadow (as if light always arrives later than the shadow, too late for the shadow). This shadow is that of the *pharmakon*,[46] and of the effects it has on the noetic soul (science *and* non-science, light *and* shadow), such that clear, enlightened consciousness can arise only from an always obscure unconscious, at once shadow and fire.[47]

As for stupidity, I think, at once, at the same time:

- of those *stupid things* that Epimetheus does, his actions, and firstly of that act that would be the original default of origin of the pharmacological beings that we are,[48] constituting a preindividual fund on the basis of which Deleuze tried to think stupidity,[49] and in which Derrida saw a groundless ground (*fond sans fond*, '*un Urgrund et un Ungrund*');[50]
- of that 'great stupidity' (*grosse Dummheit*) to which Heidegger confessed, to describe his blindness in the face of that regression through which the self-destruction – referred to by Polanyi as well as by Adorno and Horkheimer – of Germany was then taking place.

And I think as well of an expanded stupidity, all that nonsense and all those mistakes of which Flaubert wanted to take an inventory, that are perpetually spoken or written, ultimately, at one time or another, by every one of us, including the greatest among us, that is, the 'least stupid'. And we sometimes spout such nonsense at the very moment when we speak about the stupidity surrounding us – as if it were not just difficult but actually impossible, when speaking about stupidity, not to talk nonsense.

Insofar as they are derived to some degree (both shadow *and* fire, that is, light, enlightenment) from what is called *thinking*, and should thus contribute to 'harming stupidity',[51] academic institutions (schools and universities) would be composed of beings who are reason-able in actuality, and who are *for this reason* called teachers, masters and professors. More and more often, however, not only do the pupils and students of these teachers and professors, as well as the parents of these young people, doubt that their teachers and professors are *in fact* rational, but also, finally and especially, it is these professors themselves who harbour such doubts – and I am referring here especially to university professors.

This is true to such a great extent that the philosophy of the twentieth century, particularly in France, has consisted in challenging, in casting into doubt, that beautiful construction of the spirit that saw modernity, and the social and historic process in which it has consisted (modernization), as a political and economic realization of the goals of the *Aufklärung*. Challenging this construction of modern philosophy, of which the *Aufklärung* would be the culmination, brings with it the wavering of its fundamental concepts: subject, reason, truth, responsibility, sovereignty, and so on. And eventually, in particular in Derrida at the end of his immense journey, it is the idea of stupidity itself, and knowledge itself as the possibility of struggling against it, that are placed into question.[52]

13 Idiocy, stupidity and foolishness

In his final seminar, published as *The Beast and the Sovereign*, Jacques Derrida devoted lengthy analyses to questions of the animal, the beast [*la bête*], stupidity [*la bêtise*] and sovereignty. To what extent might these analyses enrich a new reflection on the current crisis of sovereignty, confronted with the current destruction of political sovereignty by financialized capitalism? My response is clear, immediate and harsh: I fear they offer very little, and that this means that, faced with the catastrophe that is presently unfolding, (1) we are poorly armed, and (2) it is urgent to reconstitute our conceptual arsenal.

Derrida refers in this seminar to a work by Avital Ronell, *Stupidity*, in which she questions the very possibility of struggling against stupidity. She questions this possibility in part because of the limits of language, as Derrida points out, limits that for example prevent translating the French word '*bêtise*' into English in any way other than as 'stupidity'. These purely factual and 'stupid' limits are insurmountable: this impossibility of thinking *bêtise* in English other than as stupidity is tied to the idiocy of idioms, and to their irreducible idiomaticity, which is always also in some way their facticity as insurmountable *bêtise* or stupidity – for example, all those mistakes [*bêtises*] due to errors of translation that mask the impossibility of translation.

Derrida meditated on all this on the basis of a fault [*défaut*]: the shibboleth, that faulty pronunciation that afflicts the Ephraimites, just as, indeed, Moses can speak only by stuttering. From this idiomatic state of affairs that can send all minds, *in advance*, into stupor, this *stupor* that (often due to a state of shock) leads to this *stupidity*, Ronell posits as the point of departure of her reflection that any struggle against stupidity, in particular by public authorities, will literally be in vain, not to say stupid:

The temptation is to wage war on stupidity as if it were a vanquishable object [...]. One could not easily imagine circumstances in which an agency of state or government, even a U.S. government, would declare war on stupidity in the manner it has engaged a large-scale war on drugs. [T]he presumed object of the drug wars offered a hint, at least, of materiality. Stupidity exceeds and undercuts materiality [...], wins a few rounds [...] and returns.[53]

These statements presuppose:

1 that for a war to be a war it must be capable of being won, and that it is impossible to struggle against that which perpetually returns – which is clearly false: it is possible to 'wage war' in the sense of struggling against a situation, a state of fact, for example against injustice, and this is in principle the goal behind many of our understandings of the reasons to organize politically, but it does not mean we believe injustice can ever be overcome;
2 that stupidity is not tied to materiality; yet if one accepts the Platonic proposition that the *pharmakon* of writing produces a state of *bêtise* as much as of stupidity (of stupor), and thus that sophistic practices impede thinking, then it is clear that in at least some cases stupidity proceeds from a certain materiality, that of the trace, from what Derrida called the supplement, and it could perhaps be posited that in general, stupidity is tied to exteriorization in traces, that is, that it comes from the fault of Epimetheus, and makes possible what Marx would later call proletarianization.

If this last statement is true, then one might suggest that it is in principle possible to struggle (while under no illusions about the possibility of victory) against stupidity. This is the perspective I would like to defend here, and I would like to do so in order to struggle against an economic and political situation that leads to the reign of stupidity, and has led philosophy and the university to abandon the struggle against this situation – confronted in particular with this state of shock, this perpetual state of shock, that industrial society has been for spirit.

Ronell also posits, and as the foundation of her first statement, that it is impossible to *oppose* stupidity and knowledge: 'stupidity does not allow itself to be opposed to knowledge in any simple way, nor is it the other of thought'.[54] If I radically disagree with the idea that it is not possible to struggle against stupidity, I *do* think, like

Ronell (who owes her point of view here to Nietzsche), that knowledge cannot be separated from stupidity. But in my view: (1) this is a pharmacological situation; (2) stupidity is the law of the *pharmakon*; and (3) the *pharmakon* is the law of knowledge, and hence a pharmacology for our age must think the *pharmakon* that I am also calling, today, the shadow.

It is in the *pharmakon* that the resources to struggle against stupidity must be found: we must practise positive pharmacology, just as poetry, for example, practises the idiocy of the idiom on the basis of which it produces *idios*, that is, singularity, individuation.

And I believe Nietzsche, who, while positing that stupidity is constitutive of knowledge, also defined philosophy as that which wants to 'harm stupidity'. I am in this respect on the side of Nietzsche and Deleuze rather than Derrida and Ronell, and all the more resolutely insofar as their doubts about the very possibility of struggling against stupidity do not prevent these professors from *professing*,[55] in the sense that this is, for Derrida, the profession of the professor, and as professor of the *truth*. Such doubts, for instance, did not prevent Derrida from claiming this as a right, and even as a sovereign right:

> The value of sovereignty is today in thorough decomposition. But one must beware that this necessary deconstruction does not compromise, not too much, the university's claim to independence, that is, to a certain very particular form of sovereignty that I will try to specify later.[56]

Therefore, all things considered – 'all things being equal', as one says – the fact remains that the relation instituted through the reason of these teachers and professors would ultimately always be *a right and thus a sovereign duty*, which to that extent confers an altogether exceptional responsibility – at a time when unreason, but also stupidity and baseness, and above all, doubt, seem to be dominating the world, and seizing hold of everyone, with the result that education has become, in the France of 2011, the premier concern of French citizens:

> For sixty per cent of French respondents, education was their top priority for public action. This was nearly twenty per cent higher than in the previous survey (dating from 2010), when the highest priority was given to jobs and the struggle against unemployment (which now comes in second position).[57]

14   The 'downgraded generation' addresses the 'lyrical generation'

As for education, François Hauter, like all of us reasonable in potential or in actuality, would do well to read what was said in 2008 by
the authors of the 'Open letter to the generation who refuse to grow
old',[58] who present themselves as constituting the 'downgraded generation' [*génération déclassée*],[59] and who address themselves to the
'lyrical generation'[60] to which their parents belong.

This downgraded generation is no longer exactly the 'generation
of youth'. Rather, it is a generation that lies between the new generation (that of the so-called 'digital natives') and the generation of
baby-boomers and 1968 – I will explain later why we should understand this as the generation of 'analogue natives'. It is, in other words,
a generation of young adults who are addressing their parents, who
may in turn have recently become young grandparents.

These anonymous authors, as we can see from the style, vocabulary and tone of their open letter, are not part of that 10 per cent of
the population who are supposedly pathological, confrontational and
frightening. Rather, they are young graduates, who see themselves –
as do some Tunisian youth at the beginning of 2011, or those in the
Occupy Wall Street movement[61] – as insecure graduates:

> As insecure graduates of higher education, whose personal and profes-
> sional aspirations are revised downwards on a daily basis [...], as
> incurable addicts abandoned since childhood into the arms of con-
> sumer society [...], we will say what no one dares to say [...], scream
> out what has not been said, and you shall listen, your eyes and ears
> open.[62]

This 'downgraded generation' want everything that the 'lyrical
generation' rejected,[63] the latter thereby having contributed to liquidating (perhaps by rationalizing a situation that had established itself,
and thus in the belief they were creating some new law or right)[64]
this 'younger generation' who have since become adults. But this
downgraded generation were previously children, the children of this
so-called lyrical generation, who in general had great difficulty taking
care of them. It is not that this downgraded generation wants to
frighten, or believes in frightening, the preceding generation, that is,
the lyrical generation, who are themselves becoming older and who
became adults around 1968 (for instance, François Hauter and
myself).

This downgraded generation does not feel that it received attention from the kind of responsible parents that Hauter believes today's parents to be. On the contrary, they feel that they lack the *means* to become a generation of responsible parents, because they were themselves abandoned by their own parents. And in this feeling of abandonment, this younger generation has become afraid, and more than that, truly despairing:

> We are afraid, [...] we dare not even speak among ourselves. [...] You question us about our career plans when we struggle every day against the urge to throw ourselves in front of a train. [...] We have neither time nor money, nor the strength to do anything for the planet.[65]

This generation feels it has been downgraded firstly because it feels that it lacks fathers, and is thus deprived of the possibility of elaborating its desires, cast instead into the drives incited and exploited by the factory of nightmares and desensitization that the society of the spectacle has become:

> *Fight Club*: the mirror of our generation without fathers, given to taking pleasure in banging against something until we bleed in order to feel something. [...] We did not need to break down any walls in order to pick up the opposite sex. Pornography is on display at newsstands.[66]

The downgraded generation did not receive from the generation that engendered them – and from whom must come that knowledge which makes it possible for intergenerational conflict to be overcome by being sublimated – that conflict and transmission of knowledge without which it is not possible to become adult. Failing this, and thus not having become adult, the downgraded generation is inclined to the worst (and thus tends towards what I have tried to analyse as negative sublimation):[67]

> At the point we have come to now, we hope this is the worst. [...] No, we are not happy. [...] You failed to teach us how to swim, and now you blame us for drowning. [...] We are not a generation. [...] We ask you what it took for you to bring us up and you reply, 'I don't know.'[68]

These *parents who don't know*, who are now becoming grandparents incapable of feeling shame, have consumed their children while blaming them for their lack of 'political consciousness':

We, your children, we are unlike anything that has gone before: we resemble nothing. [...] You have consumed us. [...] You tell us that we have failed, you truly have no shame. [...] We will not explode: we have imploded. [...] We are the first generation in history to have been poorer than our parents. [...] We are spent.[69]

This open letter, addressed to their ageing parents who are now becoming grandparents, is signed in the name of this cultivated but downgraded young generation, a generation who, living in insecure circumstances and unable to become adults in reality, that is, autonomous in actuality, lack the means to be and the knowledge to be, if one may put it this way, and as they put it themselves. But those who signed this letter also challenge psychoanalysis, in a manner that resembles that of Christopher Lasch, namely, as constituting a tool of de-politicization and de-socialization – Lasch having accused his own generation of psychologizing and narcissizing everything, and as such of regressing:[70]

The notion of collectivity has given way to individual consciousness, which is the very subject of psychoanalysis. [...] Social conscience and collective problems are replaced by individual neurosis [...]. Nowadays, anyone who tries to explain, formulate or analyse personal problems by seeing them as related to the social plane is systematically dismissed as neurotic [...]. But after twenty years of psychoanalysis, you still haven't solved your problems with your own parents [...]. When will it dawn on you that the problem is you?[71]

The narcissistic psycho-centrism of this generation (a narcissism that is no doubt not equally distributed between the employees and workers of the 'lyrical' generation – and one has the impression that the signatories are mainly the children of teachers, intellectuals, artists, therapists or executives who have come through the protest movement, in brief, the generation of those sometimes referred to as '*bobos*')[72] rendered the education of the downgraded generation both impossible and non-existent:

You were wild parents. Your education: a complete failure. [...] We were unable to live out our own adolescence, because the adolescent in the house was you.[73]

It is important to read this small volume that speaks of terrible suffering, and what it says is often correct, and provides much food for thought, even though it also seems to me to be based on a serious misunderstanding of the causal chains that led to the things it denounces.

For in fact the origin of the carelessness of these parents, who are not terrible but rather sick, lies in a situation in which they themselves are among its effects. This at least is what I have tried to show in *Disbelief and Discredit*. The destruction of the systems of identification and sublimation, without which no social investment is possible, is not *caused* by the purported narcissism of this generation, as Lasch claims. It is on the contrary the industrial system – which captures, channels and deforms desire, investment, sublimation and *therefore reason* – that creates and exploits this narcissism. And, in any case, the concept of narcissism employed by Lasch is rather rudimentary – a mishmash of psychoanalysis.

Consequently, the authors of the open letter are exactly what they condemn: they blame the flawed psycho-centrism of their parents, and therefore the psychic itself, as constituting the origin of their own socio-affective problems. It seems that in this way they themselves put the psychic question at the heart of the social, and hence, even though they themselves make clear the pointlessness of opposing the psychic and the social, this is precisely what they end up doing. They make the psychism of their parents the cause of their own misery, but when it comes to the processes that have created this situation, they prove just as blind as were their parents, failing to see that these causes are not merely psychic, but psychosocial.

If they are unable to perceive these processes, it is because academics, including myself, we who taught, trained and formed these young graduates, have failed to show them – and because we ourselves are yet to perceive these processes, or to respond to the questions posed by, for instance, Adorno, Horkheimer and Polanyi.

15   From the doctrine of 'shock and awe' to the chronic state of shock in the global economic war

These misunderstandings of the causal chains involved are the result of blindness to the logic, weapons and goals of the economic war that Naomi Klein calls 'disaster capitalism', one of the main weapons of which is the so-called 'shock doctrine' – this war being at once psychological, economic and ideological.

Naomi Klein described and theorized this shock doctrine above all by showing how the Bush administration took advantage of the catastrophic consequences of Hurricane Katrina to demolish the

American public education system, and to do so by following the
recommendations of Milton Friedman, summarized by Klein in the
following terms:

> Instead of spending a portion of the billions of dollars in reconstruction
> money on rebuilding and improving New Orleans' existing public
> school system, the government should provide families with vouchers,
> which they could spend at private institutions, many run at a profit,
> that would be subsidized by the state.[74]

The notion here is thus that the state of shock created by Hurricane
Katrina should be exploited to complete the demolition of the education system, a system that has already been undermined: by a mass
media that diverts and monopolizes the attention of pupils and students; by the discredit afflicting all forms of knowledge (knowledge
of how to do, how to live, and how to theorize), and thus also afflicting the professors in charge of transmitting and teaching it; and, more
broadly and significantly, by a delegitimation of older generations
and a destruction of intergenerational relations.

Now, it is thanks to this logic of definitive liquidation that, according to Klein, the 'charter schools' really took off – those schools
celebrated by François Hauter. In the wake of Katrina:

> The administration of George W. Bush backed up their plans with tens
> of millions of dollars to convert New Orleans schools into 'charter
> schools', publicly funded institutions run by private entities according
> to their own rules. [...] Within nineteen months, with most of the
> city's poor residents still in exile, New Orleans' public school system
> had been almost completely replaced by privately run charter schools.
> [...] New Orleans was now, according to *The New York Times*, 'the
> nation's preeminent laboratory for the widespread use of charter
> schools'.[75]

And Klein cites the American Enterprise Institute, a think tank
inspired by the Chicago School, who were pleased to report that
'Katrina accomplished in a day ... what Louisiana school reformers
couldn't do after years of trying.'[76] In other words, shocks and disasters of all kinds are exploited to demolish and disintegrate the social
systems that were developed in the wake of both the Enlightenment,
which made education a crucial republican ideal, and the New Deal.
Such is the economic war referred to by Naomi Klein:

I call these orchestrated raids on the public sphere in the wake of cata-strophic events, combined with the treatment of disasters as exciting market opportunities, 'disaster capitalism'.[77]

We shall see in the following chapters,[78] however, that it is more generally *technology* that, especially after the conservative revolution (of which Milton Friedman was one of the main ideologues), serves to create shocks and destruction, psychological as well as social and economic, and through that to paralyse thinking and nip any alterna-tive possibilities in the bud.

The disaster capitalism that implements this strategy is a 'funda-mentalist version of capitalism' inspired by Friedman and his disci-ples. The strategy: 'waiting for a major crisis, then selling off pieces of the state to private players while citizens were still reeling from the shock'.[79]

This economic war is global, and the weapons and tactics were to a large extent tested out by Friedman in Chile after Augusto Pino-chet's 1973 overthrow and assassination of Salvador Allende. They were then pushed, via the International Monetary Fund, into debt-burdened developing countries in the postcolonial era,[80] and eventu-ally implemented in the United States itself after September 11 and then again after Katrina. According to the strategists of this economic war, 'only a crisis – actual or perceived – produces real change'.[81] Klein comments: 'once a crisis has struck [...] it was crucial to act swiftly, to impose rapid and irreversible change before the crisis-racked society slipped back into the "tyranny of the status quo"'.[82]

This shock doctrine conducts its psychosocial war by profiting from collective trauma: 'it was clear that this was now the preferred method of advancing corporate goals: using moments of collective trauma to engage in radical social and economic engineering'.[83] But as we shall see, it is technology that makes it possible, far beyond the doctrine of 'shock and awe',[84] not only to exploit trauma but to *provoke* it, and eventually to make the global economic war that capitalism has become simply a matter of daily life. And this began to occur from the moment that Schumpeter's theory of capitalism as 'Creative Destruction', which was the foundation of the consumerist model that originated in the United States in 1910, was combined with the conservative revolution – that is, beyond all limits, to the point that the state and public authorities in general then became, in the eyes of Ronald Reagan, 'the problem and not the solution'.

Technological shocks make it possible for 'disaster capitalism' to conduct its global economic war, to provoke those traumas through which both the social and the psychic are destroyed, and knowledge along with them, the latter being that which connects the psychic to the social. But as we shall also see, technological shocks make this possible *only because reason, and more generally thought, and political thought in particular,*[85] *have themselves totally failed to think technics and technology in general,* these being *pharmaka,* that is, both remedies and poisons.

In this respect, the invention of new educational models and new 'forms of knowledge', in the context of the extraordinary shock that the implementation of digital technological systems has constituted in relation to all modern social structures, is imperative, and only by doing so will it be possible to struggle against simplistic models such as charter schools. The latter have often been created on the initiative of parents, who approached teachers to try to devise solutions to the situations that confronted them, situations that were clearly failing. Whatever may be the causes of these failures, parents have no interest in sitting around waiting for institutions to find the time to work out alternative institutional pathways in order to care for their children. And these parents have good reason for preferring not to wait around, even if their analysis of the problem and how to respond to it may be deficient. It is therefore certainly not good enough, in the face of attacks on public education, simply to deny that it no longer serves its mission, regardless of what the causes of this obvious fact turn out to be.

Having myself established, with my wife, a kind of school that lies outside the public system, albeit with assistance from the Regional Council of the Centre, I would like here to propose a more complex approach. Naomi Klein's analysis is undoubtedly relevant to this, and I shall return to her account of the shock doctrine and disaster capitalism in more detail in subsequent chapters. I believe she is absolutely correct to re-evaluate the emergence of charter schools from within this context. But the fact remains that we must invent something new, and that new collaborations are in the process of being developed between public authorities, academies, scholarly and scientific societies, civil society and citizens, in the context of digital networks and what they make possible, namely, a contributory society founded on the production and sharing of what I call tertiary retentions.[86]

This society, which is struggling to emerge, wants to invent a new socio-therapeutic system founded on a new division of responsibilities, that is, on *a new conception of majority,* from both a psychic perspective and a political and economic perspective, which will also be the basis for another industrial model and a new economic form: an economy of contribution.[87]

How and why these questions could and should be brought into the heart of the academic mission, and more precisely the responsibility of universities, is the subject of the second part of this work, where I offer specific proposals.[88] Before doing so, however, we must examine how so-called poststructuralist thought, which echoed or failed to echo the warnings of Adorno, Horkheimer and Polanyi, will or will not make it possible to move along this path, and will or will not take *and share in* these new responsibilities.

2

Doing and Saying Stupid Things in the Twentieth Century

But knowledge is far weaker than necessity.

Aeschylus[1]

Stupidity is a scar. [...] [A]t the point where its impulse has been blocked a scar can easily be left behind, a slight callous where the surface is numb. Such scars lead to deformations.

Theodor Adorno and Max Horkheimer[2]

'I believe you are very good.'
'So I am', said the monster. 'But besides being ugly, I have no sense [*point d'esprit*]; I know I am only a beast.'
'One is not a beast', replied Beauty, 'for believing they have no sense. That is what a fool never knows.'

Jeanne-Marie Leprince de Beaumont[3]

If I am asked, whether such an one should not rather be considered an ass than a man; I answer, that I do not know.

Benedict de Spinoza[4]

16   'Do we know who we ourselves are?'

In relation to responsibility, baseness, reason and unreason, that is, both madness and stupidity, the twentieth century would, in philosophy, be the century of the 'great stupidity' of Heidegger – a stupidity that has everything to do with the *baseness* of thinking, and which, here, must necessarily be related to *horror* – to that which confronts humanity with the shame of being human.

What would be this stupidity – this *'grosse Dummheit'*? It would consist in both saying stupid things and doing stupid things – for example, in making philosophical speeches in a political context where saying was doing, and letting happen, and even *encouraging* to happen, for example in 'The Self-Assertion of the German University', subtitled 'Speech given on taking solemn charge of the rectorate of the University of Freiburg, 27 May 1933', where Heidegger (before himself referring to Prometheus while forgetting his brother Epimetheus, the forgotten forgetful one who does stupid things) asks: 'But do we know *who we ourselves* are, this body of teachers and students of the highest school of the German people?'[5]

There are times when to say is to do, and this is what John Austin called the performative dimension of language. In certain circumstances, saying something does something to those one is addressing, and thereby creates a new situation: one's speech is an action. Jacques Derrida long meditated on Austin's philosophico-linguistic discovery, and we shall see that he relates this performativity to the profession of professing that is proper to the university professor.[6]

I would like for the moment merely to point out that in the case of performative utterances, saying something stupid amounts to doing something stupid, and that it is also and especially for this reason that, today, the question of the *responsibility of the university*, or of professors professing their profession through more or less performative statements, authorizing their own autonomy and their self-assertive sovereignty, arises as never before. As never *before*: that is, since knowledge began to move from being 'Promethean' technics towards becoming technology, the latter in turn becoming the weapon of a global economic war that is ruining the planet, and that leads reason to self-destruction through a 'torrent of events'.

17   Prostitution of theory, reification and proletarianization

If regression (*Rückschritt*, to step back) is induced *by reason itself* when it becomes rationalization (including that of mass death), leading to 'the tireless self-destruction of the *Aufklärung*',[7] then this self-destruction (*Selbstzerstörung*) rests for Adorno and Horkheimer on a *prostitution of theory*[8] that denatures it and sends it into decadence:

> In the operations of modern science, the major discoveries are paid for with an increasing decline of theoretical education.[9]

The eighteenth-century philosophy which [...] put the fear of death into infamy, joined forces with it under Bonaparte. [...] Such metamorphoses of critique into affirmation do not leave theoretical content untouched: its truth evaporates [...] the official spokesmen, who have other concerns, are liquidating the theory to which they owe their place in the sun before it has time to prostitute itself completely.[10]

Progress (the *Aufklärung* understood as progress of reason)[11] in this way inverts its sign (through this prostitution, and as rationalization): 'progress is reverting to regression'.[12] The *Aufklärung* has failed and requires a leap, a jumpstart, because, according to Adorno and Horkheimer, it has abandoned the development of the theoretical understanding of its inverted destiny:

By leaving *reflection* on the *destructive side of progress to its enemies*, [...] the mysterious willingness of the technologically educated masses to fall under the spell of any despotism, in its self-destructive affinity to nationalist paranoia, in all this uncomprehended senselessness the *weakness of contemporary theoretical understanding* is evident.[13]

This theoretical weakness was present in 1947,[14] but it seems in 2011 to be even more present, and seems to be *more present than ever in the eyes of the younger generations, and not just to the younger generation of philosophers* trained in France at the École normale supérieure or in universities. This weakness seems to be present in 'all layers of the population',[15] all struck (in all three senses of this expression: 1) shocked, including and firstly in Naomi Klein's sense of the term; 2) 'completely stricken'; and 3) in the sense that a coin is struck) by what I have analysed as *systemic* stupidity.[16] But this theoretical weakness has also emerged, in an historic way, from the prostitution of the *Aufklärung*.

This prostitution of reason and theory consists in making them serve rationalization, not only as the secularization of society (in the Weberian sense) but as legitimation, that is, as rationalization in the sense of Ernest Jones and Sigmund Freud.[17] And this inversion of sign, through which reason leads to unreason, progress to regression, is justified under the cloak of reason itself, rationalization then consisting in positing and in having accepted as a conclusion that 'nothing can be done', that is, that *there is no alternative*.

This prostitution arises, moreover, from a vast subservience of individuals to apparatus, which induces a regression to minority affecting 'all layers of the population'. This subjugation and regression derive from what Adorno and Horkheimer referred to as *reification* (*Verdinglichung*), through which the economy (including today's economy of 'cognitive capitalism') disindividuates individuals:

> The individual is entirely nullified in face of the economic powers. [...]
> While individuals as such are vanishing before the apparatus they
> serve, they are provided for by that apparatus and better than ever
> before.[18]

What is here called 'reification' refers to what I, along with Ars Industrialis – counter to the dominant understanding of the discourse of Marx and Engels – have tried to understand as a process of generalized proletarianization (on the basis of an interpretation of Marx by Simondon),[19] a process that liquidates all forms of knowledge, including and especially, today, theoretical knowledge (and not only savoir-faire and savoir-vivre).

The process involved here is that of grammatization:[20] the proletarianization of thinking and of that understanding that hence escapes reason, that escapes the 'kingdom of ends'[21] (and this is essentially what Weber's account of rationalization means), may well produce a kind of pragmatic intelligence, *mētis*, ingenuity, a shrewdness or a cunning through which everyone seems to be becoming 'cleverer',[22] yet what it in fact leads to is *generalized stupidity*, which, in 1944, is imposed along with the still very recent advent of the culture industry:

> [The mind or intellect] must perish when it is solidified into a cultural
> asset and handed out for consumption purposes. The flood of precise
> information and brand-new amusements make people smarter and
> more stupid at once.[23]

Hence regression forms a cocktail of ingenious stupidities brought about by cultural consumerism.[24] In a more general way, however, stupidity is a *scar of desire*[25] – of which regression is precisely the return to its primordial stage, which is that of the drives.[26]

The fact that reason can regress and self-destruct, that is, lead to its opposite, which is unreason as stupidity or even madness, is not unique to our age: the 'tendency toward self-destruction has been inherent in rationality *from the first*'.[27]

Stupidity is *never* foreign to knowledge: knowledge can itself become stupidity par excellence, so to speak. And this is so because knowledge, and in particular theoretical knowledge as passage to the act of reason – or more broadly, *noēsis* – can occur only *intermittently* to a noetic soul that is constantly regressing, and that, as such, is like Sisyphus, perpetually ascending the slope of its own stupidity, given that, as stated by Simonides and cited by Aristotle, 'God alone enjoys this privilege',[28] that is, the privilege of being always in actuality, of never being stupid, of never going down the path of disindividuation, reification and proletarianization.

This is why not only can knowledge make thought base, but it is essentially a matter of thought's own baseness – ever threatening, ever the threat.

18   Epimetheus and Sisyphus – 'the most cunning of mortals'

Stupidity is not error or a tissue of errors. There are imbecile thoughts, imbecile discourses, that are made up entirely of truths; but these truths are base, they are those of a base, heavy and leaden soul. The state of mind dominated by reactive forces, *by right*, expresses *stupidity and, more profoundly, that which it is a symptom of: a base way of thinking.*[29]

One would clearly understand nothing of these lines by Gilles Deleuze extracted from *Nietzsche and Philosophy* if one did not posit, with Dork Zabunyan, that 'stupidity must therefore be understood as my own stupidity'.[30]

This is above all a question of *my* stupidity such that it is capable of making me ashamed, that is, such that I am capable of being ashamed of myself: a stupidity such that *I perceive my own being-stupid*. Without which (for want of being stupid, of being *able* to be) I would not be able to be affected (pained, struck) by the stupidity of others, or to have shame for myself (as if their stupidity necessarily and immediately becomes mine): without that, I could not be made ashamed.

It is on the basis of this experience of shame that I begin to philosophize, writes Deleuze in reading Nietzsche – and this means that stupidity is 'a properly transcendental question: how is stupidity (not error) possible?'[31] This is the question of individuation and disindividuation. If we are able to be stupid, it is because individuals individuate themselves only on the basis of preindividual funds (or grounds) from which they can never break free: from out of which, alone, they can individuate themselves, but within which they can also get stuck, bogged down, that is, disindividuate themselves.

[Stupidity] is possible by virtue of the link between thought and individuation. [...] Individuation as such, as it operates beneath all forms, is inseparable from a pure ground that it brings to the surface and trails with it. [...] Stupidity is neither the ground nor the individual, but rather this *relation in which individuation brings the ground to the surface without being able to give it form.*[32]

That is, it cannot produce what Simondon called 'taking form'.[33] Such a fund or ground may be that of knowledge itself, of knowledge that has become 'well known',[34] and of the *best* thoughts – those that *make* knowledge, that open what I describe as a new circuit of transindividuation. And yet even the best thinking always remains susceptible to regression.

The question of stupidity is the question of regression (of lowering, of baseness) in relation to this solemnity [*gravité*] with which thought progresses, that is, raises itself in climbing [*gravissant*] that which is high, in advancing towards what Simondon called 'key points'[35] – but always with the risk that inevitably accompanies elevation, the constant imminence of the fall, of which the tightrope walker is the figure.[36] One who thinks can think noetically only intermittently, and this means that the one who thinks, *this one* who thinks, always ends up falling back again, that all thinking can become stupid, eventually becomes stupid (again), and that any knowledge can end up justifying and rationalizing the worst stupidity.[37]

This relation, stupidity/knowledge, *bêtise/savoir, Dummheit/Wissenschaft*, means that knowledge will never be done with stupidity insofar as it is firstly and above all its own stupidity, that stupidity proper to knowledge, that is, the *impropriety* of knowledge (which is taught to us by the figure of Epimetheus and by *ēpimethēia*, which thinks only on the basis of its own stupidity, making stupidity its point of departure, and which provided the name for the collection 'Epiméthée' founded by Jean Hyppolite at Presses Universitaires de France). This relation, stupidity/knowledge, is what is at stake in what, relying especially on Jacques Derrida and Paul Valéry, I have to tried to think as the *pharmacological condition* of knowledge, that is, of *noēsis* as that existence which is possible for non-inhuman beings faced with the fact of being-inhuman (faced with the shameful, and as deficiency of shame, absence of shame, of *aidos*).[38]

The pharmacological (that is, Epimethean) condition of knowledge and *noēsis* is also that of the university insofar as it is an institution in constant struggle against stupidity, and more particularly against its *own* stupidity (which is always already expropriated, beginning

with what Derrida analysed as exappropriation), constantly recon-
quering the gravity of this pharmacological condition – in order to
refound, like a 'happy Sisyphus',[39] the meaning and value of the
universal that derives its name from *universitas*, that is, such that, in
the universe, something has still not happened, remains still to be
climbed [*à gravir*]... and to be engraved [*à graver*], according to
the mnemotechnical condition described in the 'Second Essay' of
Nietzsche's *On the Genealogy of Morality*.[40]

19 Derrida plays the fool – and Deleuze is not *exactly* Derrida

Derrida has commented on this passage in which Deleuze asked how
stupidity is possible firstly in relation to the question of the animal,
and bases his response on the beginning of Deleuze's argument, where
he proposes that 'Stupidity [*bêtise*] is not animality. The animal is
protected by specific forms which prevent it from being "stupid"
[*bête*].'[41] Following the 'well-known' method of deconstruction,
Derrida, in *The Beast and the Sovereign* – a work that derived from
a seminar that was part of a series dedicated to the question of
responsibility[42] – tries to reduce Deleuze's reasoning to a classical
opposition between the human and the animal. He thus challenges
the possibility of identifying this stupidity that according to Deleuze
would be 'proper to man'.

Now, I cannot help but think that Derrida, here, is playing the fool
[*fait la bête*, acts the beast, plays the fool, makes a blunder] – when,
for example, he writes that 'Deleuze intends to separate man from
animality as to *bêtise*, saying without equivocation, decidedly and
determinedly, that "*bêtise* is not animality." '[43] It is hard to understand why, if this is the case, Derrida himself declares, at the beginning of the first session of his seminar devoted to the beast and the
sovereign, that 'the beast is not exactly the animal'.[44]

One could no doubt respond that Derrida reproaches Deleuze by
saying something that is *close* to what Deleuze says, but that is not
exactly what Deleuze says, just as the beast, according to Derrida, is
'not exactly' the animal. This odd animal who is Deleuze is not
exactly Derrida, however much the latter plays the fool: Deleuze does
not say exactly what Derrida says, Derrida tells us, because he says
it 'without equivocation, decidedly and determinedly'.

Besides the fact, however, that decided and determined clarity,
which is not always useless or harmful, does not necessarily always

lead to a logic of opposition – it can and even *must* be the clarity of a *distinction* – beyond the fact, also, that the verb 'to be' in Deleuze, as in Derrida, is a copula[45] *that we cannot do without* at the very moment when we want to deconstruct, and to deconstruct this very impossibility of doing without it, as, for example, when one says that '*bêtise is not* animality', or that 'the beast *is not exactly* the animal' (and it would here be necessary to deconstruct the question of exactitude,[46] and everything that this raises – a thousand necessary tasks that, equivocating, could nevertheless end up resembling what Hegel called *Räsonieren*),[47] beyond all this, I believe that, here, Derrida totally misinterprets the discourse of Deleuze, and that he profoundly misunderstands the provenance of this discourse on individuation (and disindividuation) in repetition that is the book *Difference and Repetition*.[48]

Deleuze tried to think stupidity on the basis of individuation. Individuation, he writes, is 'inseparable from a pure ground that it brings to the surface and trails with it'.[49] And it is in relation to this inseparable ground that stupidity takes place as a transcendental structure of thinking.

To develop his argument against this analysis, Derrida focuses on a sentence in which Deleuze posits that animals 'are in a sense forewarned against this ground, protected by their explicit forms'.[50] But what is this ground? Is it, for example, what Derrida called the 'groundless ground (*Urgrund* as *Ungrund*)', taking this question up in the terms Heidegger used in *An Introduction to Metaphysics*?[51] Nothing is less certain. It is a matter of the ground of what Deleuze named *individuation of any kind whatsoever*, that is, whether it be animal or human, that 'operates beneath all forms, [and that] is inseparable' from such a ground. Animals, however, would according to Deleuze be 'in a sense forewarned against this ground, protected by their explicit forms'.

To this assertion Derrida objects that 'if they are forewarned, then they must be in a relation, in some relation, with this ground and the threat of this ground'.[52] Deleuze would not, of course, deny this, and he himself speaks of relation, 'as we're shortly going to show'.[53] But what are these forms that 'forewarn' or 'forearm' animals from their ground, of which we continue to ask (we have not yet had an answer) in what this ground (or fund) consists? And why are they 'explicit'?

All individuals (humans, animals, vegetables and crystals, that is, minerals) are individuated through an individuation process. In the vital individuation process, the true individual is the animal group that forms the species insofar as it is affected by that which, in its vital preindividual fund (or ground), constitutes the mark of a phase difference (that molecular theory, for example, relates to copying errors that give rise to singularities, which, within their milieu, may in extreme cases lead to monstrosity or to a mutation of species): the phase shift is marked not in the vital individuation process at the level of the animal, but at the level of the animal group that constitutes and individuates the species.

The individuated species constitutes the vital unit, writes Simondon:

> The group is integrative. The only concrete reality is the vital unit, which in certain cases can be reduced to a single being and in other cases corresponds to a highly differentiated group of many beings.

This is particularly visible in termites:

> Hence termites construct the most complex edifices in the animal kingdom, despite the relative simplicity of their nervous system: they act almost as a unique organism, working as a group. [...] What we refer to as the individual in biology is in reality in some ways a sub-individual more than an individual; in biology, it seems that the notion of individuality is applicable at several stages, or at different levels successively included within each other. [...] The unity of life lies with the complete group, not the isolated individual.[54]

In *Civilization and Its Discontents*, Freud highlighted that 'we should not think ourselves happy in any of these animal States or in any of the roles assigned in them to the individual'.[55] In the language of Simondon taken up by Deleuze, it could be said that we are fortunate in being able to find material with which to individuate ourselves psychically – and not just vitally.

20   Repetition as individuation

Derrida does not understand the meaning of the words *fond*, *rapport* and *individuation* as they are used in *Difference and Repetition*. That animals are 'forewarned against this ground' does not mean for Deleuze that they *are not* in relation to this ground. Rather, it means that their relation to this ground passes through *specific organizations*, where the word 'specific' means that which characterizes an animal species, as specific relations typical and determinate for this or that animal species. These relations thus constitute, as such, 'explicit forms', that is, forms that are recognizable (including by the animals themselves as *imago* – which makes it possible for the locust to adopt its 'gregarious' form, as Lacan says in 'The Mirror Stage')[56] and describable, through which the preindividual fund from which they come individuates itself diversely and specifically – that is, at the level of the living group that constitutes a species – and without the isolated animal individual itself being affected by *indetermination*.[57]

It is here completely impossible to follow Deleuze's reasoning without referring in detail to the Simondonian philosophy of individuation – which Derrida seems totally to ignore. The 'explicit' forms that species form (as 'taking form') are processes of vital individuation, of which the 'concrete' forms consist in processes of specification. In the first chapter of *Difference and Repetition*, 'Difference in Itself', specification and individuation are linked together by Deleuze, both with reference to Simondon, as when Deleuze paraphrases Simondon by asserting that 'the individuating is not the simple individual', and against Duns Scotus, about whom he nevertheless states: '[Duns Scotus was] not content [despite this] to analyse the elements of an individual but went as far as the conception of individuation as the "ultimate actuality of form." '[58]

If it is necessary to pass through the thought of Simondon, this is because:

> We must show not only how individuating difference differs in kind from specific difference, but primarily and above all how individuation properly *precedes* matter and form, species and parts, and every other element of the constituted individual.[59]

One of the main aims of *Difference and Repetition* is precisely to think this link *other than* according to tradition and everything that follows it up until Heidegger (who was also a reader of Duns Scotus) and beyond: it is a matter of thinking *with Simondon beginning with the animal* and, more generally, with the vital – the animal and the vital being themselves thought beginning with the crystal, that is, with the individuation of the mineral.

The regimes of individuation, here, are kingdoms, that is, forms of sovereignty, of which the juridico-social form would therefore be merely a case – given that individuation is in general sovereign.

In the passages of *Difference and Repetition* on which Derrida comments (which it is hardly possible to read without referring to the passage from *Nietzsche and Philosophy* – published six years before *Difference and Repetition* – that I have already cited, which is also to say, without referring to what Nietzsche wrote about the relation between philosophy and stupidity in *The Gay Science*),[60]

Deleuze speaks of a process of vital individuation on the ground of which, *from out of* the *funds* of which, and *in* which appears an individuation process *of a new type*: psychic and collective individuation, which no longer has the same relation to this ground or fund because it constitutes, precisely, a new regime (that is, a new kingdom) of individuation.

Individuation in general must be thought as relation and process and not as stasis and identity. What is new here is the relation between the determined and the undetermined, and the way in which they are instantiated in different types of individuation (mineral, vital, psychosocial).[61] Deleuze in *Difference and Repetition* poses the question of the undetermined above all in reference to Kant – and to the question of the 'I think'. In Simondonian thought, this becomes the question of the 'phase shift' that constitutes the dynamic principle of the process itself, and that is concretely expressed as the 'taking form' of an individuation in an individuating being.

There is a ground or fund common to all individuation processes, which are not at all opposed to one another by this thought, contrary to what Derrida would have us believe. But there is a new relation to this ground with each new type of process (mineral, vital, psychosocial), this relation consisting in the distinction and the inscription of a difference – and which is, in addition, a new regime of différance – and which itself derives from a repetition (and I shall return to this later).

This is why Deleuze can write:

> The animal is protected by specific forms which prevent it from being 'stupid' [*bête*]. Formal correspondences between the human face and the heads of animals have often been composed; in other words, correspondences between individual differences peculiar to humans and the specific differences of animals. Such correspondences, however, take no account of stupidity as a specifically human form of bestiality.[62]

Between the human and the animal there is a change of regime of individuation, which is a change of relation to its preindividual funds. Humans individuate psychically, whereas animals individuate specifically.

If 'individuation as such, as it operates beneath all forms, is inseparable from a pure ground that it brings to the surface and trails with it',[63] this is because it is always associated with its milieu, which must be understood as a potential for individuation, that is, as a preindividual fund. This potential constitutes possibilities, and it is on the basis of these possibilities that we must think being, and not the other way around.[64]

21   Indeterminacy and determination – *The Wanderer and His Shadow* in psychosocial individuation

The preindividual is conceptualized by Simondon through the analysis of crystallization as the individuation of the mineral:[65] the crystal congeals (crystallizes) and stabilizes a tension coming from a metastable milieu that Simondon thinks in terms of the pairs 'wave or particle, matter or energy',[66] whereas a living thing is an incomplete and unfinishable form of mineral. A living thing is a crystal *that does not take*, which is 'in between', in a situation of metastability, between stability and instability, engendering a succession of specific metastable forms that concretely express this 'perpetuated individuation'.[67]

This vital incompleteness that perpetuates the individuation process, rather than congealing it as a crystal, establishes and metastabilizes a situation of différance. This différantial situation, constantly forming and de-forming, that is, differentiating itself, and thus perpetually individuating itself, and in struggling thus against its crystallization, that is, against its pure stabilization, against its hardening, if not its 'stupidity' ('stupidity' being a psychic and transcendental trait in that it is not a specific trait, not the trait of a *species*: the animal head is an incorrect representation), results in the passage from the mineral to the biological.[68]

Since 'stupidity' is a transcendental trait, that is (in Deleuze), psychic rather than specific, 'cowardice, cruelty, baseness and stupidity are not simply corporeal capacities or traits of character or society; they are structures of thought as such'.[69] Nevertheless, these structures *of thought* must be thought on the basis of a psychosocial (that is, both psychic and social) preindividual ground or fund:

> The individual distinguishes itself from it, but it [this psychic and social preindividual fund] does not distinguish itself, continuing rather to be wedded to that which divorces itself from it. It is the indeterminate, but the indeterminate in so far as it continues to embrace determination, as the ground does the shoe.[70]

That the psychic individual cannot individuate itself psychically without individuating itself socially is, in Simondonian theory, the trait specific to (in this case in the logical sense of the word 'specific') psychic and collective individuation. But this dual individuation, however, always operates in an intermittent tension between the psychic individual and the social group from which the former cannot be separated: from which it can distinguish and 'divorce' itself only while remaining 'wedded' to it.

It is also in this sense that we must read *The Wanderer and His Shadow*, where man 'is *always* living in manifold dependence but regards himself *as free* when, out of long habituation, he *no longer perceives* the weight of his chains'.[71] This freedom, however, consists in *forging and adopting new chains*. If animals 'are in a sense fore-warned against this ground, protected by their explicit forms', this is because they are not chained in this way – given that it is possible to *have* chains only if it is possible to *not be* chained, and therefore to *make* and *adopt*[72] new ones. Animals, through their species, 'are' not a species: they *are* this species.

If man can suffer (from having that which he is not), then it is 'only from *new chains* that he suffers: – "free will" really means nothing more than not feeling his new chains.'[73] Now, there are such chains because, from out of psychosocial preindividual funds, psychic individuation and collective individuation are simultaneously arranged, according to Simondon, and where all this presupposes, as I feel compelled to add at this point, *technical* individuation. Psychic individuation and social individuation (of the group) can, however, be turned against one another, and nullify one another: their confusion is their mutual disindividuation, and it is precisely this confusion that leads to stupidity, *bêtise, Dummheit*[74] (baseness), yet psychic individuation and social individuation can never individuate without each other – which is what in the eighteenth century was called *understanding*.

It is by separating in a new way that which links them together (as a new relation), thus establishing a new form of phase difference in the process of individuation (which is always changing phase, since otherwise it would not be a process, that is, a dynamic system rather than a determinist system), it is through this binding separation (the purest form of which is friendship, in the sense given to this by Blanchot)[75] that these psychosocial preindividual funds make possible a new type of incompleteness and constitute through this a new regime of individuation, producing the *transindividual* – that is, meaning.

Even though he did not himself thematize the need for psychosocial individuation to be supported by technical individuation, Simondon did suggest[76] that the transindividual presupposes artefacts, technical objects, which are also object-images[77] that must be understood as hypomnesic supports, *hypomnēmata*, *pharmaka* and everything that Derrida analysed as *supplementarity* in that history of the supplement that Derrida did not himself ever actually carry out. Derrida did not carry out this history of the supplement even though he announced it, a history that, in the language of Simondon, pursues individuation – into what we should perhaps call the *psychosocial kingdom* – by compensating for an incompleteness that is *other* than that of the living, even though that is its provenance, just as the provenance of the vital lies in the mineral.

22   Différance and repetition

Simondonian thought overcomes the oppositions between types of individuation by referring to traits common to all individuation processes – always constituted through the pair *individual/super-saturated milieu* (crystalline, vital, psychosocial), which exceeds the opposition *inside/outside* – and such that these traits individuate themselves through *types* of individuation and as *relations* within what Simondon called an 'ontogenesis'. My own preference is to call this a genealogy: the genealogy of different regimes of individuation (different kingdoms that are different forms of sovereignty – including within species, including within that species called human, or rather non-inhuman-within-inhuman-being, including between psychic individuals, and so on) as local individuations within a much broader process binding and connecting them all together.

Such a thought of individuation as process is not foreign to that process that différance also is – this 'kind of gross spelling mistake'[78] on the basis of which alone it is possible and necessary, in the eyes of Derrida (and I found this convincing from the moment I began to read it), to think 'gross stupidity'. And this includes that gross stupidity through which was expressed, historico-politically, that hyper-metaphysical sludge in which Citizen Heidegger got bogged down (and disindividuated himself, that is, betrayed himself, in both senses of the term). This relation between individuation and différance is something of which we can easily be convinced if we re-read, for example, the following lines:

> *Différer* [...] is to temporize, to take recourse, consciously or unconsciously, in the temporal and temporizing mediation of a detour that suspends the accomplishment or fulfillment of 'desire'.[79]

'To differ' is in this sense, which is that of différ*a*nce, to implement the structural incompleteness of the vital or psychosocial (but not mineral) individuation process such as it was thought by Simondon: 'this temporization is also temporalization and spacing, the becoming-time of space and the becoming-space of time'.[80] In other words, this individuation that is différance gives a difference that spatially concretizes this différ*a*nce 'to be not identical, to be other, discernible, etc.'.[81]

The individuation of differences by différance is possible only through an originary phase difference that is also a default of origin that spaces itself (out) by repeating itself (from out of a primordial repetition[82]):

> When dealing with *differen(ts)(ds)*, a word that can be written with a final *ts* or a final *ds*, as you will, whether it is a question of dissimilar otherness or of allergic and polemical otherness, an interval, a distance, *spacing*, must be produced between the elements other, and be produced with a certain perseverance in repetition.[83]

23 The problematization of the living

Within the broader process of individuation, regressions are always possible. This does not mean that psychosocial individuation may devolve into vital individuation, that is, specific individuation, or that vital individuation may devolve into mineral individuation.[84] It means, rather, that psychosocial life oscillates between dynamic possibilities that characterize types of individuation without separating them:

> The psychic and the vital cannot be distinguished like two substances, nor even as two parallel or superimposed functions; the psychic acts as a brake, decreasing the speed of the individuation of the living, a neotenic amplification of the first state of this genesis.[85]

As is now well known, neoteny is thought, in the theories of Kapp and then of Canguilhem and Leroi-Gourhan, in terms of 'organic projection' and 'process of exteriorization', that is, as the technicization of the living and as a 'technical form of life'. Neoteny does not just mean that the living requires artefacts in order to live – which is already the case for certain living things that modify their vital milieu by imprinting their form of life upon it. It means that, 'if the living being could be *completely peaceful and satisfied in itself*',[86] as 'the animal does not reason or work',[87] and is in this sense sovereign – in a sense that is not that of the psychosocial kingdom, where sovereignty derives on the contrary from a primordial in-quietude and dis-satisfaction – 'there would be no appeal to the psyche'.[88]

Psychic and collective individuation is what occurs when 'life problematizes itself'.[89] This problematization results in a decoupling between perception and action, that is, it means behaving *differently, otherwise* than merely a reaction, becoming through that an act, an action as *passage* to the act. And this constitutes a transformation of affectivity: affectivity itself becomes *emotion* as the différance of the effect from the affect, a différance that retains (a retention) and reflects, which psychically individuates – but in trans-individuating as the work of the psychosocial regime of différance.

Psychosocial différance translates into a slowing down of life in the sense that, instead of a reaction (a response to a stimulus in a sensorimotor loop, such as Jacob von Uexküll described),[90] there is an action that itself derives from a reflection that begins with an auto-affection. Psychosocial individuation (that is, psychosocial différance) is not a substance or function distinct from vital individuation, because it is on the contrary a kind of *sprouting out* from the 'stem' of vital différance, and the two types of individuation are poles within the process of meta-individuation and meta-différance in which evolution has consisted ever since the primordial incompletion of the crystal that became life.

Hence:

[It is not that there are some] beings that merely live, and others that are living-and-thinking: animals probably occasionally find themselves in a psychic situation. Such situations that lead to acts of thinking are, however, less frequent in animals.

For human beings, on the contrary, it is 'the purely vital situation that is [...] rare':

There is no nature, no essence on which to found an anthropology; simply, a threshold is crossed: *animals are better equipped to live than to think, whereas humans are better equipped to think than to live.*[91]

Dissatisfaction is a new modality of incompleteness (of différance) through which the living individual becomes a psychic and social individual. Psychic différance is immediately social individuation because 'the vital functions can no longer solve the problems posed by living'.[92]

To the extent that he posits explicitly and in principle that technical concretization is the condition of appearance of the transindividual, it is quite surprising that Simondon does not delve into the process of exteriorization theorized by Leroi-Gourhan as the consequence of neotenization, that is, of the *technical problem* – of technical problematization – in the différance of psychic life.[93] For the psychic individual individuates itself only when the resolution of the problems of life become *psychic* problems – because the neotenic living thing that is the psychic living thing can no longer solve them – and can thus be dealt with only by participating in the transindividual, which the psychosocial constitutes and which itself presupposes technical objects that, as image-objects, are the supports of the transindividual.

The transindividual occurs to the strict extent that 'entering the path of psychic individuation requires the individuated being to surpass itself',[94] and this surpassing of the psychic individual is a trans-formation not only of the self. The self can trans-form itself psychically only to the extent that it trans-forms its social milieu. In order that its psychic trans-formation can *in fact* become its own, it must trans-individually surpass itself as social trans-formation, that is, as social différance:

> The psychic results in a transindividual order of reality [...], the psychic is born of the transindividual [...], psychic reality is not closed in on itself [...], the resolution of the intra-individual psychic problem [...] occurs at the transindividual level.[95]

That the psychic individual may, however, get bogged down in the transindividual, and therefore function as a quasi-specific individuation, is not only something that *can* happen to the psychic individual, including to Citizen Heidegger: it is a *condition* of its psychic individuation to the extent that it must become collective individuation, and it is in this *necessity* that the 'transcendental' character of stupidity lies.

This does not mean that stupidity would be a fall of the psychic individual into a disindividuation that would be the passage to the social – as is the case in Heidegger with the 'falling prey' (*Verfallen*) of *Dasein* – since, as we have seen, this passage to the social is on the contrary, as collective individuation, the condition of psychic individuation. It does mean, however, that participation in the transindividual can in fact fall into an *interindividuality* within which individuation is suspended:

> Interindividuality is an exchange between individuated realities who remain at their level of individuation, and who seek in other individuals an image of their own existence parallel to this existence.[96]

It is on the basis of such a degradation of the transindividual into interindividuality that psychosocial individuation may regress to a stage that is neither animal, nor vegetable, nor mineral. This regression of psychosocial individuation constitutes a deficient relation to the potential that its preindividual funds constitute (at once as crystalline, vital and psychosocial: the psychic individual that disindividuates suffers psychically but also somatically, which means that he or she also tends to disindividuate vitally, that his or her organs are in contradiction, and may even mean that they no longer metabolize, that is, assimilate minerals, and so on – this being the preindividual potential for vital individuation).

24 Three types of psychic disindividuation

In psychosocial individuation the specific group gives way to what Freud described as the horde, then – in constant and functional relation to the prehistoric, then proto-historical and finally historical evolution of the hypomnesic supplement – to what Leroi-Gourhan referred to as the socio-ethnic group, which itself gives way to the socio-political group.[97] Psychosocial individuation is thus characterized by the fact that it constantly techno-logically modifies the conditions of its individuation – that is, of its *trans*-individuation.

But these successive stages have a perpetual tendency to return to vital forms of individuation, which constantly polarizes them – they have a perpetual tendency to put themselves into the mode of the specific group, and to operate the technical envelope of this group as an animal society in which the psychic and the social de-compose (and disindividuate) through being superimposed in an interindividuality of the group, which thus becomes more like a herd. This does not mean that technicity is regressive. It means that it constitutes a polarity at once regressive and progressive.

Hence Simondon says of the collective formed by psychic and collective individuation:

> [It is a] transindividual reality obtained through the individuation of preindividual realities associated with a plurality of living things

[becoming through that psychic individuals], distinguished from the *purely social* and from the *purely interindividual*; the purely social exists, in fact, in animal societies; it is not necessary for a new individuation to exist to expand vital individuation; it expresses how living things exist socially; it is vital unity at the first degree that is directly social.[98]

In its interindividual modality, and when this spreads to the totality of the social group (through some kind of mimetic contagion), the transindividual psychosocial tends thus to rejoin the 'purely social' of animal societies insofar as they are conditioned by specific individuation (that is, herd-like – in the sense that Lacan refers to the *grégarisation* of the locust, the way it is able to take on its 'gregarious' form) rather than psychic individuation.

Now, stupidity always passes through this tendency, insofar as it seeks to stabilize in the form of an *identity* that which is in reality always a metastability with the potential for altering. As such, it is also what conditions the formation of an *I*, or of an ego, that is, of a narcissistic structure that sees itself through the mirror of other similarly interindividual structures. Hence the fantasy of identity is constructed as a 'narcissism of minor differences',[99] founded on those paralogisms conceptualized by Kant[100] long before Freud began to refer to the psychic apparatus and psychic functions.

In the epoch of psycho-power and psycho-technologies, and even more recently with neuro-power, marketing exploits such tendencies in order to take control of the processes of transindividuation – thereby setting off massive processes of disindividuation. Given that the projection of a phantasmatic identity polarizes the interindividual, and that the interindividual always haunts the transindividual, the *I* and the ego are thus moments of disindividuation. But this does not mean that we ought to try and reduce or dissolve them (that is, raise them into a dialectical synthesis), if only because disindividuation is the condition of a new individuation, which itself consists in the fabrication of 'new chains'.[101]

We must in fact distinguish three types of disindividuation:

- *that which derives from interindividuality*, wherein the social group regresses to the purely social, through which it again takes on specific traits (in the sense that they characterize that species of vital individuation) that then pervade the *I* or the ego;
- *that which occurs as a divestiture by technics* – what Simondon described as proletarianization;

- *that which is necessary for individuation* as the *epokhē* of an earlier individuation,[102] through which the psychic individual accomplishes a 'quantum leap', that is, crosses a threshold in their psychic trans-formation.

This third form of disindividuation, as condition of the continuation of individuation, itself presupposes *emotion* as the psychic modality and différance of affectivity. It is the 'capacity of the individuating being to temporarily disindividuate'.[103]

My own position is that, in the final analysis, these three forms of disindividuation can never be separated, and always constitute three necessary moments of psychic individuation as that which leads to the formation of the transindividual, that is, of the psychosocial collective individual. They must be thought in terms of a doubly epokhal redoubling over-determined by technical evolutions.[104]

These moments are not dialectical because the poisonous aspect of this pharmacology is irreducible. For example, if individuation occurs as rational knowledge, this knowledge may always some day or other come to serve stupidity: there is no absolute knowledge.

This is because 'the I or the Ego', as a fantasy of identity (as the purely psychic as well as the purely social) is the point of articulation of these three dimensions of disindividuation that Deleuze called 'indices of the species'.[105]

As such, it is necessary to posit that the psychic individual is the individual *capable of disindividuating* (just as, according to Canguilhem, the technique of healthy living lies in '*the power and the will to fall sick*')[106] through a disindividuation due, not to an act of will, but to the artefactual (factical) and pharmacological situation through which alone it is possible to say and do stupid things, and where *saying* often means *doing* – stupidity being also and perhaps especially performative (and we should perhaps read Gabriel Tarde from this perspective).

3

Différance and Repetition: Thinking Différance as Individuation

We dream of reinventing invention on the far side of the programmed matrices.

Jacques Derrida[1]

25   The future of individuation and the question of repetition

Disindividuation is a deficient relation to potentiality, a failure of individuation, an inability to pass into action, that is, in the language of Simondon, an inability to individuate this potentiality as actuality, and through that to be an individual that individuates itself (in movement) rather than an individuated individual (hardened, in the sense that Adorno and Horkheimer describe stupidity as a hardening).[2] Nevertheless, disindividuation may and often does pave the way – and as an individuation that is pending, an individuation in waiting [*en souffrance*], that is, an individuation suffering as dis-individuation – for a *new form* of individuation, that is, for other chains.

Deleuze described this as a 'relation in which individuation brings the ground to the surface *without being able to give it form*'.[3] And it is this relation that he referred to as 'stupidity'.

It is because stupidity is the condition of individuation that it is possible for systemic stupidity to be established on a planetary scale.[4]

If systemic stupidity now dominates – and in some way rules, and even seems to be sovereign, even if this sovereignty is seen as regressive by many of those it crushes, who thus refuse to recognize it – this means that stupidity has reached such heights that its trans-formation seems impossible. But this feeling is possible only because, as I shall try to show in the remainder of this work, consumerist capitalism has taken control of the transindividuation process through a hegemonic monopolization of the retentional supports and systems that condition all psychic and collective individuation.[5]

This is what Deleuze described as the 'realization' of the universal by the market – and by marketing, which creates 'the market' and imposes its rule, the range of which itself extends across the planet. Marketing organizes the globalization of ways of life and the destruction of both psychic and collective individuation processes, processes that, as singularities, are obstacles to this 'universal'.

To think today's reign of stupidity, we must *think différance as individuation* in the Simondonian sense that inspired Deleuze.

Simondonian thought (and the Deleuzian thought that follows it) deconstructs oppositions and tries to conceive new kinds of relations (above all by surpassing the hylomorphic oppositional scheme, itself opposed to substantialism),[6] where what counts is not being, that is, the state, but the relation, that is, the process (which Simondon somewhat imprudently called *onto*-genesis). This makes it possible to think the conditions of appearance of new regimes of individuation – and to say why, for example, the mineral is not the vital, which in turn is not the psychosocial (rather than 'the human'). It thus also makes it possible to think the process of disindividuation and the new possibilities of collective individuation it thereby prepares – sometimes at the cost of horrific conflicts.

It is better to refer here to the psychosocial rather than the human. The wish constantly to track down and deconstruct the 'metaphysics of the proper of man' risks locking oneself in, and locking oneself into the question of man and the rights of man. Consider for example the following statement by Derrida in relation to the responsibility of the university in the context of globalization (of 'mondialization', of the universal as market), and especially of what he then called, in the American context in which the speech was delivered, the 'new Humanities'. It is a statement that, after 2008, seems truly stupid:

> The conceptual networks of man, of what is proper to man, of human rights, of crimes against the humanity of man, organizes, as we know, such a *mondialization* or worldwide-ization.
> This *mondialization* wishes to be a humanization.[7]

To *say* this is to *do* something stupid – given that today, a few years after the onset of the crisis and almost fifteen years after the speech in which Derrida pronounced these words at Stanford

University,[8] 'mondialization' has turned out to be the complete opposite of 'humanization'. This does not mean that we should instead
describe it as 'dehumanization' – a word that has never meant very
much. Rather, it must be understood as a massive, planetary-wide
disindividuation that, as we shall see, is caused by an immense process
of dis-apprenticeship in every sphere.

This question amounts to that of the future of individuation – of
psychosocial individuation, but also of vital and even mineral individuation (given that applied quantum mechanics now seems to individuate matter in new ways), in an age of globalization in which the
categories that were derived from classical cosmopolitanism are
becoming tragically ineffective. It is from this perspective, from this
question, and at this moment when there reigns, over the entire
planet, a systemic stupidity wherein all of us can say and do just
about anything, that I turn to this reading of Deleuze by Derrida.
This reading was ultimately a missed encounter, and this is a cause
for infinite regret, and even sadness, given that it is precisely through
these two great thinkers that we will need to try – in particular
through what initially brought them together, which was the
question of repetition – to repeat in other terms the questions asked
by Adorno, Horkheimer and Polanyi, and to do so in order to make
a difference.

26   Individuation and regression

Derrida argued in 2002 that Deleuze opposes animality and stupidity,
and he saw this as a repetition of a more general opposition between
humanity, for whom stupidity would be 'proper', and the animal. Yet
aside from the fact that stupidity is properly the improper – 'Well,
you're in the shit' [*Bah, te v'là propre*] – and even if Deleuze speaks
of 'stupidity as properly human bestiality',[9] I believe that the question
of the proper has *nothing* to do with Deleuze's concerns, precisely
because he thinks with Simondon.

Who, for that matter, has ever truly argued, for example – at least
since the collapse of the authority of Revelation in such matters, that
is, since the beginning of the age of the *Aufklärung* – that the vegetable is *opposed* to the mineral, which would mean that they have
nothing to do with each other? To do so would obviously be ridicu-
lous: plants are *made* of minerals. And who does not know that the
animal's regime (its rule or its sovereignty) is a kind of colony of
diverse cellular forms (in some way vegetative forms), more or less
governed by a neurovegetative organization, and dependent on

various mineral elements (such as magnesium and calcium, deficiencies of which, or the defective assimilation of which, may predispose one to suffering depression, which would thus be a matter of the vital organology of melancholy) – a cellular colony organized according to the rules of a species, and where in the animal kingdom the species would be, according to Simondon, the true individual?

Only a fool could be unaware of this. This is why Derrida states:

> I am not saying this to discredit the discourses that are doing everything they can to specify humanity as much as possible, a properly human character of bestiality and *bêtise*. Nor am I saying it to confound, to say that there is no difference between animals of a non-human type and human animals. On the contrary, it is to refine differential concepts that I am emphasizing a non-pertinence of the concepts and the logic that are employed to reserve the privilege of what one thinks one can define as *bestiality* and *bêtise*.[10]

Despite this, he seems to comprehend neither the concepts nor the logic involved in *Difference and Repetition*, and ignores the fact that Simondon supplies the preindividual funds on the basis of which Deleuze thinks, that is, individuates himself as a psychic individual. On the contrary, Derrida concludes his critique by suggesting that Deleuze's entire approach is in the final analysis founded on a profound misunderstanding.

Deleuze asks himself how stupidity is possible (a question that he thus says is 'properly transcendental'), and he answers, 'by virtue of the link between thought and individuation'. And he adds: 'This link is much more profound than that which appears in the "I think."'[11]

This question of the 'I think' is, we recall, the central subject of *Difference and Repetition*. Derrida, however, takes no account of this in the reading he proposes of the passage on stupidity – as if he had not even read the book from which he has extracted this quotation. Deleuze says that the individuated *I* is in some way an obstacle to psychic individuation, which is precisely *not reducible* to the *I*. As we have already seen: 'the I and the Ego are perhaps no more than indices of the species: of humanity as a species with divisions'.[12] If this is so, however, it is because of the following:

> The I [which is not] a species [...] implicitly contains what the species and kinds explicitly develop [...]. Individuation, by contrast [it is a matter here of *psychic* individuation as conceived by Simondon], has nothing to do with specification [the process through which a species individuates itself], that protracted [specification typical of the vital

individuation of a species as 'perpetuated individuation']. [Psychic individuation] consists in fields of fluid intensive factors that no more [than the specific form] take the form of an I than of an Ego.[13]

This does not mean that the psychic individual cannot be an *I*. But it is when it tends to be *reduced* to this being-an-*I* (in interindividuality) that it becomes stupid.

We have seen that the type of individuation that 'differs in kind from all specification [...] precedes and renders the latter possible'.[14] What this means is that to think the psychic individual *on the basis* of the individuated *I* is to miss the individuation *process* through which alone it is possible to think this individual. The *I* is the individuated outcome or fall-back position of individuation, its inevitable (re)lapse, and in this sense its disindividuation.

It is clear, therefore, that Derrida completely misreads *Difference and Repetition* when he writes of Deleuze:

This is to recognize *bêtise* as a thing of the 'Ego' or the 'I' [...], it is not to name something as a form of psychic life (whether or not one calls it ground or fund) that would not have the figure of the I or the Ego.[15]

What Derrida here says contra Deleuze – that there is a psychic form that does not have the figure of the *I* or the ego – is very clearly *precisely what Deleuze said*. It is thus absurd to accuse Deleuze of any 'egological' leanings, as Derrida does in the following:

One cannot reduce the whole of psychic or phenomenological experience to its egological form, and one cannot reduce the whole of the life of the Ego, all egological structure, to the conscious self.[16]

Derrida, here, goes totally astray:[17] *Difference and Repetition*, like Deleuze's work in general, is constituted precisely *against* such a perspective.[18] And when he speaks here of the *I*, it is by thinking the 'I think': he thinks and combats precisely the privilege given to the figure of consciousness insofar as it grounds the modern metaphysics that Derrida himself deconstructed, and in a way that was always kindred to the works of Gilles Deleuze and Félix Guattari.

27 Pharmacology of repetition as pharmacology of the unconscious

It is on the basis of Kierkegaard, Nietzsche and Freud, and on the ground of a Simondonian conceptuality that he very rarely cites

– although the bibliography of *Difference and Repetition* includes Simondon's *L'Individu et sa genèse physico-biologique*, published by Presses Universitaires de France six years before *Difference and Repetition* – that Deleuze thinks repetition as a 'selective test' that is not contemplation, but action.

> [It is a matter of making] something new of repetition itself; connecting it with a test, with a selective test; positing it as the supreme object of the will and of freedom. Kierkegaard specifies that [...] it is [...] a matter of acting, of *making* repetition [...] a novelty; that is, a freedom and a task of freedom. And Nietzsche: liberate the will from everything *that chains it* by making repetition the very object of willing.[19]

It is a question of links and chains – and these chains are *pharmaka*:

> No doubt repetition is already *that which chains*; but *if we die of repetition we are also saved and healed by it* – healed, above all, by the other repetition. The whole *mystical play of loss and salvation* is therefore contained in repetition, along with the *whole theatrical play of life and death* and the whole *positive play of illness and health* (cf., Zarathustra ill and Zarathustra convalescent by virtue of one and the same power which is that of repetition in the eternal return).[20]

Hence repetition presents itself as the pharmacological object par excellence.

As such, it is also what frames language and writing: it 'forms the real power of language in speech and writing'.[21] In short, this pharmacology of repetition has everything to do with the Derridian question of iteration (see the 'Introduction' to Husserl's 'Origin of Geometry'), of the trace, of archi-writing, of the supplement (see *Speech and Phenomena*, *Of Grammatology*) and of différance (see *Of Grammatology*, 'Différance'). *Difference and Repetition* was published in 1968, the year in which Derrida published his 'Différance' essay in *Tel quel* (a journal that Deleuze evidently read, citing it for example in *Difference and Repetition* in reference to Philippe Sollers), and one year after *Of Grammatology* and *Speech and Phenomena* – moreover, *Nietzsche and Philosophy* was published in 1962, as was Derrida's 'Introduction' to Husserl's 'Origin of Geometry'.[22]

Simondon posited that the great philosophical error consisted in wanting to think individuation (genesis) on the basis of the individual (being). It is, on the contrary, from the process (individuation) that it is possible to know the individuated (that individuals are), which this individuation exceeds and to which it is never reducible, precisely because it carries within it, or along with it, preindividual funds. Yet it remains inherently impossible to know individuation,[23] because it is always unfinished, that is, 'différante'.

This is the perspective from which Deleuze *begins*, when he tries to think difference as constituted in repetition, and he does so in a way that is quite close to that of Derrida during the same period: repetition and iterability are questions of différance, and the latter is another name for individuation – even if Derrida is unaware of this – insofar as it puts to work a difference that is always 'older' than any identity.[24]

It is thus tremendously disappointing that by 2002 Derrida seems to have become insensitive to Deleuzian questions – and that his argument that Deleuze thinks the psyche on the basis of the ego or the *I* seems so ill-judged. For repetition (of which the *I* and the ego are instances) is what Deleuze thinks as the very question of the unconscious, on the basis of the repetition compulsion that Freud discovered in 1920 while treating the traumatic neuroses of those wounded in the First World War, and through which he will then think the death drive and the relations between Eros and Thanatos.

In *Beyond the Pleasure Principle* (of which in 1980 Derrida will himself propose a reading, in *The Post Card*), according to Deleuze:

> The death instinct is discovered [...] as a result of a direct considera-
> tion of repetition phenomena. Strangely, the death instinct serves as a
> positive, originary principle for repetition; this is its domain and its
> meaning. It plays the role of a transcendental principle, whereas the
> pleasure principle is only psychological.[25]

Through the 'relation between repetition and disguises [...] disguises found in the work of dreams or symptoms',[26] the question of
the id is constituted. But, Deleuze continues:

> [The] disguise is then understood [by Freud] from the perspective of a
> simple opposition of forces; disguised repetition is only the fruit of a
> secondary compromise between the opposed forces of the Ego and the
> Id.[27]

Deleuze was no doubt too hasty in presuming that Freud *opposes* the ego and the id, given that in 1923 Freud, repeating and paraphras-ing Georg Groddeck, posited that 'what we call our ego behaves essentially passively in life, and that, as he expresses it, we are "lived" by unknown and uncontrollable forces'.[28]

With Groddeck, Freud defined the id as precisely what in some way *embraces* both the ego and the unconscious, and in particular the necessarily non-conscious part of the ego, which censors on behalf of consciousness insofar as it submits the pleasure principle to the reality principle. *Beyond the Pleasure Principle* received this title because it was in fact a matter of going beyond not just a principle but an *opposition*, and an opposition not just of the reality and pleasure principles, but of those functions of which the psychic apparatus is constituted that put these principles to work.

Freud did not begin to pursue this path until 1920. And it was not until 1923 that, in 'The Ego and the Id', he would write that 'an individual [is] a psychical id, unknown and unconscious, upon whose surface rests the ego, developed from its nucleus the *Pcpt.* System'.[29] In analysing these texts, what Deleuze laments is the place of repression, which in Freud in some way unifies the ego and the id. Freud does indeed write:

> The repressed merges into the id as well, and is merely a part of it. The repressed is only cut off sharply from the ego by the resistances of repression; it can communicate with the ego through the id.[30]

In objecting to this, Deleuze responds that the true question is the pharmacological interpretation of repetition. This, he claims, is the basis on which repression must be thought, not the other way around. Whereas:

> Freud interpreted the death instinct [which was his point of departure for thinking the repetition compulsion] as a tendency to return to the state of inanimate matter, thereby maintaining the model of a wholly physical or material repetition.[31]

That is, he did not confer upon it any pharmacological positivity, which is the issue in Kierkegaardian and Nietzschean styles of thought.

Deleuze's whole point is to begin with repetition, with a pharmacological field of possibility (*'loss and salvation* [...] *illness and health'*), and to think the process of repression *on the basis* of these possibilities and this field as structured by the play of the drives, and especially by the death drive that governs the repetition compulsion. Deleuze, however, is not unaware of but apparently overlooks the fact that, on the basis of repression, Freud did assert that in principle the ego and the id are not opposed: the id exceeds any simple opposition between the ego and the unconscious, and in a way encompasses them.

Be that as it may, for Deleuze, what is at stake behind this question, from which emerges a form of disindividuation as repression, is a way of thinking repression as a case of repetition:

> I do not repeat because I repress. I repress because I repeat [...]. I can live certain things or certain experiences only in the mode of repetition. [...] *Eros must be repeated, can be lived only through repetition, whereas Thanatos (as transcendental principle) is that which gives repetition to Eros, that which submits Eros to repetition.*[32]

Deleuze thus returns to the pharmacology of repetition as pharmacology of the unconscious, and where the pivot is transference:

> Becoming conscious counts for little. The more theatrical and dramatic operation by which healing takes place – or does not take place – has a name: transference. Now transference is still repetition: above all it is repetition. If repetition makes us ill, it also heals us; if it enchains and destroys us, it also frees us, testifying in both cases to its 'demonic' power.[33]

The individuation that is the history of the psychic apparatus – constituted through the sedimentation of experience – is here in some way a pharmacological linkage of repetitions, which are chains as well as unchainings.

Having recalled all this, we cannot follow Derrida when, after having reproached Deleuze for 'reducing the whole of psychic or phenomenological experience to its egological form, and [...] reducing all life of the Ego, all egological structure, to the conscious self',[34] he suggests that Deleuze *would not know* that 'a form of psychic life (whether one call it ground or not) [...] would not have the figure of the I or the Ego',[35] and that 'in the self-relation of the living being, there is some non-ego, on the one hand, and there is even, Freud would say, some of the Ego that is unconscious'.[36] Deleuze is indeed, of course, aware of this, and it is precisely what he problematizes – even if it is indeed unfortunate that Deleuze was not clearer about the position of the id.

Behind all these questions, it is for Deleuze a matter of thinking time no longer on the basis of consciousness, but on the basis of a passive synthesis carried out by repetition (as condition of the unconscious):

> Time is constituted only in the originary synthesis which operates on the *repetition* of instants. This synthesis contracts the successive

independent instants into one another, thereby constituting the lived, or living, present. [...] [T]his synthesis must be given a name: passive synthesis.[37]

But it was also on the basis of the question of a passive synthesis – which he located in Husserl – that Derrida began his own career, with his first research work in 1953, entitled *The Problem of Genesis in Husserl's Philosophy*.[38]

I have myself tried to return to these first steps and to think passive synthesis on the basis of tertiary retention[39] – and I shall return to this subject in the second part of this book in order to think the pharmacological and organological situation of the contemporary university, and, on the basis of these considerations, to think its responsibility at the moment when tertiary retention has become the main product of an industrial system that is itself globalized.

28 Shadow zones: the *Aufklärung* after the discovery of the unconscious

Why insist on all these questions here? Because behind the questions of reason (actualized as rational knowledge and maturity) and unreason (stupidity and madness), which cannot simply be opposed, there lie the play and the role of the unconscious, which the *Aufklärung* was obviously incapable of thinking – the play of Light and Shade, Enlightenment and Darkness, and of shadows, which Nietzsche tried to think several years prior to Freud.

The discovery of the unconscious was the true break between classical philosophy and twentieth-century thought. In Derrida and in Deleuze, this discovery is combined with that of passive synthesis. But the philosophical work needed in order to think with Freud and after Freud remains, today, still largely incomplete. And so too is the work that psychoanalysis needs to do in order to think with philosophy – even if Jacques Lacan travelled some distance along this path.

But whereas 'French theory' failed to create much public debate around the differences between the various analyses of the question of the Shadow, of shadows and of Enlightenments, entirely new questions for philosophy and for rational knowledge in general, at the very same time psycho-technologies were being developed, making it possible to set up a psycho-power that drew upon the discovery of the unconscious in the most pragmatic way possible:

- by establishing, through marketing, the *global consumerist model*, in taking control of behavioural models, that is, processes of transindividuation (I return to this in the second part);
- by leading an ideological war against the state (the public thing) and disarming all forms of public authority that might impede the *spread of privatization* advocated by neoliberal ideology, through a strategy of shock that goes beyond the 'shock doctrine' described by Naomi Klein – and does so by taking Schumpeter's 'Creative Destruction' to extremes.[40]

In 1944, Adorno and Horkheimer warned that 'if enlightenment does not undertake work that reflects on this regressive moment, it seals its own fate'.[41] Some twenty years later, at almost the same time, and in terms and from perspectives that were ultimately very close, Derrida and Deleuze both 'undertook' such 'work'. Two careers were thereby inaugurated that, while continually evolving, increasingly left the critique of political economy in the shadows, as well as the critique of this critique, that is, discussion of its fundamental concepts, such as that of knowing in what consists the relations between reproduction, work, supplement and repetition. Or again, they left in the shadows any discussion of how to interpret the propositions and counter-propositions concerning the concepts of ideology and hegemony in relation to these notions of supplement, repetition, différance and individuation, and of how to do so in the context of an industrialization founded on grammatization and repetition, and so on.

The new critique of political economy absolutely demanded by this approach never saw the light of day, despite the preliminary attempt that was *Capitalism and Schizophrenia*.[42] And no theoretical dialogue between Louis Althusser and Jacques Derrida ever took place, as Derrida testifies in his interview with Michael Sprinker, published under the title 'Politics and Friendship':

> I was thus paralyzed [before Althusser, declares Derrida], silent, before something that resembled a sort of theoreticism, a hypostasis of Theory with a capital 'T', before a bit too emphatic or grandiloquent use of capital letters with regard to *the* theory, with regard to *the* science. All of that seemed to me quite worrisome, problematic, precritical [...]. I thus found myself walled in by a sort of tormented silence.[43]

> I would have liked to have had a long discussion with him and his friends and ask them to respond to questions I felt necessary. The fact is, as strange as it might seem, this discussion never took place. [...] An intellectual sociology of this dimension of French intellectual or

academic life remains to be undertaken and notably of that *normalien* milieu in which the practice of avoidance is stupefying.[44]

But is this merely a matter of sociology? And, what is more, of a merely French sociology? I believe otherwise: I believe it is a matter of the philosophical problem of the epoch itself, localized in France, and of which these peculiarities are symptoms.

In this way 'churches' were established, as one says – and between them lie the shadow zones within which we still wander:

> There were *camps*, strategic alliances, maneuvers of encirclement and exclusion. Some forces in this merciless *Kampfplatz* grouped around Lacan, others around Foucault, Althusser, Deleuze. When it had any, that period's diplomacy (war by other means) was that of avoidance: silence, one doesn't cite or name, everyone distinguishes himself and everything forms a sort of archipelago of discourse without earthly communication, without visible passageway.[45]

We, almost seventy years after *Dialectic of Enlightenment*, and more than forty years after the publication of *Of Grammatology* and *Difference and Repetition*, wandering among the ruins of warring capitalism like shades in the shadow zones, have the impression that *nothing* has yet truly taken place in terms of thinking this regression and this unreason. We have come to believe (falsely) that these works and projects have ultimately come to nothing, have led to nothing, to nothing decisive, that nothing has been learned, that nothing good has been turned into 'action' by repetition, nor by acting from within repetition, that is, within différance. That nothing can be done to counteract this situation that leads to the self-destruction of reason, that is, to generalized disindividuation.

And that is not all: some among us have come to believe that these poststructuralist projects have only aggravated the situation, or that they could even be, if not the only cause, then at least one of the causes. And if this is indeed the case, as some sincerely believe (as Rainer Rochlitz undoubtedly did, when he defended critical theory against deconstruction),[46] then this is because this work and these projects ground to a halt while still en route. They have stumbled at difficult hurdles; those who encountered these difficulties became tired; they aged; they died; in one case they committed suicide. The general feeling is that, despite having prepared for countless calamities of every kind, each more disarming than the last, this thought found itself in some way disarmed in advance: its weapons had been laid down and the struggle abandoned.

Thinking, and especially philosophical thinking, is a struggle – and firstly, particularly in philosophy, a struggle against oneself and with oneself, that is, with one's shadow, in reckoning with it, and in counting on it. In this shadow, the social dimension of the unconscious and the collective dimension of psychic individuation are in play: this is what Nietzsche said, then Simondon, and it is what Deleuze and Guattari in turn repeated.

Is a rearmament possible, presuming that a disastrous disarmament of thinking did effectively occur (which can be vigorously and legitimately contested in a thousand ways: all kinds of other thoughts the future of which remain invisible to us are yet to take place), after the old arms have become obsolete (this is what Deleuze implied through his call, five years before his death, to 'look for new weapons')?[47]

29   The pharmacological arsenal beyond reason

This rearmament of thinking is possible only on the condition of grasping that the *pharmakon* – that is, repetition, which is also to say technics in general, and the mnemotechnics constituting tertiary retention in particular – is the *condition of articulation* of Light and Shade, Enlightenment and Darkness, consciousness and the unconscious, psychic individuation and collective individuation, and on the condition of grasping that psycho-power, in its economic and ideological struggle, and put at the direct service of financialization[48] after the 'petrol shock' of the 1970s, has seized hold of this articulation. Here, the 'body without organs' has disarmed many readers of *Capitalism and Schizophrenia* – and has for a long time set up a misunderstanding between deconstruction and schizo-analysis.[49]

To rethink and rearm thought is to rethink the *pharmakon* itself as arm, as weapon – and, of course, as a double-edged sword. And this means that the feeling that ultimately nothing came to pass in France in the final quarter of the twentieth century is an illusion – even if this illusion was provoked by real impasses. The critique of reason insofar as it can engender unreason was the very object of what eventually came to be called 'deconstruction': this way of philosophizing typically shows that everything that poses itself to thought, and imposes itself on thought as that which claims to found it, inevitably tends to engender its contrary, and that what is thereby posed is not opposed to, but *is already* ('always already') itself *in, that which thus opposes itself*. I hope I have shown that the perspective of *Difference and Repetition* is very close to this way of thinking.

Precisely because this trait typifies deconstruction, it seems to many that this led to an exhaustion of critical power itself (and with it of theory, understood for example in Althusser's sense of the term). Critical power, so it seems, became incapable of 'passing into action', deconstruction having *dazzled* thought (broken its limbs, immobilized it by fascinating it) by establishing within it an undecidable situation. This undecidability was constantly and increasingly claimed by Derrida throughout his writings on deconstruction, as if the fate of post-metaphysical philosophy was to become foolish, in fact to become an ass, and not just any ass: that of the accursed and sceptical scholar and priest, Jean Buridan, who returns in Spinoza as an ass, and who kept waiting for a thought of metastability.[50]

The philosophical concept of metastability is Simondon's main contribution to the philosophy of freedom, that is, of autonomy and responsibility, and it is a concept sorely lacking in deconstruction. And perhaps the metaphysical concept par excellence, of all the concepts of 'metaphysics', is *equilibrium*. A crisis is an instance of disequilibrium in which a critical necessity arises as the need for decision – that is, above all, for discerning. Deconstruction, however, cultivates great ambiguity about the critical possibility itself, including about the concept of crisis itself.[51] There is in this regard an immense amount that remains unsaid, and this is undoubtedly one of the most disarming and paralysing factors in relation to this thought.

Using this as a pretext to give up teaching deconstruction and more generally what in America is called poststructuralism would, however, amount to a new calamity, and a new step in the regression of reason. I do not at all believe that the thinkers of that epoch, in France, ever abandoned either reason or critique – even if they continually challenged, interrogated and denounced the oppositional schemes on which, since Plato, these have been grounded.

This is the case, for Deleuze and for Derrida (this at least is what I attempt to show in this chapter), precisely because each of them unearthed a pharmacological dimension of reason, and of that which constitutes its condition, beyond reason as the power of unifying, namely: *difference* – as différance and as repetition.

This enterprise may indeed, at least on certain points (but on the decisive points), have to a certain extent slowed down: it has not come to a halt, but it has in a sense got bogged down 'midway', and it must be dug out of this bog and recovered. Such statements may in some quarters seem shocking. But those who would be shocked are those who do not want to hear that the fate of any thought is to call up other thoughts that it alone would have been able to incite, but that it was not itself capable of thinking – because the time had not yet come: philosophy is that dove that, always in the end partially deaf to itself (in its metastable situation), in times that themselves 'come on doves' feet', needs air to fly, and always comes too late to its becoming-an-ass, discovering itself very nice/an owl [*très chouette*].[52]

This *air* is what Marx called both matter and history, and it is what, since Galileo, must be observed (as matter in History) by means of instruments, which are *pharmaka*.[53]

A recovery and a de-bogging, or a *repairing* of thought (which has accidents when it runs out of fuel),[54] on the basis of that thought referred to as poststructuralism, is possible only by trying to understand what, when and how elements of fatigue, disarmament and loss of vigilance could occur along its route.

After the critical approach of Adorno and Horkheimer, the 'post-critical' approach of poststructuralism in some way opened up a site for a pharmacology of that historical reason that was the *Aufklärung*. The need for such a pharmacology of reason was foreshadowed by Adorno and Horkheimer themselves, given that for them rationality appeared self-destructive in its origins. Nevertheless, they themselves, in 1944, still left in obscurity the pharmacological dimension as such – as passing from an inherently heterogeneous *pharmakon* to reason itself defined as autonomy – by ignoring, for example in the chapter devoted to those industries of cultural goods that they saw as a major cause of regression, the always artefactual dimension of the imagination, and by returning to the Kantian question of transcendental imagination and the schematism.

Some years later, Marcuse, in his critique of what he called the 'performance principle', would himself fail in his attempt to think the articulation of the Freudian libidinal economy with the consumerist capitalist economy, because he too was unable to see the organological and therefore pharmacological dimension of desire itself[55] – which constitutes, I argue, the very horizon of *Difference and Repetition*.

The Frankfurt School seems to have locked itself into a conception of reason that remains very metaphysical, despite its Marxist claims (and according to Derrida this was a problem that he still found in certain respects in Althusser). Because of this, when, in 1968, the thinkers of critical theory became central to the social critique and student movement under way in France, Germany and California, the poststructuralist philosophies tended not only to rid themselves of the Frankfurt School's way of formulating these questions, but in fact to ignore them altogether – and ultimately to forget them, and to forget at the same time the kind of *vigilance* for which the Frankfurt School had been calling.

30   Decisions, incisions, discouragement

Deconstruction unfolded along these lines because from the outset Derrida conceived this work not as a decision *of* thought (for example, of *his* thought), but as thinking generated by a process that operates prior to thought, and that works *outside the subject*, if one can put it like this (after Jean Hyppolite),[56] and as the work of différance through the history of the supplement. And it would thus be a process that is in a way the preindividual condition of this thought called 'deconstruction', even if the process would therefore also produce itself[57] *through* this thinking, *with* it and *in* it, by individuating itself, and above all as the test or event of disindividuation, one translation of which would be the critique of the subject.

> Perhaps patient meditation and painstaking investigation on and around what is still provisionally called writing [...] are the wanderings of a way of thinking that is faithful and attentive to the ineluctable world of the future which proclaims itself at present, beyond the closure of knowledge. The future can only be anticipated in the form of an absolute danger. It is that which breaks absolutely with constituted normality and can only be proclaimed, *presented*, as a sort of monstrosity.[58]

The 'monstrosity' of what will occur is therefore not a failure of reason, Derrida writes here, but, so to speak, 'revelation'. It takes place through the contemporary history of what *Of Grammatology* called the 'supplement', that supplementarity that would always already inhabit reason and its knowledge. Knowledge and reason are here declared closed for this very reason, and this would also be true because rationality, having become techno-logical (in this instance a generalized programmatology through the extension of the 'concept of programme'),[59] has reached a stage of rationalization, reification and proletarianization that explodes the great conceptual divisions of metaphysics (intelligible/sensible, inside/outside, subject/object, and so on, oppositions characteristic of the 'metaphysics of presence', the 'modern subject', and so forth).

Such an analysis thus requires a wholly other problematic than that of the Frankfurt School, which remains a philosophy of 'mastery'. Supplementarity, which is always a kind of incision, thus deconstructs long before 'deconstruction' and its 'decisions' (which therefore aren't). Supplementarity: that is, facticity, artificiality and prostheticity (themes taken up in *The Beast and the Sovereign* in a way that must one day be analysed,[60] and that concern the State, the Leviathan, that is, that sea monster that is the Whale, politics as power, and so on). Facticity, artificiality and prostheticity have always inhabited, and have always been the condition of, all critique, all *logos*, all *Aufklärung*, all subjectivation, all autonomy and all responsibility, all existence, all *Da-sein*, and so on and so forth.

The fact remains that, re-reading Adorno, Horkheimer and Polanyi in 2011, that is, at the moment when the 'ratings' of various nations, including the United States, are being lowered by 'ratings agencies', as if nations were children – that is, minors – to be marked and graded by the 'rationality of the market', that is, by the international rationalization and destruction of reason (and here I am clearly intending the double genitive); re-reading Adorno, Horkheimer and Polanyi in 2011, therefore, and then re-reading Derrida and all the thinkers who would constitute so-called French thought,[61] one cannot help but wonder if they too let slip an 'unthought' of the *Aufklärung*, to which Adorno and Horkheimer referred. And one wonders if, ultimately, this poststructuralist period, including Deleuze and Foucault as well as Derrida and Lyotard (who is often confounded with so-called 'postmodern' thought),[62] did not sometimes constitute, rationalize[63] and ultimately legitimate this backwards step, this withdrawal and this regression.

One might be tempted to say, and in certain respects I do not hesitate to state it myself: in its great unfinished state (and the magnitude of incompleteness – constitutive of any process of individuation – that thinking makes it possible to sense, is what pushes thinking further along, even if it cannot make this incompleteness intelligible to itself), that thinking elaborated in France between 1960 and 2000 through these imposing personalities has left its heirs disarmed, and in a way the inheritance of this thought has indubitably led to a veritable sterilization of thinking itself. This sterilization often gives the impression of rationalizing and legitimating the abandonment of any thought of an alternative, by suggesting, for example, that there is in fact *no* alternative to the state of fact leading to universal unreason other than 'resistance', confronted with a kind of inevitability of stupidity and of performance imposed as a new regime of knowledge-become-'informational commodity'.[64]

'Stupidity always triumphs, it is always, in the war we are talking about, on the side of the victor.'[65] So says Derrida in his final seminar.

Such a thought, which is in fact a kind of testament, is profoundly discouraging.

If we must now inherit the thoughts left to us by these thinkers, if we must build upon this heritage, we must move on from it via the question of a positive pharmacology, by breaking with the discourse of 'resistance'. And this must be done via the question of invention, and according to a non-metaphysical conception of invention, thought as a quantum leap into individuation within and beyond reason, in a complex of moments that weave a threefold process of individuation: at once psychic, social and technical – wherein repetition, supplementarity and tertiary retention together constitute the primordial element, an 'element' that is always already 'supplementary', an *elementary supplementarity*.

31   Alternatives, imagination and invention

Tertiary retention is what, in *Imagination et invention*, Simondon referred to as the object-image – an instance of which would be what I myself have called the image-object:[66] 'Almost all objects produced by man are in some degree object-images.'[67] Like that *pharmakon* that text is for Plato, these object-images disseminate and proliferate. And throughout this dissemination, they bring about psychic individuation processes and collective individuation processes:

> Object-images are almost like organisms, or at least the germs capable of living and developing within the subject. Even outside the subject, through exchanges and group activities, they multiply, propagate and reproduce in the neotenic state.[68]

Simondon thinks here (in 1965) what Derrida would later call 'dissemination'.[69] That these object-images are in the neotenic state means that they are waiting to be imagined, that is, received: the object-image is both a fruit *of* the imagination and a fruit *for* the imagination:

> Imagination is not only the activity of producing or evoking images, but also the way of receiving images concretized in an object, the discovery of their meaning.[70]

It is the mind or spirit that is here made of images:

> The generator of images that is the mind is therefore comparable to the generator of cells that is the body: the cells are in interaction with

one another; so too, images; they result, in a state of reason and wake-
fulness, in a mutual equilibrium.[71]

The retentions that form memory are composed of images, from
which protentions are projected, that is, anticipations,[72] which are
also images: time is composed of images of the past, present and
future.

Imagination is constituted through these *mental images* that
support object-images and that develop in three steps:

> First, pure and spontaneous growth [...], each image, an embryo of
> motor and perceptive activity, develops here for itself [...]. Next, the
> image becomes a way of receiving information coming from the milieu
> and a source of schemes that respond to these stimulations. [...]
> Finally, [...] affective-emotive repercussions that organize images
> according to a systematic mode of linkages, evocations and communi-
> cations; a genuinely mental mode.[73]

It is through these three stages that the 'generator of images' is
constituted, through which invention occurs:

> These images undergo successive mutations that modify their mutual
> relations by passing from a primitive state of mutual independence to
> an interdependent phase at the moment they encounter the object, then
> necessarily to a final state of systematic connection where primitive
> kinetic energies become tensions for a system. Invention could then be
> considered *a change of organization* of the system of adult images,
> bringing mental activity, through a change of level, to a new stage of
> free images, enabling the recommencement of a genesis: invention
> would be a rebirth of the cycle of images making it possible to address
> the milieu with new anticipations [...], in other words, invention
> produces a change of level; it marks the end of a cycle and the begin-
> ning of a new cycle, each cycle comprising three phases – anticipation,
> experience, systematization.[74]

These three types of mental images, supported by object-images,
are founded on *a priori images* constituted on a specific biological
basis, that is, based on the species, a vital modality that prefigures
all forms of movement, sensoriality and perception – which constitute
the matrices of sensorimotor loops. These a priori images are a kind
of biologically engrammed capacity for anticipation, and are revealed
by so-called '*Leerlaufreaktion* in ethology, empty activities' that
reflect the fact that 'in the development of species, as perhaps with

that of individuals, *motor ability precedes sensoriality*, as long-term behavioural anticipation'.[75]

From such a perspective, invention would be a reorganization of the dynamic field and thus of the potential formed by the generator of mental images, linked with object-images, on the ground of a priori images, occurring during a cycle that results in new capacities for anticipation, in which '*a rebirth of the cycle of images* makes it possible to address the milieu with new anticipations'.[76]

Such a circulation, which forms circuits (that I argue must be thought as circuits of transindividuation formed by retentions, protentions and attentions, themselves composed of images), arises from the *phase differences* constitutive of individuation – that is, of différance – and in which, in the emergence of an invention, 'solutions appear, as *restitutions of continuity*, allowing the operative procedures to progress along a previously invisible pathway of the given reality'.[77]

A linkage (a continuity) thus occurs, that is, a growth from out of psychosocial preindividual funds. This production of a phase difference, however, always results in a tension, that is, a problem between the individual and the milieu, a problem to which invention comes along as the resolution:

> Invention is the emergence of an extrinsic compatibility between the milieu and the organism, and of an intrinsic compatibility between the sub-systems of action.[78]

Derrida himself referred to invention in a way almost directly opposed to this, whereby invention seems in a way to *cause incompatibility*:

> An invention always presupposes some illegality, the breaking of an implicit contract; it inserts a disorder into the peaceful ordering of things, it disregards the proprieties.[79]

But such a perspective on invention, which is very classical, and which seems self-evident, starts from invention as origin of the dynamism of the process, and as initial disorder, whereas Simondon starts from the process in order to think the dynamic necessity of invention as cycle, and as circulation within the metastability of the process.

Nevertheless, in *Psyche: Inventions of the Other*, Derrida proposes a kind of supplementary genealogy of invention (which is always an invention of supplements), in which he emphasizes the *singularity of the question of invention today*, that is, in the context of industrial technology:

> If the word 'invention' is going through a rebirth, on a ground of anguished exhaustion but also out of a desire to reinvent invention itself, including its very status, this is perhaps because, on a scale incommensurable with that of the past, what is called a patentable 'invention' is now programmed, that is, subjected to powerful movements of authoritarian prescription and anticipation of the widest variety. And that is as true in the domains of art or the fine arts as in the technoscientific domain. Everywhere the enterprise of knowledge and research is first of all a programmatics of inventions. We could evoke the politics of publishing, the orders of booksellers or art merchants, studies of the market, cultural policies, whether state-promoted or not, and the politics of research and, as we say these days, the 'orientations' that this politics imposes throughout our institutions of higher education; we could also evoke all the institutions, private or public, capitalist or not, that declare themselves to be organs for producing and orienting invention.[80]

We shall return to this supplementary genealogy in the second half of this work. Let us merely add for now that in passing through the *ars inveniendi* of Leibniz, Derrida places tertiary retention at the heart of the question. And yet he nevertheless evacuates from this question any politics of invention capable of taking the *pharmakon* as its object – a fact that, all things considered, in the end locks deconstruction into a depressive, anti-inventive and anti-alternative discourse of 'resistance'.[81]

32   The masks of reason and the responsibility of the university

There is nothing to *do, say* or *think* to counter stupidity, which is always the foundering of reason, there is nothing to do, say or think against unreason, reversing and inverting the conquest of majority that for Kant was the whole meaning of the *Aufklärung*, there is 'no alternative' to the pigsty: this is what a herd-become-stupid has been convinced of by an enormous ideological machine. A herd-become-stupid: that is, stunned and stupefied by a shock doctrine that is the properly political dimension of psycho-power, of which so many of us, among the academics, have become the 'rationalizers' and the 'shepherds' – those who produce rationalizations as camouflage of motives and as resistance (in the Freudian sense[82] about which Derrida also speculated), those who, as Georges Didi-Huberman put it, 'take the mask of reason'.[83]

This rationalizing machine, which is being rationalized in the Freudian sense by those it rationalizes in the Weberian sense, this machine from which no one can completely escape (no one can avoid stupidity), is a psycho-power machine insofar as it has power over noetic souls. And it has this power because such souls are always fundamentally regressive and prone to stupidity, an inclination that is *systemically*[84] and *systematically*[85] exploited, not by a manipulation plotted and engineered through evil intentions, but by the blind establishment of a systemic stupidity that is inherent in a consumerist model founded on soliciting the drives.

The ideological machine that has been deliberately and systematically grafted onto this systemic stupidity – and that has also encouraged, proliferated and ultimately imposed it as its very hegemony – is in the first place constituted not as a theory but as a process. And this is all the more difficult to combat since this imposition occurs through an *immense dis-apprenticeship*.

Whereas the formation and training of the individual, as citizen, producer, designer, inventor (artist, politician, administrator, technician, and so on), is posited as an absolute priority, imperative for any modern society – that is, industrial society – founded on the democratic ideal, the *reality* of the consumerist development of this industrial society has led to the generalized de-formation of knowledge. It has led, that is, to the disindividuation and reification of knowledge, which can then do nothing but undergo a massive inversion into stupidity, and lead to universal unreason, that is, to the ruin of democracy.

Schools and universities have themselves internalized this fate, or else they have been pushed into doing so. This is the cause of that lack of well-being, that being-ill [*mal-être*], that academics and teachers have been afflicted with for a considerable time. But so too have parents and students:

> Could we agree to debate together about the responsibility proper to the university? [...] Of this I am not sure, and herein lies a being-ill [*mal-être*] no doubt more serious than a malaise or a crisis. [...] But we lack the categories for analyzing this being-ill.[86]

This being-ill derives from *disarmament* – academics are disarmed and feel bad because the 'code' is no longer relevant:

> It is an im-pertinence of the code, which can go hand in hand with the
> greatest power, which lies, perhaps, at the source of this being-ill. For
> if a code guaranteed a problematic [...], then we would feel better in
> the university. But we feel bad, who would dare to say otherwise?[87]

These lines were written in 1980: Derrida, Deleuze, Foucault and
Lyotard emerged at the very moment this malaise was installed and
began to grow, precisely as the blind establishment of systemic stupidity by psycho-power.

Together these thinkers formed – despite their misunderstandings,
and through them, and even thanks to them – one of the greatest
moments in the history of French thought, built upon the structuralist euphoria that combined Saussurian linguistics, anthropology,
Marxism and psychoanalysis, and that became widespread social
convictions, if not indeed beliefs, and ultimately dogmas. But if they
did so, they also transformed what resulted from the structuralist
approach – the question of the role of anthropological systems and
structures, and the fall into disuse of the question of the purely and
originally autonomous subject. They transformed it into deconstruction, hyper-critique, and so on, at the same time transforming the
possibility of theory (exposed to the risk of 'theoreticism')[88] and the
problem of alienation.

These new pathways attempted to think above and beyond the
theory of alienation and the struggle for emancipation. The latter
were supposedly founded, according to Lyotard, on the 'narratology'
of 'grand narratives'[89] charged with unifying the language games that
would be the different regimes of discourse in which incompatible
types of knowledge consist, and with suturing the 'differend', of
which Kantian reason, split into an archipelago of faculties, would
be the general matrix.[90] These pathways were not trodden in the
course of some touristic wandering of thought that turned out to be
more or less vaguely 'postmodern': they were grafted upon, and
pathways through the experience of, a thought of heteronomy that
seemed to have become irreducible (as repetition, simulacrum, supplement, schize, language games, technologies of power older than
any law, and so on – all the masks of reason authorizing all the
rationalizations).

It is from these paths, about which the question today is to know
where they might lead us, that Derrida reopened, at the end of the
1990s, the question of the *responsibility of the university*. For what
is the University (if we must capitalize the first letter of this word, as
is done with 'the Enlightenment') responsible? What distinguishes

and what links the responsibility and autonomy of the University or autonomy and reason *in* the University, and so on? Let us bluntly ask, instead: does the University in all its components not bear responsibility for this global unreason, if not indeed universal unreason, which seems to have taken hold of us, the latecomers of the twenty-first century, wherever on Earth we happen to be?

> The notion of responsibility would have to be re-elaborated within an entirely novel problematic. In the relations of the university to society, in the production, structure, archiving, and transmission of knowledges and technologies (of forms of knowledge as technologies), in the political stakes of knowledge, in the very idea of knowledge and truth, lies the advent of something entirely other.[91]

This excerpt from *Du droit à la philosophie*, published in 1989, but taken from a text written in 1980, was therefore delivered one year after the publication of Jean-François Lyotard's *The Postmodern Condition*, to which we must now return.

But before we do so, I would like, without delay and in concluding this chapter, to get straight to the point: that other notion of responsibility, which must be forged, passes through what I will call in the second part of this work an *organology* of knowledge, through which occurs 'something entirely other' – an organology of the trace and of repetition (and of stupidity, and of invention) conceived as a positive pharmacology in différance (which is also to say, as transference, working-through and anamnesis).[92]

4

Après Coup, the Differend

All this remains to be thought out, tried out.

Jean-François Lyotard[1]

33 Silence, language, technology, testimony

An organology of knowledge – capable of rendering an account of what affects the contemporary university, where according to Derrida 'the advent of something entirely other' is occurring – is today sorely lacking, given that it consists in the study of the organizational complexes[2] and processes of individuation and disindividuation made possible by specific forms and arrangements of tertiary retentions.

The total absence of any critique of that system of which the ratings agencies are merely the visible face, but which suddenly make clear the liquidation of all political sovereignty at any geographic scale we care to think of, is a terrible and flagrant symptom of a disarmament of thought. What thought is confronted with is a becoming, a development, wherein technology is the weapon held in common in a global economic war. The precise identities of all the protagonists in this war may remain unclear, but the outcome of the battle – which can and must lead to a peace treaty[3] – passes through the redefinition of the conditions of arrangement between psychic individuation, collective individuation and technical individuation.[4]

Such a redefinition is the very object of politics, and in particular of that grand politics that tackles the tasks of political constitution. Entry into the political sphere (into the *polis*) coincides with exit from war – *polemos* becomes logical disputation and the weapons become those of the law. The challenge of peace today is to transform the weapons of war (that is, of barbarism), supplied by technology to a psycho-power subservient to financial capitalism, into technologies of the spirit at the service of logical disputations[5] within a civil peace.

The current 'silence of the intellectuals' about the global economico-political situation, the economic war to which it has led, and the chances for a peaceful outcome of this war, is 'deafening'[6] – aside from a few notable exceptions, such as the three Portuguese economists previously mentioned from the universities of Coimbra and Lisbon, or, in France, Paul Jorion.

'Silence of the intellectuals' was a phrase used in *Le Monde* on 16 July 1983 by Max Gallo, then spokesman for the socialist government that had at that time been in power for two years. This phrase, according to Jean-François Lyotard's summary of his remarks, called on 'intellectuals' to 'open the debate on the "transformation" France requires in order to "catch up" in economic and social matters'.[7]

In March of that year, the government formed under new prime minister Laurent Fabius had 'turned to austerity'. On 8 October 1983, in the same newspaper, Lyotard analysed and commented on Gallo's appeal in the following terms:

> What exactly does he mean by 'intellectuals'? His appeal is really an appeal for ideas people, experts, decision makers. Of course it is an appeal for intelligences, but for intelligences who take on or will have to take on administrative, economic, social, and cultural responsibilities, or for intelligences who at least debate or will debate the aforementioned 'transformation' without losing sight of these responsibilities. [Such an appeal rests on] a confusion of responsibilities. He ignores the dissociations that are the basic principle of the task of intelligence.[8]

These dissociations derive from what Lyotard called a 'differend', of which we have seen that it rests both on the division of reason (thought by Kant at the end of the eighteenth century) and on the role of language and 'language games', which according to Wittgenstein (as interpreted by Lyotard) structure all noetic life. This differend makes impossible a synthesis capable of producing a 'unitotal' perspective that would ground and legitimate the historical action of a universal subject embodying the common good, and it subjects the ideality of the universal and the historical subject who embodies it to the systemic performance of capitalism.[9]

In another text published in October 1981, however – that is, two years after *The Postmodern Condition* and a few months after François Mitterand and the communist and socialist coalition government of Pierre Mauroy came to power – Lyotard claimed that we have 'ample proof that this subject [the universal subject, embodying the common good] has not arisen'.[10] And he argued that we must draw from this the consequence that is suggested by passing through Kant and Wittgenstein as read by Lyotard – a reading that he would make explicit in 1983, in *The Differend*[11] – namely, that ' "society," as one says, is inhabited by differends'.[12]

It was for this reason that Lyotard was extremely wary of the 'intellectuals' who gathered around Mitterand and the socialist government:

> The intelligentsia is not sparing with its support, its advice, its participation in the new power. [...] I believe that the activities of thought have another vocation: that of bearing witness to differends. [...] [P]olitics is only business and culture is only tradition [if] both of them are worked over by a sense of the differend, which, moreover, is nobody's special prerogative.[13]

Is this differend, however, of linguistic essence, as Lyotard argued in *The Differend* by inscribing the approach within what was at that time referred to as the 'linguistic turn'? And is he right to interpret, as he does in *The Postmodern Condition*, the development of technology as being essentially founded on 'language machines'?[14]

These questions are fundamental, given that the differend may be interpreted in two very different ways:

- either it derives from the fundamentally linguistic character of the mind or the noetic soul, in which case language would be irreducibly idiomatic, and as such immediately fractured by an untranslatability that was reflected upon by Wittgenstein in his theory of language games, interpreted here in a sense quite close to the Derridian thought of *untranslatable heterogeneity*;[15]
- or the situation of language, wherein the differend takes the form of speech in multiple, untranslatable ways, is itself *one singular dimension of a more deeply buried pharmacological situation*, the differend itself deriving from this pharmacology that shelters it by never ceasing to displace it; within this pharmacology, which is a 'pharmaco-logic', one pole does not oppose the other: therein would lie its transductive condition as potential, tension and phase difference, that is, as the *différance of the individuation process*.

My view is that in responding to Max Gallo, Lyotard moves all too quickly in relation to questions concerning technics and technology, in particular when he tends to oppose technics and language in order to justify the withdrawal into which, faced with the demands of politicians, the 'bearing witness to the differend' becomes drawn, as he is himself. Before elaborating these issues, however, we must return to the initial hypotheses that Lyotard first presented in *The Postmodern Condition*.

34 Systems and responsibilities

The Postmodern Condition is a 'report on knowledge' (according to the subtitle) written for the government of Quebec under the influence of the systems theory then dominant in North America, in particular through the writings of Talcott Parsons, and written in the context, as well, of a theoretical conflict between Jürgen Habermas and Niklas Luhmann.[16] It was this context that led him to define *performativity* on the basis of the notion of system, and to the following position:

> The true goal of the system, the reason it programs itself like an intelligent machine, is the optimization of the global relationship between input and output, that is, its performativity. Even when its rules are in the process of changing and innovations are occurring, even when its dysfunctions (such as strikes, crises, unemployment or political revolutions) inspire hope and lead to belief in an alternative, even then what is actually taking place is only an internal readjustment, and its result can be no more than an increase in the system's 'viability', the only alternative to this perfecting of performance being entropy, that is, decline.[17]

The reign of this performativity, and of the systematicity that it spreads through the development of technologies and language machines,[18] amounts to the fall into disuse of the Enlightenment model. Lyotard – here breaking radically with Adorno and Horkheimer, if not with Habermas's 'communicative action' – is somewhat hasty in identifying this fall with speculative reason, that is, with the *speculative proposition* in the Hegelian dialectic of 'substance-subject', in turn analysed in relation to its historical transformation into Marxism, that is, into historical materialism and dialectical materialism, and in the aftermath of what Lyotard understood to be its failure.[19]

Marxism appears here as the materialist combination (inverting the meaning of the terms that it combines) of the emancipatory ideal of the Enlightenment, speculative metaphysics, the dialectics of mastery in which Hegelian reason consists, and its own materialism, which lies in the notion of class struggle over the relations of production, so that on the basis of a reinterpretation of the master–slave dialectic it assigns a revolutionary role to the proletariat, who become the subject of History.

This disuse or obsolescence of the *Aufklärung*, which would be proven by the historical failure of Hegelian Marxism (from which Lyotard had only recently parted ways),[20] has as its eventual outcome the end of 'grand narratives':

> The grand narrative has lost its credibility, regardless of what *mode of unification* it uses, regardless of whether it is a speculative narrative or a narrative of emancipation.[21]

The question is indeed that of unification. Since Kant, Lyotard claims in *The Differend*, reason has been wracked by conflict – and this conflict, and its work, that is, its working through,[22] is that to which post-Kantian philosophy testifies, in having undergone this work of mourning for a unified and unifying conception of reason. 'Reason' – if we must retain this question and this word – is no longer the One, but the horizon that allows passages between the faculties of reason, forming an archipelago.[23]

After Kant, a new attempt at unification, more totalitarian and synthesizing than ever, will be attempted by Hegelianism, which Lyotard calls the 'speculative narrative' (*Phenomenology of Spirit* being indeed a narrative that leads to what Hegel called the speculative proposition). The continuation of this attempt occurs with the 'narrative of emancipation', through the historico-political fate of Hegelianism, then with Feuerbach (whose thesis was entitled *On Reason: One, Universal, Infinite*), and persists right up until Lyotard himself,[24] in passing through Marx, Engels, Lenin and various others, notably Althusser. This dual attempt, both epistemological and historical, will eventually fail on both counts, while thought, continuing into phenomenology where it appears to itself, will ultimately run up against its limits, in the face of which it will mourn for the One – and confront the differend.

In other words, the obsolescence of the *Aufklärung* – which, according to *The Postmodern Condition: A Report on Knowledge*, takes effect in an epoch defined as that of *post-industrial society*[25] – is the result not just of the performativity stemming from technological development, which transforms science and 'knowledge forms' in general into a commodity[26] to be exploited by that system that is capital: this obsolescence is preceded and foreshadowed by transformations in art, literature and philosophical and scientific thought:

> But in order to understand how contemporary science could have been susceptible to those effects long before they took place, we must first locate the seeds of 'delegitimation' and nihilism that were inherent in the grand narratives of the nineteenth century.[27]

These seeds are the precursors of what, according to Lyotard, constitutes a new epoch – the epoch that, coming after the emancipatory ideal, that is, after modernity, must consequently be named *postmodernity*, a postmodernity supposedly post-industrial.

In such an epoch, 'science [...] is incapable of legitimating itself, as speculation assumed it could [and] the principle of unitotality – or synthesis under the authority of a meta-discourse of knowledge – is inapplicable'.[28] This discovery was made in the late nineteenth and early twentieth centuries, hence long before the advent of the post-modern era, following the crisis of the foundations of mathematics and the advent of Viennese thought. This occurred, according to Lyotard, because after Kant reason was torn between these islands that are the faculties, and that together form an archipelago. Reason (if we must and if we can still refer here to reason) passes through these islands, opening passages[29] in which languages form, over and above which there is no universal language, as the classical thought of the seventeenth century believed, nor any 'synthesis', nor any 'meta-discourse of knowledge', nor a universal subject, as idealist speculative thought believed, and as did, later, the materialism of the nineteenth century.

This crisis of knowledge occurred at the end of the nineteenth century in mathematics and physics, and also in literary language and artistic perception. On the basis of this crisis, the Kantian archipelago can and must be translated into a *heteronomy of language games*, as Wittgenstein thought: 'nobody speaks all of those languages, they have no universal metalanguage, the project of the system-subject is a failure, the goal of emancipation has nothing to do with science'.[30] And the final clause of this sentence would also be a kick aimed at Louis Althusser.

All these negations result in *mourning*, which is an ordeal of *de-legitimation*. By the time Lyotard was writing this, however, this mourning was already done with, and it will no longer do:

> Turn-of-the-century Vienna was weaned on this pessimism: not just artists such as Musil, Kraus, Hofmannsthal, Loos, Schönberg, and

Bruch, but also the philosophers Mach and Wittgenstein. They carried awareness of delegitimation, and theoretical and artistic responsibility for it, as far as it could be taken. We can say today that the work of mourning has been completed. There is no need to start all over again.[31]

I cannot help but find this suspicious, and I see in this statement a denial – a statement that, after the fact, it is hard not to find peremptory (over thirty years later, in the aftermath of an age that presents itself to us as a story, our story, and as the story of a disaster). I see a denial, that is, a resistance to the necessary experience of melancholy and, perhaps, of the form of intelligence to which, sometimes, it alone can give rise. And I am thus quite surprised to find, in the end, and as the horizon opened by this statement, a discourse deriving from the Frankfurt School, even if in its later version – namely, that of Jürgen Habermas.

If we must mourn the 'grand narratives of legitimation', writes Lyotard, we must still not give up the search for 'a kind of legitimation not based on performativity'.[32] This other kind of legitimation, it turns out, is *linguistic and communicative*, and while 'most people have lost the nostalgia for the lost narrative', nevertheless, contrary to the belief of Adorno and Horkheimer, 'it in no way follows that they are reduced to barbarity', since for 'most people', 'legitimation can only spring from their own linguistic practice and communicative interaction'.[33] Hence this amounts to a repetition of the position taken by Habermas, even if it is here being taken as the possibility, in this linguistic and communicative practice, of affirming *dissensus* – rather than the *consensus* that Habermas continues to seek.

Nostalgia (for the 'lost narrative' and for so many other things that went along with it), then, may be 'lost for most people', but they would not be 'doomed to barbarism' so long as their 'linguistic practice' can reconstruct legitimation – this is what I find absolutely doubtful. And I am doubtful along with the 'downgraded generation' that addresses the 'lyrical generation' of 1968, sixty-five years after Adorno and Horkheimer, in 1944, addressed a world struck by unreason: I am doubtful in the aftermath of all this at once – and of yet more things.[34] And I fear that the credit and debt crisis in which the twenty-first century has become mired again raises up the same doubt, which strikes more or less the whole world and everyone it contains, leaving each of us, throughout the world, caught in terrible isolation.

The problem is that 'communicative interaction' has been *reduced to a pulp* for reasons that Lyotard loftily ignores (but this is not the case for Habermas,[35] even if he does consistently ignore the technicity of language).[36] This has been brought about by what I call dissociation, in a sense completely different from that of Lyotard. Dissociation: that is, the *destruction of associated milieus*,[37] which constitute symbolic fields in general – and where such symbolic fields are clearly not reducible to language and communication, and are *always* technologically over-determined.

The grammatization of practices and of knowledge in general, including savoir-vivre, has led to generalized proletarianization. But this is also a de-symbolization, that is, a destruction of the dialogism in which all individuation consists: a process of massive disindividuation has been installed, the result of which is a situation of systemic stupidity. We, the latecomers of that twenty-first century that Lyotard would never know, are the ones who must undergo this terrible ordeal, and the result is that we can no longer take such statements totally seriously, statements that on occasion seem almost playful, and that, by privileging language in this way, avoid a critique of economics with respect to the hegemony it exercises over technological becoming, that is, pharmaco-logical becoming.

In particular, one cannot fail to notice here that what is said about the system seems to leave no room for the question of the *limits of the system*, for the fact that any dynamic system has limits, and that a time will inevitably come when these limits are reached,[38] philosophy consisting perhaps always and firstly in thinking such passages to the limit.[39]

Hence one reaches the conclusion that it may be time to re-read – and to read completely otherwise – the philosophy of the nineteenth century, and in particular to examine:

- the difference (in repetition) between predicative proposition and speculative proposition;
- the meaning of 'proletariat' and 'proletarianization'.

In his Marxist past, and in his passage to the pragmatic of the differend inspired by systems theory, Lyotard takes up the concept of the proletariat *as is*, that is, in classical Marxist fashion. I argue that it is precisely by misinterpreting the meaning of proletarianization, as Lyotard continually does, that materialism perpetuates a metaphysical point of view in its interpretation and reappropriation of Hegelianism, and at the same time fails to think the becoming of capital.

Before returning to this point, which will conclude the first part of this book, we must again take up Lyotard's response to Gallo on the silence of the intellectuals and on their responsibility in the epoch of 'change' (Gallo) induced by 'language machines' (Lyotard).

35 Technologies of responsibility and responsibilities before technology

If the differend is essentially linguistic, it is nevertheless accentuated by the 'new techniques' and 'new technologies' that shift and differentiate responsibility, writes Lyotard in *Le Monde* in 1983:

> New technologies, essentially linked to the technosciences of language, along with the concentration of civil, economic, social, and military administrations, have changed the nature of intermediary and higher responsibilities and have attracted numerous thinkers trained in the hard sciences, high technology, and the human sciences.[40]

These technologies, 'essentially linked to the technosciences of language', have given rise to *knowledge performance agents* that, contrary to that to which the differend bears witness, and contrary to a sense of responsibility founded on an experience of this differend, turn knowledge into a question of performance. That is, they subject this knowledge to economic criteria, and such criteria are established at the moment, furthermore, when neoliberalism begins to liquidate that public thing that the modern state had, hitherto, embodied.[41] New technologies are put to work by competences in the service of performances, the goals of which conflict with those of a noetic and *rational* act in the Enlightenment sense:

> [For] these new cadres [the] professional exercise of their intelligence is not directed toward the fullest possible embodiment of the universal subject in the domain of their competence, but to the achievement of the best possible performance in that domain.[42]

Their criteriology is 'technical'. And 'a mind engaged in such responsibilities can and probably must be led to invent new devices [...] but [it] does not question the limits [of these *dispositifs*]'.[43] Such minds are unaware, I would add, of their own pharmacological character: they do not practise negative pharmacology. They do, however, engage in a positive practice of *pharmaka*, but, because they are unaware of the toxicity of *pharmaka*, they ignore the pharmacological dimension in general – that is, the differend that the latter, in fact, inevitably contains. Furthermore, did not Lyotard himself ignore these limits in his presentation of a performative system that would render narratives of legitimation obsolete, as we saw earlier?[44] And does he not continue to do so here?

In the differend, technology shifts the boundaries between those who bear witness to the differend and those whose work is in some way conducted in terms of performance – even if unwillingly. Lyotard admits that 'the proliferation of new technologies continually destabilizes this compartmentalization'[45] between the 'witnesses' and the actors (for example, the 'new cadres') of this differend. Nevertheless, he concludes that this shift changes nothing in relation to performativity: it does not in any way alter the fact that the technologization of language in all cases results in the submission of responsibility to performance – which could also be called *efficiency*, or even, the 'reality principle'. I would argue on the contrary that this 'technologization' is a grammatization that opens language to the very possibility of 'bearing witness', and to many other possibilities.

For Lyotard, technologization inevitably leads to the submission of responsibility to performance:

> When a writer, an artist, a scholar, or a philosopher takes on this kind of responsibility [as would Max Gallo in relation to a change in course that it would be a matter of analysing], they accept ipso facto the conditions of that responsibility: the requirement to perform in the assigned domain.[46]

Is it not surprising to see posited in principle the impossibility of redefining the sharing of responsibility in the face of a technological mutation of responsibility – which may have been precisely what Gallo expected *without realizing it*, what he *waited for without expecting*? Could there be an ontology – necessarily, in some way, unitotal – of the differend, which would also be an ontology of responsibility?

Does all this also imply that it is inevitable that such technologies can be placed *only* in the service of *this* 'performativity'? Would no other politics of such technologies (and of the responsibility that is evidently always tied to technics and technology insofar as it constitutes the instruments of all power, beginning with the power to kill possessed by anyone who gets their hands on even the smallest knife) be possible? Could there not be a politics, for example, that would enable an *individuating performativity*, such as, as we shall see, Derrida claimed?[47]

This is my hypothesis, but Lyotard seems to have given it no consideration. And yet, as we shall see,[48] he himself opened up certain prospects at the very end of *The Postmodern Condition*, but he did so, in a way, without knowing it. Or more exactly: he did so, but in the belief that he knew *something else* (something that I myself came to believe – afterwards, and in the après-coup that separates us from that time – has become false).

To ask this another way, and to put it bluntly: is this *pharmakon* of performativity, understood as efficiency, that is, in the sense in which, according to Plato, the Sophists understood and explained their own role (and of which 'high-performance culture', a 'culture of results', would be the grotesque variant found in our own miserable age), is this *pharmakon* inherently and exclusively toxic? Or could and should there be a pharmacology that leads to a complete rethinking of the technology of responsibility, that is, of autonomy and reason, as well as the responsibility of technology, and by 'technologies of power',[49] given that these three terms – autonomy, reason, responsibility – are inseparable from heteronomy that might be the root, or the default of origin, of what Lyotard called the 'differend' (as trace, repetition)?

36 Anamnesis as après-coup

In a chapter of *The Inhuman* entitled 'Logos and *Techne*, or Telegraphy', Lyotard himself outlines such a hypothesis – just barely opening the possibility, and with great reservation – by distinguishing between writing and telegraphy. This response is strangely close to Heidegger's discourse in 'Traditional Language and Technological Language'[50] (on which I commented in *Technics and Time, 2*),[51] where telegraphy is defined as a 'technicization of language' – that is, as a *denaturation* of language.

Lyotard distinguishes three types of 'memory-effects':

> Breaching [*frayage*], scanning and passing, which coincide more or less with three very different sorts of temporal synthesis linked to inscription: habit, remembering [*rémémoration*] and anamnesis.[52]

Having done so, and having specified the contemporary history of scanning as typifying the *tekhnologos* that is implemented along with digitalization, and that was already analysed in *The Postmodern Condition*, a history of scanning thus redefined here as telegraphy, and based essentially on the development of language machines that in some way set up automated understanding,[53] Lyotard addresses what he calls *passing [passage]*, for which the model is what Freud called *Durcharbeitung* (working through), and which constitutes *writing as that which would be irreducible to telegraphy*:

> Finally, a few words about 'passing'. This is another memorization, linked to a writing which is different from the inscription by breaching or experimentation, different from habitual repetition or voluntary remembering. I use the term 'passing' with an allusion to the third memorizing technique that Freud opposes to the first two in his text on 'psychoanalytical technique': the (infinitive) 'passing' here is the German *durch*, as in *Durcharbeitung*, or the *through* of the English *working through*, the passing through of *trans*- or *per*-laboration.[54]

This writing is irreducible to any telegraphy whatsoever, that is, to any technicization or technologization of language whatsoever, because perlaboration (or translaboration) would 'pass beyond synthesis in general. Or, if you like, [...] the point would be to recall what could not have been forgotten because it was not inscribed.'[55] And only writing *as anamnesis* – which, for Lyotard, is *not* telegraphic, that is, hypomnesic, that is, a technics of scanning – can support 'what has not been inscribed': 'I see only writing, itself anamnesis of what has not been inscribed, as capable of supporting a comparison with this a-technical or a-technological rule'[56] that would be anamnesis. And it must not be forgotten that the latter was in Plato the founding question of philosophical knowledge,[57] and I will return to this in the second part.[58]

> This is the whole question of Freud's *Nachträglichkeit*: was the first blow – which [...] was not recorded and only comes back as second blow, disguised – struck on the same surface on which the second and following blows will be inscribed, differing from them only in that it is undecipherable?[59]

Anamnesis would thus have the structure of a repetition of what has not yet taken place, which as such constitutes the question of writing – that is, of what Derrida called archi-writing – as irreducible to telegraphy: 'I am talking here about what psychoanalysis called anamnesis, what so-called "French thought" has for a long time called *writing*.'[60] Besides the fact, however, that I doubt that Derrida would have seen writing and telegraphy in oppositional terms, and besides the fact that the Hegelian speculative proposition *too* derives from such an après-coup (as we shall show in a moment), would it not be necessary here to return to Lacan and to the question of the Thing – *das Ding*?

In Lacan's analysis,[61] *das Ding* constitutes a process of substitution without end, a primordial and interminable supplementarity, and in this sense a différance, the object of desire always masking *another* object – *das Ding*, which never presents itself, which is never present, and which is thus what knows no present and is therefore tempting to understand as transcendence.[62] *Das Ding*, which is in this way the a priori structure of desire, is that Thing of which there will never be an experience.

I myself, however, propose a slightly discordant reading of Lacan's analysis (and as such a reading slightly closer to Deleuze). Whereas Lacan suggests that this substitution without end should be thought as having the structure of a lack, this could also be interpreted as that of a default of origin. And it would be this default that condemns us to a repetition that can and must become that which is necessary, and in that to make a difference: as a prostheticity, neoteny and primordial exteriorization that would not be preceded by any interiority, and that can be interiorized only via that primordial *pharmakon* that is, in the construction of the psychic apparatus, Winnicott's transitional object.[63]

The transitional object is *in no way linguistic*; quite the contrary: pre-ceding access to language, it is the object of the *infans*. And what this object allows us to understand is that *das Ding* constitutes the *horizon of consistence in general* – that is, of what neither exists nor subsists, but consists,[64] and as such finds itself infinitely desired. This necessary default is the pharmacological consistence (sickness and health, say Deleuze and Canguilhem) of that which *makes* fault(s)/ absence as object(s) of desire [*ce qui fait défaut(s) comme objet(s) d'un désir*], *das Ding* appearing only in the mode of always being yet to come (and as such forming the structure of what Derrida called the promise).

37   Invention and resistance: the dilution of responsibility

The conclusion drawn by Lyotard from this opposition between technics and language, or telegraphy and writing, is that in the field of performance, of language machines, and of the technologies of a purportedly postmodern and post-industrial world, the witnesses to the differend can invent nothing: they can only resist – invention being on the side of the 'new cadres' and other technicians caught adrift in an efficiency without end.

The witness to the differend resists '(in what I think is a non-psychoanalytical sense, more like that of Wilson in Orwell's *1984*) [...] the syntheses of breaching and scanning. A resistance to the clever programmes and fat telegrams.'[65] This is why, even if Lyotard says he tries to envisage the possibility that passing – that is, anamnesis – is possible, 'possible with, or allowed by, the new mode of inscription and memoration that characterizes the new technologies', he nevertheless asks, in relation to this 'breaching' and 'scanning' proper to the digital (which is what we nowadays call those technologies that today support most of our activities, regardless of who we may be, or whether or not we are aware of it), the following:

> Do [these technologies] not impose syntheses, and syntheses conceived still more intimately in the soul than any earlier technology has done? But by that very fact, do they not also help to refine our anamnesic resistance? I'll stop on this vague hope, which is too dialectical to take seriously. All this remains to be thought out, tried out.[66]

So ends '*Logos* and *Techne*, or Telegraphy'.

Yet is this hypothesis – in which Lyotard in 1986 clearly does not believe, and which he seems almost to have inserted just to please the addressee[67] – really so 'dialectical'? What exactly is being referred to here as 'dialectical'? And is he really being serious if he invokes the latter simply in order to toss it aside without discussion? Is he seriously saying that the dialectical is not a serious question?

A feature common to all 'French thought' of that era – as mark of a definitive break with Althusser, and more generally with Marxism, of which Lyotard was initially a thinker and a militant – was anti-Hegelianism, where Hegelianism was rejected on the grounds of being 'totalizing'. And for Lyotard, synthesis in general here represents this totalization, and the very idea of universality, as he says elsewhere, is a worn-out fantasy: 'The decline, *perhaps the ruin*, of the universal idea can free thought and life from totalizing obsessions.'[68] It is in this possibility that, at the end of his response to Gallo, Lyotard places his hopes that responsibilities will disseminate and multiply:

> The multiplicity of responsibilities, and their independence (their incompatibility), oblige and will oblige those who take on those responsibilities, small or great, to be flexible, tolerant, and svelte.[69]

Such would be the 'good side' of the postmodern condition.

One feels here the dawning of that political flabbiness that typified the end of the twentieth century, bringing with it great threats, and that became in the first part of the twenty-first century literally unsustainable – at a time when sovereignty, democratic or republican, has, as 'universal idea', been literally and dangerously ruined. This flabbiness of philosophy's political and economic propositions seems, after the fact, to amount to a terrible blindness to what was beginning to transpire with the conservative revolution and the first steps towards financialization, which in April 2002 proved very costly for Lionel Jospin (who attended Lyotard's funeral) and for all of us along with him. But aside from all this, which must be clearly explained, it is utterly misleading to relate those syntheses referred to as 'breaching' and 'scanning' to the Hegelian synthesis by passing through Kant, as does Lyotard in relation to 'telegraphy'.

Should we be content with 'flexibility', 'tolerance' and 'svelteness' as we confront the systemic limits with which we are being tested in the twenty-first century? This test is a *catastrophē*, that is, a denouement,[70] wherein it seems that what we have called postmodernity, the history of which more or less coincides with that of the conservative revolution, turns out to have been the epoch of financialization, that is, of the structural separation of financial capitalism and industrial capitalism. The financial oligarchy is delivering us over to a systematic economic war against all forms of investment, that is, against any way of immobilizing capital or limiting its mobility, and it is thus a war against all forms of public power or authority insofar as the latter is the mutualized organization of investment. This war, however, has led to this ruin that is the *systemic dilution of responsibility*, which in turn leads the system in its totality towards its self-destructive limits.

'Flexibility', 'tolerance' and 'svelteness' would, according to Lyotard, be beneficial, as we can expect a decline in that unifying power that would be synthesis. Kant distributes this power to unify between understanding (which produces concepts) and reason (which produces ends), via the intermediary of the syntheses of the transcendental imagination and of what Kant called the schematism. It is clear that this unifying power must be thought otherwise – especially given that knowledge has put these syntheses to work by exteriorizing them in prostheses that automate them and make them commensurable and calculable, which has become a major factor in this economic war. And it is equally clear that Kant failed to think these syntheses on the basis of a primordial heteronomy from which they would undoubtedly always be constituted, and which would thus always introduce and reintroduce the differend into these syntheses.[71]

That the *one*, then, never occurs except as dissemination in multiplicity is what Deleuze tried to think as repetition, and what Derrida tried to think as writing, and as différance and dissemination. Nevertheless, it remains the case that:

- the unifying power of the Kantian syntheses, which '*Logos* and *Techne*, or Telegraphy' presents as the model for the syntheses of breaching and scanning,[72] is of a wholly other nature than Hegelian and 'unitotalizing' dialectical synthesis;
- what has been thought as subject-substance and as speculative proposition must be thought afresh, and in terms of the question of individuation.

In thinking individuation, however, Simondon gives a new twist to the question of proletarianization: he makes it a question of *disindividuation*, produced by the loss of knowledge that results from the exteriorization of knowledge in machines and apparatus.

In this respect, what *The Postmodern Condition* describes is a new stage of proletarianization – but neither the work nor the author show any awareness of this. Because of this, this work is incapable of anticipating or thinking the dilution of responsibility typical of this 'postmodernity', a dilution founded on a total loss of economic knowledge. Economic knowledge has become an automatism without decision, while simultaneously presenting itself as an inevitability without alternative – a destruction of decision similar to that brought about by nuclear weaponry, which must for this reason be understood, according to Derrida, as an 'absolute *pharmakon*'.[73]

Lyotard wrote these texts at the precise moment when the conservative revolution began to be implemented in the West, ten years after the 'experiments' of the Chicago School in Chile and elsewhere. It can now be seen how the logic dictated to the IMF by Milton Friedman and his team – to subject developing countries to 'disaster capitalism', that is, to 'fundamentalist capitalism' – is now being applied, via ratings agencies, in Europe and North America (just as it was thirty years ago in South America). Hence the industrialized continents are entering a path of underdevelopment: a complete regression imposed by the reign of stupidity.

Perhaps like no other philosopher of 'French thought', Lyotard felt coming *something* of what was brewing on the side of capital: 'After thirty years of expansion, [capital] has entered a new phase of overcapitalization.'[74] Lyotard may have had perfectly understandable reasons for the flat-out refusal he addressed to Gallo,[75] and it is no doubt all too easy to be critical after the fact. Nevertheless, Lyotard's response does seem to lead to the suggestion that it is in principle impossible to imagine an alternative, and thus to be in agreement with Thatcher's infamous statement: his rejection suggests that it is in principle impossible to invent, leaving the inventive operation to technocrats in the name of the differend, and the 'witnesses' to take refuge in 'resistance'.[76]

38   From dialectics to poststructuralism and beyond: re-reading

Faced with such a situation, it is not enough just to serve notice on the dialectical synthesis – as leading to the speculative proposition – in order to escape from a totalization of 'commensurabilities'. Quite the opposite: we must *re-read* those speculative propositions that attempt to say what a speculative proposition is, not to dispense with them, but to see where they lose sight of that which works through them, namely, an 'idealist' attempt to think the subject afresh, on the basis of the process and not the individual.

The critique of political economy that began with Marx, as the thought of a so-called materialist process understood in terms of an 'inverted' dialectic, was abandoned by 'French thought' from the 1960s until the end of the twentieth century. During these years, the Althusserian enterprise was respectfully but definitively turned into a museum piece – as if the thought of Marx no longer had any substance to it, as if the economy had become a vulgar affair unworthy of thought, as if dialectics was of no significance in the history of philosophy and had no practical importance in history in general.[77]

Dialectics, become materialist, is in reality that which formulates, according to a framework that remains metaphysical, the new questions that arise with industrial technology from the standpoint of individuation and disindividuation, and in a situation that is clearly pharmacological. But dialectics has, precisely, also prevented these questions from being thought *as such* (as pharmacological, that is, without dialectical sublation and without unitotal synthesis).

Only through the possibility of elaborating alternatives, and especially in the fields of politics and economics, can there be any possibility of any responsibility whatsoever. According to Derrida, however, as according to almost all the thinkers of his time, including Althusser, responsibility should be thought 'as no longer passing, in the last instance, through an ego, the "I think", intention, the subject, the ideal of decidability'.[78]

This obsolescence of the 'I think' first occurs with Hegelian dialectics and becomes definitive with Marxism. And it will be reinforced by structuralism and everything that makes those collective individuation processes that are structures – language, kinship systems, the law, and so on – the structural condition of any psychic individuation, as, for example, the utterances of a subject, that is, the subject thought on the basis of the signifier.

Nevertheless, this reference to structure, like the dialectical synthesis, would fail to think the conditions of emergence of singularities, because the methodology that was a major feature of structuralism (which fascinated Althusser and his students) rested on an opposition between genesis and structure, that is, between diachrony and synchrony.

It was in this general context, outlined too quickly here, that 'poststructuralism' emerged. Like structuralism, however, the latter failed to think what nevertheless made Derrida's thought possible in the first place, namely, technics as the surface on which memory is inscribed, and as such exteriorization, and therefore disindividuation as well as individuation – which was exploited by capital in an extreme way in that epoch analysed by Lyotard in terms of postmodernity. But in order to understand this, we must re-read Hegel, Marx *and Simondon*.

Derrida may be right in wanting to think responsibility without passing through 'the subject, the ideal of decidability', but only to the extent that this new way of thinking responsibility raises up a politics of tertiary retention as the heteronomy that conditions all autonomy and all sovereignty. Or only to the extent that the subject becomes a psychic individual that can individuate only at the core of a collective individuation itself made possible and impossible by a technical individuation, which, as hypomnesic (as object-image, as Simondon puts it in 1965), is also, always and necessarily, a disindividuation – psychic and collective individuation being in constant struggle with, against, right up against, disindividuation, that is, against and with that stupidity in which it results.

This new way of thinking responsibility consists as well in thinking the school not just as a place of breachings, or even scannings, as does Lyotard, mourning the *Aufklärung* in *The Postmodern Condition*.[79] The school must be thought as the institution of a new process of psychic, collective *and technical* individuation, where tertiary retention becomes, as *pharmakon*, the object of a positive pharmacology, that is, of a therapeutic experience of anamneses – countering the short-circuiting of democratic and political forms of sovereignty. This positive pharmacology is woven through those long circuits of transindividuation that knowledge constitutes: this is what will be developed in the second part.

This thought presupposes the conceptualization of technics, that is, in our time, technology, and ultimately industry. This in turn presupposes the rethinking of the place of the university in the industrial world – in the new industrial world that has begun to unfold since the beginning of the twenty-first century, but that is yet to find a sustainable direction or to bring forth a global future. And this requires us to engage in an anamnesic practice in relation to the immense impact that Hegel and Marx have had on all twentieth-century thought.

5

Reading and Re-Reading Hegel After Poststructuralism

What is it to read? [...] [O]ur age threatens one day to appear in the history of human culture as marked by the most dramatic and difficult trial of all, the discovery of and training in the meaning of the 'simplest' acts of existence: seeing, listening, speaking, reading.

Louis Althusser[1]

39   Four reasons to take Hegelian dialectics seriously

Spirit in its formation matures slowly and quietly into its new shape, dissolving bit by bit the structure of its previous world [...]. The frivolity and boredom which unsettle the established order, the vague foreboding of something unknown, these are the heralds of approaching change.[2]

The Hegelian dialectic must be taken *seriously*, and so must dialectical materialism. We must take them seriously, that is, critique them – not just repeat them like trained monkeys. The motive for this new critique is the status of desire in Hegelian thought:

The true shape in which truth exists can only be the scientific system of such truth. To help bring philosophy closer to the form of Science, to the goal where it can lay aside the title '*love* of knowing' and be *actual* knowing – that is what I have set myself to do.[3]

This laying aside of love [*désamour*],[4] which Hegel himself claims to be the price of 'absolute knowledge', must be taken seriously, more seriously than anything else, given that this has established itself in the current world as the destruction of desire, as desublimation and the spread of drive-based capitalism – in a way that is undoubtedly the inversion of what Hegel imagined. We must take this, and many other aspects of Hegel, seriously, and for a variety of reasons that we cannot go into here (and we will also need, one day, to state the reasons for taking the Platonic dialectic seriously).[5]

As for us, the latecomers who arrive after poststructuralism, we must take the Hegelian dialectic and its speculative proposition seriously, for four reasons:

1 Hegel thinks the life of spirit as dia-lectic – that is, as movement of spirit – on the basis of the Aristotelian conception of *nous*: as (auto-)movement induced by an object of desire – the object of all desires that Aristotle calls *theos* (which is not *heteros*, since it is the community of all desires, and which it is tempting to equate with the big Other, even with *das Ding*).

2 Hegel conceives this auto-movement of desiring spirit as a process of exteriorization, and it is to think this process that he elaborates its dia-lectic, the kernel of which is the speculative proposition as exceeding the predicative proposition, that is, as exceeding the fixed determinations of the understanding.

3 What Hegel calls the speculative proposition is the enunciation of the movement that is spirit as movement of a substance that is the becoming-subject in itself and for itself of a subject that thinks, and for a subject that is, in this, this substance as *power of exteriorization*. Substance, here, designates that which is in the movement of its becoming, and one of the fundamental aspects of this dialectic is that it *exceeds the opposition between being and becoming* as well as between subject and object.

This 'exceeding', however, is one of the fundamental problems of the dialectic: it is translated, as the auto-movement of this dialectic, into the dissolution of becoming (and of future) into being as 'uni-total' synthesis. This is why the dialectic, conceived in this way as the dissolution of oppositions, is what all so-called poststructuralist thinkers reject. This rejection comes despite the fact that exceeding oppositions is also a typical feature of poststructuralism, especially in Derrida and Deleuze, but in poststructuralism this 'exceeding' is not a dissolution, that is, a synthetic resolution.

Nevertheless, the Hegelian dialectic of substance-subject is an attempt to think individuation on the basis of a process – as process of exteriorization – and not on the basis of a constituted individual.

4 The materialist version of the speculative dialectic understands exteriorization as materialization, and the latter as the technical self-production of humanity by its 'means' of production, while for the first time it explicitly poses the question of proletarianization, that is, the question of the destruction of knowledge that results from its exteriorization, even though the latter is also the fundamental condition of the constitution of all knowledge.

In this way, dialectical materialism rediscovered the initial question of the *pharmakon*. And yet this materialism produced no pharmacology: it continued to understand technics as a means, and hence 'toxic' processes (such as proletarianization, or its consequence, pauperization) would be understood only as translations of class struggle, as the relations of production.

Even though the process of exteriorization, as we shall see, is described in Marx's work as grammatization (but this is not thought *as such*), and even though the *Grundrisse* describes the materialization of knowledge in the form of what I call tertiary retention, the general question of knowledge in industrial society is not truly posed by dialectical materialism: technics is not thematized as a factor in both knowledge and non-knowledge, nor is there an organology of knowledge, or any economy of knowledge (that is, of sublimated desire).

It is the failure to pose either the question of the toxicity of the *pharmakon*, or that of its curativity and the therapeutic this requires (which is always a system of de-proletarianization), that leads the negativity of the Marxist dialectic to the doctrine of the dictatorship of the proletariat rather than to a political project of de-proletarianization, that is, to a reacquisition of knowledge in the service of the individuation of citizens.

This outcome was due less to the fact that Marx was wrong than to the fact that philosophy is collective work, and those who contribute to its individuation are able to do so *only in their time* – and *as* their time becomes the time of everyone. This is just as true for Foucault, Deleuze, Derrida and Lyotard. If it is now imperative to think grammatization and knowledge from an organological perspective, and as an economy, this presupposes concepts forged by Nietzsche (shadow), Freud (libidinal economy), Husserl (retention and protention) and Simondon (individuation and transduction), hence from all those works from which poststructuralism emerged – that is, those works from which structuralism emerged and, before that, the Saussurian method of linguistic investigation.

Marx, of course, could not have conceived any of this or the way that it would and should come to modify his own concepts. Because these concepts were unavailable to him, and because exteriorization itself had not yet reached the stage that would require thinking grammatization as such (as the pharmacological spatialization of time in the form of tertiary retention), Marx was not able to pose the question of a curative pharmacology, that is, a positive pharmacology. The failure of poststructuralism to pose this question, on the other hand, seems to lie rather in the fact that it is unaware of the scope of the Marxist understanding of technics, despite the analyses of Kostas Axelos.[6] As for Marx, he could not envisage this curativity as techno-logical and industrial individuation, reconstituting knowledge and participating in the struggle against proletarianization.

The complete assumption [*assomption*] and then the speculative exceeding of the idealist dialectic of master and slave, its re-reading, and the counter-thrust [*choc en retour*] that it must produce, beyond Hegel himself, lead to this question, as we shall see.

As for Lyotard – whose arguments get caught up, after the works of his that date from the early 1970s (*Dérive à partir de Marx et Freud*, 1972, and *L'Économie libidinale*, 1974), in the 'linguistic turn' – he reverts, in certain respects, if not to Hegelianism, then at least to a pre-Marxist position. That is, Lyotard regresses in relation to the critical elements that Marx formulated against Hegel's idealism, to the extent that, from *The Postmodern Condition* onwards, he privileges language. And as such, he can no longer be counted as in any way a materialist (at least not in the Marxist sense).

40   Hegel à la lettre

The phenomenology of spirit is for Hegel a process in which the mind or spirit enunciates itself, that is, exteriorizes itself logically in this element of *logos* that is language as the *power to determine*. What this phenomenology shows, insofar as Hegel claims to reconstitute it as this process, is that the subject of the statement – that which is said, and as to its being, that is: the *what* – is always in some way the subject of enunciation – the one who speaks: the *who*. And this subject becomes who he is or she is through the restating of the statement, a restating that, as we shall see, is a written statement. The subject is therefore – and essentially – a reader.

This saying can in fact appear to itself, that is, *for itself*, and in the aftermath of the sedimentation that is its *in itself*, only by itself being trans-formed à la lettre: this saying of the self is a writing of the self[7] as well as a reading of the self. In other words, this phenomenology (which passes through the becoming of the proposition) can occur only in a linguistic milieu that has been alphabetically grammatized, making it possible to consider the proposition *as such*, that is, as a sentence (verbal or nominal) that begins with a capital letter and ends with a full stop, conventions or standards of which the languages of electronic document files, and then the languages of the web, such as SGML, and today HTML and its derivatives, are extensions.

That this *literal condition* was under-thematized by Hegel, if not concealed (by himself, from himself), did not prevent this literality of spirit from being expressly claimed on numerous occasions in his work, and as condition of this phenomenology of spirit as the possibility of re-reading à la lettre. It is only on the basis of such a possibility of repetition and difference, granting a regime of *specific* difference (specific to an epoch of the history of the supplement), that the subject of the statement (that is, the *what*, and the predicative *what*) can proceed from the subject of enunciation, as Hegel argues in relation to what he names, for this very reason, the speculative proposition. In the speculative proposition, that is, the literal proposition, the *what* appears to proceed from the *who* insofar as it itself individuates a process – which Hegel called spirit, and of which he analysed the individuating hearth that achieves its completion as the speculative proposition.

In other words, the phenomenology of spirit (spirit appearing to itself) is its exteriorization as knowledge, that is, as that constitution of knowing that is the subject who inherits the exteriorized (of what has been determined by the understanding via language) by interiorizing it – by individuating. This is why the movement of the *for itself* of the subject that is the spirit appears, *to itself*, to itself[8] discover *its own, proper knowledge* in the subject of the statement (but without knowing this insofar as Hegel did not think *as such* the speculativity of the speculative proposition, that is, the dia-lectical mirroring of the subject in its statements – those it listens to as well as those it speaks or writes – a specular experience leading to 'absolute knowledge'). It discovers the subject of enunciation that it is, and through which knowledge individuates itself – as 'phenomenology of spirit'.

We shall see in the next section that this collective individuation of knowledge, in order that it may coincide with that of psychic individuation (as substance becoming subject and subject becoming substance, in Hegelian terms), must be thought in terms of transindividuation.[9]

This subjectivity is speculative in the sense that it is *its* knowledge that is reflected in what it at first believes (wrongly) is received from the exterior through this or that inherited statement (inherited from science, which is not distinguished here from philosophy), but which proves to be, in the speculative proposition – but this does not appear to the subject in the predicative proposition – what it pro-duces as this moment that becomes *its* moment (a moment of its knowledge), and a production that is both *its* individuation and the individuation *of knowledge* insofar as it coincides with substance itself: this speculative phenomenology of spirit is the process of the individuation of spirit, that is, of knowledge in movement, through reading writing and as a moment of writing, that is, as a moment of the *individuation of the exterior*.[10]

This phenomenology of spirit is a processuality, wherein it is a matter of abandoning the individual as point of departure (as Cartesian subject, as the transcendental subjectivity of the *I think*). In this respect, the phenomenology of spirit anticipates the Simondonian perspective: the subject of enunciation is knowledge that occurs only by individuating its preindividual funds, which appear to it firstly as exteriority – precisely because these preindividual funds have been exteriorized (produced) by the spirit, and precisely as its phenomenology, its appearance to itself and its sedimentation (which is also a *disappearance* to itself, that is, a *blindness* to itself). For Hegel, in other words, it is a matter of overcoming the opposition between the psychic and the collective – a philosophical imperative that, by thinking the individual on the basis of the process, contrary to transcendental idealism, and as historical idealism, leads to the question of the substance-subject.

41   Spirit as exteriorization

The process of exteriorization and of interiorization in return[11] that is the origin of the life of the spirit is an 'emergence from the immediacy of substantial life'.[12] Substantial life is life alienated from its immediate needs. Mediacy – as a mode of *différance* – is the condition of this liberation, yet equally a loss and an alienation: spirit produces itself as freedom only by chaining itself in some way to itself, insofar as it exteriorizes itself:

> The power of Spirit is only as great as its expression [*Äußerung, extériorisation*], its depth only as deep as it dares to spread out and lose itself in its exposition [*Auslegung, déployant*].[13]

What Lyotard describes in *The Postmodern Condition* is the epoch of the industrial systematization and exploitation of this exteriorization.

Phenomenology of Spirit already felt coming this absolutely new mode of exteriorization that industrialization will soon constitute: 'Besides, it is not difficult to see that ours is a birth-time and a period of transition to a new era.'[14] And Hegel understands this period of transition in terms of shock: 'The onset of the new spirit is the product of a widespread upheaval in various forms of culture.'[15] In this upheaval, all previously inherited forms of spirit are rearranged and must be reanimated, de-sedimented and fluidized.

> Those various shapes and forms [...] become its moments [moments of that which happens now, that is, in this new stage of exteriorization that is spirit whose power 'is only as great as its expression'], and [...] will now develop and take shape afresh.[16]

This moment is what Simondon called a 'quantum leap' in collective individuation, consisting in a trans-formation of the very conditions of individuation (a new epoch of the self), but a trans-formation the full process of which has yet to unfurl itself.

This is so because this upheaval interrupts the preceding configuration of the spirit, whereas the consciousness that this spirit traverses is still attached to and framed by this legacy. This is why this unfurling can be accomplished only by *contradicting* consciousness, which thus lags behind that which constitutes it as being itself a process of individuation – a process that is out of phase and destabilized:

> The wealth of previous existence is still present to consciousness in memory. Consciousness misses in the newly emerging shape its former range and specificity of content, and even more the articulation of form whereby distinctions are securely defined, and stand arrayed in their fixed relations.[17]

This consciousness, on its way to a new age of spirit, which will be a new metastability, is disoriented because it has lost the network of 'fixed relations' that grants it its east and west, that is, precisely, its network of relations metastabilized by the preceding stage of collective individuation, which has been destroyed, and which constituted what Simondon named the *transindividual* (meaning), forming 'the wealth of previous existence'. This disorientation is the *inquietude* of consciousness, a consciousness that is on the way to individuating the contradiction of the 'negative' (what Simondon described as a phase-shift),[18] but that nevertheless initially finds itself disindividuated.

From the pharmacological perspective that I defend here, one must say that the exteriorization through which spirit appears to itself is not merely logical, that is, spontaneously projected through the categories of language that grammar helps to identify as such, and as predication, and for consciousness itself. From the pharmacological perspective, this exteriorization is also and above all technical – which is clearly not a perspective that is tenable for Hegel. But as we shall see, it will indeed be Marx's perspective – and it is in the encounter of dialectical materialism with its historical subject, which for Marx is the proletariat, that Lyotard calls into question what he calls the 'speculative narrative', a narrative that leads firstly to the *speculative proposition*, and then, with Marx, and as the critical and anti-idealist continuation of the Enlightenment project, to the 'emancipatory narrative'.

The pharmacological perspective is no more Marx's than it is Hegel's, because for Marx the means of production, even if they are often described in ways that seem pharmacological, are not *pharmaka* (if that were the case, he would have posed the ecological question, which is the ecology of spirit as much as it is the ecology of the environment). But from the pharmacological perspective, the process of destruction that Hegel described as the negativity or negative side of the phenomenology of spirit is, in fact, the first moment of the doubly epokhal redoubling. The doubly epokhal redoubling is that to which technical exteriorization gives rise in a psychosocial individuation process. The doubly epokhal redoubling occurs when exteriorization causes the technical system to change, a technical system that concretizes and materializes all preceding exteriorizations, and that as such and *according to its pharmacological characteristics* supports the transindividual (through those object-images that are, for Simondon in 1965, technical artefacts).[19]

42   Re-reading I – *Phenomenology of Spirit*

Hegel did not discover the *technicity* of this exteriorization, which therefore remained transparent to him (that is, soluble in the self of the spirit), just as it did for Kant:[20] its technicity is only an accidental[21] moment of the spirit, and its opacity for the spirit is a contingent state of affairs that the spirit, acceding to its pure speculative rationality, can and must dissolve.

This dissolution constitutes the horizon of the speculative proposition, such that, substance appearing there as subject, it is truth itself that becomes speculative, and where what becomes possible and necessary is 'grasping and expressing the True, not only as *Substance*, but equally as *Subject*. [This Substance] is the movement of positing itself, or is the mediation of its self-othering with itself.'[22] Hitherto (that is, until Hegel), this substance-subject had not yet appeared *as such* to itself, because it was held in exteriority in relation to its own enunciation; hence 'God is the Eternal', the predicate of a preacher [*prédicateur*], for whom 'the Subject is assumed as a fixed point to which, as their support, the predicates are affixed by a movement belonging to the knower of this Subject, and which is not regarded as belonging to the fixed point itself'.[23]

The substance-subject does not yet know either subject or substance because it does not yet know that the subject of the statement is the subject of the enunciation in its becoming-other – which will be discovered in the speculative proposition thinking itself as such – and that the reader of the proposition, and not just its author, is an enunciator. The substance is still enclosed here in the predicative form of proposition, such that it lies outside of this subject of the enunciation who is the reader of the statement, who does not know (not yet) that he or she becomes the subject of the enunciation by reading – that to pass in actuality to the act of reading[24] is to become the author of that which is read. The non-speculative ('predicative') reader of the proposition still believes they are merely a passive reader of this written statement: they are unaware that the text they read is pro-duced.

That this reading is a pro-duction, that is, a kind of writing, and not just a reception, is due to the fact that any true reading (passing to the act of reading) is a selection from among the *primary* retentions (what I retain in what I read) operating according to those criteria that *secondary* retentions constitute for the reader, that is, according to memories that are themselves woven together as *this* reader, and not as another. It is because the secondary retentions of each reader are different from those of every other that each time someone hears or reads a philosophical statement, they do so singularly: a proposition is philosophical only insofar as it puts in play and in question the singularity of the associated milieu[25] that the secondary retentions of a psychic individual constitute for this individual.

And this is because philosophical works, according to Hegel, are books that are written in a way that makes them incomprehensible to those who are unable to put back in play the knowledge they contain, put back in play as a fabric of secondary retentions, of memories, through which is woven the experience that is the book – and which it replays through each new experience. This is why philosophical books are seen as being essentially and irreducibly difficult to read.

The philosophical work thwarts calm, quiet reading, that is, reading that just flows along. The reader is put to work, made to contribute, that is, forced to individuate themselves by individuating what they read on the basis of themselves, and by reading themselves through what they read (which is the Proustian definition of reading). Calm, quiet reading relates on the contrary to what Hegel referred to as the predicative proposition.

It is the contradiction of calm, quiet reading that causes philosophical works to be difficult, and this contradiction is described by Hegel as a brake on or inhibition of [*Hemmen*] this form of reading – an inhibition that necessitates repetition, and that thwarts and disquiets the reader:

> This abnormal inhibition of thought is in large measure the source of the complaints regarding the unintelligibility of philosophical writings from individuals who otherwise possess the education requirements for understanding them. Here we see the reason behind one particular complaint so often made against them: that so much has to be read over and over before it can be understood.[26]

Predicative proposition keeps *exterior* to itself that which *is* itself: its predicative determination separates the subject of the statement from the subject of the enunciation that the reader always is.

The speculative proposition, insofar as it says the essence of the subject of the statement through the predicate of this subject, on the contrary requires the reader to admit that it predicates itself on this subject of the statement by passing through the proposition, triggering an active selection on its part, a selection that constitutes the actual or effective content of the predication by the subject of the enunciation that in this way the reader is. And it does so in such a way that the subject of the statement then becomes the necessary trans-formation of the subject of the enunciation itself, and as a new experience of this subject, through the acquisition of the new secondary retention that the proposition then constitutes for them.

In reading the speculative proposition, the proposition that is philosophical in actuality, the subject of the enunciation who is the reader is trans-formed, individuated and, ultimately, transindividuated through the individuation of the subject of the statement, with which the reader joins, and doing so at the same time as other readers, who together form a 'social body', and thereby contribute to the emergence of the substance-subject: to its 'phenomenology'.[27]

But this subject of the enunciation may not know this and thus may not pass to the act of reading – that is, to the act of reading the proposition that is philosophical only insofar as it is speculative, in the sense that the reading subject mirrors itself in the read subject by gaining knowledge and, therefore, by trans-forming itself, that is, by trans-individuating the substance that it is. This subject may not pass to the act of reading because it solidifies the knowledge it has inherited as the sediment of the past life of the spirit – such knowledge then becomes the type that Hegel calls 'well known'.[28] And the effect of such knowledge is to solidify the reader's own retentions (his or her own experience), because the proposition, read as predicative, confirms the solidity and the solidification of the reader's predicative determinations for a reader who is incapable of re-reading and replaying themselves through their selection criteria. Such a reader does not individuate – because the predicative proposition is, on the contrary, disindividuating.

This disindividuation is possible because the retentional funds from which the individual is constituted, to which it is linked, which it inherits, and which support its own retentions, have been amortized in the sense that they have become dead, as well as mortifying. This mortification is the negativity of exteriority:

> We find that what in former ages engaged the attention of men of mature mind, has been reduced to the level of facts, exercises, and even games for children; and, in the child's progress through school, we shall recognize the history of the cultural development of the world traced, as it were, in a silhouette. This past existence is the already acquired property of universal Spirit which constitutes the Substance of the individual, and hence appears externally to him as his inorganic nature.[29]

This inorganic nature that is *in itself* cannot individuate *for itself*; it remains calm, quiescent. That is, it cannot be put to work, it cannot work towards and contribute by itself to its self-movement. It constantly generates, therefore, a form of stupidity.

The history of universal culture is that of its exteriorization, an exteriorization that must be re-internalized and re-individuated. But during the period when *Phenomenology of Spirit* was written, that is, in the modern epoch, and unlike antiquity, this internalization occurs as the predicative 'ratiocination' that results from the fact that 'in modern times [...] the individual finds the abstract form ready-made'.[30] In modern times, the work of forming the spirit 'in the whole wealth of the developed form', through the relations that have been established by the understanding in the course of this formation, reaches the point where the spirit seems to have become fixed (for example, through the formalist or spiritualist effects of the Kantian heritage).[31]

The task, therefore, consists in fluidifying this form, that is, 'in freeing determinate thoughts from their fixity so as to give actuality to the universal [as self-movement]'.[32] Determination is the fruit of understanding, as the power of discretization and analysis through exteriorization, that is, as spatialization and objectivation of the temporality of spirit, which Hegel called *objective spirit*. But this destination (determination as objective spirit), which is essential to the life of spirit, is also an obstacle to the life of this spirit: it presents itself to it as 'lifeless Understanding and external cognition'.[33]

This 'formal Understanding'[34] is concretely expressed as a process of grammatization through which tertiary retentions are configured that short-circuit the subject insofar as it is speculative, that is, an individuating subject, one capable of passing, anew, into the noetic act.

Formal understanding as exteriorization is therefore the principal cause of proletarianization. But we shall see that this is only because it is realized in the form of those material systems and machines that are retentional systems.[35]

43   Re-reading II – Objective spirit and the unthought in Hegel

Obviously this is not what Hegel says. And nor is it what he thinks: it is, precisely, his *unthought*. But in *Phenomenology of Spirit*, as in the *Aesthetics*, *Philosophy of History* and the *Encyclopedia of the Philosophical Sciences*, he is constantly describing the genesis of this element that forms the understanding concretized through its discretizing exteriorization, so that it can be bequeathed and inherited as objective spirit – and in this case as literalization, that is, as the spatialization 'to the letter' of time that is this process whereby spirit appears to itself by exteriorizing itself.

Hence it is that according to his lectures on history, the true objective history of a people begins when it becomes written history.[36] This perspective, which will be analysed from the angle of social psychology by Jean-Pierre Vernant,[37] is by no means ethnocentric, as hasty readers of Derrida rush to claim.[38] For here, on the contrary, Hegel attributed to a technical invention, that is, an *accidental* invention, and not to 'Western genius' or to its 'essence', the fact that his phenomenology of spirit becomes a worldwide process.

Leroi-Gourhan objected in the same way to the racial theorists of Nazi archaeology, arguing that if Europe was really the central point of a global diffusion of technics in concentric circles, this was the result not of some European (Aryan) genius, but of a concentration of arable land and a great number of other favourable conditions, including climate, and other elements of good fortune that were beneficial for the West and fatal for the civilizations that would be destroyed as a result.[39]

Phenomenology of Spirit describes the constitution of spirit by its exteriorization through historical examples of many kinds. And yet it grants no status to technicity itself in the dialectical process that is exteriorization internalizing itself. Hegel may describe this dialectic as a logic, but not as a techno-logic, a mechano-logic or an organo-logic, and still less as a pharmaco-logic.

The phenomenology of spirit is on the contrary that of its actualization as absolute knowledge, so that philosophy 'can lay aside the title "*love* of knowing" and be *actual* knowing'.[40] Exteriority appears here for what it was from the beginning: a transitory, accidental reality, a reality that is soluble into spirit as ab-solute knowledge (achieved through and as this dissolution). But at the same time, when desire attains its goal, it no longer desires. Knowledge [*savoir*] then becomes insipid: flavourless [*sans saveur*]. Which is to say, *non-knowledge* – and since it is not known as such, it is no longer desired or respected: this is the true ground of the false questions that will be asked by François Hauter.[41]

That absolute knowledge is flavourless, without savour, is for Hegel inconceivable. He does not realize that what he refers to as absolute knowledge would thus be an absolute exteriority that would make absolutely impossible, in its idealist mode – that is, in the denial of its pharmacological dimension – any psychic individuation and any collective individuation, or any philosophical speculativity, since it would be, rather, a process of psychic and collective disindividuation that would be not only massive, but total. Hegel is unaware of this because he ignores the fact that exteriorization is technical, and that its technicity itself derives from a process of technical individuation that is a primary element of a dynamic that he himself understands as a purely spiritual process.

He ignores this, but in ignoring it he unintentionally announces what will actually take place, namely, a totalization effected through a synthesis that is certainly not dialectical, but precisely techno-logical. This totalizing and disindividuating synthesis both absolutely confirms and radically refutes Hegel: what he believed would occur, and would do so as the final reason of History, presents itself as its unreason. Cut off from psychic individuation as from collective indi-viduation, knowledge, grammatized through technical individuation, becomes flavourless because it leads not to absolute knowledge but to the total destruction of knowledge, that is, to its unlearning, to dis-apprenticeship and proletarianization – and as *generalized* proletarianization.

This generalization of proletarianization is completed when specu-lativity becomes that of speculators (and does so for precise historical reasons, which constitute a milestone in the history of capitalism, that I have tried to describe in a number of previous works)[42] and of 'economic rationality'. And this economic rationality puts the *phar-makon*, that is, grammatized material (becoming through that hyper-material),[43] at the service of its speculative auto-concealment: it eliminates the third element, which is precisely the *pharmakon* and its pharmacological dimension, a dimension that would otherwise open all kinds of alternatives to this speculation. The result is an economy of carelessness and neglect.

Generalized proletarianization results, therefore, in an unreason that is a *diseconomy*, wherein speculativity, dissimulating and dis-solving the thickness of its exteriority, becomes 'immaterial', that is, divests all objects and liquidates all desires through a rationalized knowledge in Weber and Adorno's sense: a knowledge without love of knowledge, because without object (and without transitional object),[44] and which *as such* becomes a systemic stupidity.

The phenomenology of spirit leads to this absolute exteriorization that, as proletarianization, makes processes of individuation impos-sible, that is, processes of trans-formation. It is this absolute exteri-orization that constitutes the horizon of *The Postmodern Condition* (and also of *Of Grammatology* and *Capitalism and Schizophrenia*). There is no alternative to this situation so long as the phenomenology of spirit is not reinterpreted as a pharmacology of spirit, which itself presupposes a genealogical (Simondon says 'ontogenetic') organology of spirit.

It is a question not of dismissing Hegel but of re-reading him in order to take the 'step beyond' what he would himself anticipate perfectly well – absolute knowledge as the absolute non-knowledge of systemic stupidity – but by inverting the sign. The dismissal of Hegel and the 'speculative narrative' has on the contrary consisted in repeating the gesture without retaining the greatness. And as we shall see, the same thing occurs with Marx and the 'emancipatory narrative'.

What must pharmacology make of the speculative proposition (and, after that, of the universal subject that is the proletariat)? In what way does it allow or prevent thought of what Lyotard called 'anamnesis'? In what way does it allow us to think beyond the opposition between writing and telegraphy that Lyotard sets up in opposing, precisely, the speculative proposition?

Contrary to Lyotard's assertions, it is necessary to re-read, after Lyotard and poststructuralism in general, those propositions that set out the theory of the speculative proposition, because what Hegel said through these statements on the proposition consists precisely in a rejection of any reading of the proposition by scanning, and in making repetition, which the hypomnesic textuality of the proposition alone makes possible, the very possibility of such an anamnesis, apprehending itself as such, that is: the possibility of a difference wherein the reader remembers what has not yet been experienced, pursuing the movement of différance by constituting *a new turn*.

The speculative proposition is a phenomenology of reading that, if it does not problematize writing as such, does hold not just that the element of the phenomenology of spirit gains access to the speculative proposition through written and difficult-to-read philosophical works, but that so too does sense-certainty, by making writing the experience of that night through which is revealed the day:

> 'What is Now?' [...] 'Now is Night.' [...] We write down this truth; a truth cannot lose anything by being written down, any more than it can lose anything through our preserving it. If *now, this noon*, we look again at the written truth we shall have to say that it has become stale.[45]

Insofar as it is philosophical, predicative proposition is written. But predicative proposition, by solidifying and freezing determinations, short-circuits knowledge, given that the latter is always, first and foremost, the individuation of the subject-becoming-mature, not by receiving knowledge, but by trans-forming it through (trans-) forming oneself.

Hegel, here, does nothing other than reformulate the Kantian injunction in relation to the book as a factor in 'laziness' and 'cowardice' (an injunction that itself reformulates the Platonic view-point on the *pharmakon* that is writing):

> It is so convenient to be immature! If I have a book to have under-standing in place of me, a spiritual adviser to have a conscience for me, a doctor to judge my diet for me, and so on, I need not make any efforts at all.[46]

The necessity of writing lies in the repetition that it makes possible as difference, and thus precisely in the fact that what repeats itself is that which has yet to occur. This is highlighted by Catherine Malabou:

> The specific nature of the philosophical proposition lies in something which could not be available to the first reading. What seems obvious at the first grasp of the proposition is in reality its fundamental unread-ability [...]. At the moment when the reader suffers the 'counter-thrust' [*choc en retour*], 'instead of being for itself, the reader has to remain associated (*zusammensein*) with the content itself' of the prop-osition, in other words to join its backward movement. [...] But at this place of return, the reader finds *nothing*. As the origin was never there the first time, the reader cannot discover any substantial presence or substratum waiting to be identified.[47]

Such is the *philosophical state of shock* in relation to which there is no philosophical thought. But this shocked state of spirit is possible only as a return effect of a technological state of shock. If it is true that the understanding, as determination operating (without knowl-edge) through grammatization, is what tends to freeze the deter-mined, and somehow to impose it as a *state of fact of an exteriority without law*, and as the objectivation of spirit, then this operation, in its effective reality, consists in a production of tertiary retentions that tend to automatically and by themselves link themselves together, outside of any knowing subject, and to do so as cognitive objects – what are today referred to as cognitive technologies, communicating objects, the internet of objects (or of things),[48] and so on.

The speculative proposition, which anticipates this situation, this state of fact, affirms on the contrary the possibility of a new individu-ation in grammatization, which is also an anamnesic movement of the de-proletarianization of what, after Hegel and after Marx, must be understood no longer as a subject, or as a subject-substance (which prevent thinking the techno-logical substrate of determinations as indeterminations, that is, as individuations), but as a process of indi-viduation at once psychic, collective and technical.

If Hegelianism does not by itself allow us to think individuation, this is because it conceives de-proletarianization as an assimilation of exteriority by interiority. And this is what it describes as absolute knowledge laying aside its title 'love of knowing'. But this dissolution of love, grounded in an assimilation of exteriority, completely ignores the constitution of desire through the *transitional* object that is here, insofar as it is neither interior nor exterior, the foundation of all anamnesis (if not of anamnesis apprehending itself as such).[49] And it equally ignores the role of desire in all individuation – as the negentropic principle (in the sense that Canguilhem gives to this term, after Schrödinger) that is short-circuited by absolute knowledge.

Such short-circuits lead to absolute non-knowledge and to generalized proletarianization. They do not, however, spring from some 'essence of technology': they are the result of a war of capital, *become speculative*, that is, a war that ignores the inevitability of material limits, which have now become limits to investment, that is, to individuation. It is for this reason that we must re-read the propositions on the speculative proposition by preliminarily re-reading Marx's *Foundations of the Critique of Political Economy*, the so-called *Grundrisse*.

But to read the latter correctly, we must first re-read the dialectic of the master and the slave, which is its source.

6

Re-Reading the *Grundrisse*: Beyond Two Marxist and Poststructuralist Misunderstandings

The increased productive force of labour is posited rather as the increase of a force [*Kraft*] outside itself, and as labour's own debilitation [*Entkräftung*]. The hand tool makes the worker independent – posits him as proprietor. Machinery – as fixed capital – posits him as dependent, posits him as appropriated. This effect of machinery holds only in so far as it is cast into the role of fixed capital, and this it is only because the worker relates to it as wage-worker.

Karl Marx[1]

Disembrain them, devitalize them, cut off their ears, confiscate their money and drink yourself to death, that's the life of a Salopin, that's happiness for the Master of Phynances.

Alfred Jarry[2]

Only from history in thought, the theory of history, was it possible to account for the historical religion of reading: by discovering that the truth of history cannot be read in its manifest discourse, because the text of history is not a text in which a voice (the Logos) speaks, but the inaudible and illegible notation of the effects of a structure of structures. [...]

Returning to Marx, we note that not only in what he says but in what he does we can grasp the transition from an earlier idea and practice of reading to a new practice of reading, and to a theory of history capable of providing us with a new theory of *reading*.

When we read Marx, we immediately find a *reader* who *reads* to us, and out loud.

Louis Althusser[3]

44   Re-reading III – Mastery and servitude: on the 'dictatorship of the proletariat'

The problem with the Hegelian dialectic is that it makes the exterior 'moment' a transparent milieu, that is, a milieu the heteronomy of which is auto-soluble (ab-solute) into a *Science of Logic* wherein the real ultimately proves to be that which is effectively, actually, rational. This idealism is incapable of seeing, since it postulates the transparency of the 'objective spirit', that to conceive rationality in this way can lead only to an *absolutely irrational rationalization*, that is, to a universal unreason that will manifest itself as stupidity and madness.

In this Science of Logic, which is not a Science of Technology [*technologique*] or of Organology [*organologique*], the exteriority of spirit is not a supplement – it remains an element.[4] It is not pharmacological – it remains purely logical. As such, this exteriority must inevitably be dissolved into the science of logic, within which heteronomy would be but a moment of a negativity that is itself soluble. Or, to put it in terms closer to Nietzsche, it is not tragic.

Exteriority is sublatable, that is, it can be synthesized into a uni-totality: this is what dialectics posits as a principle. To us, however, the latecomers, this synthesis shows itself to be techno-logical, and not dialectical: having reached the stage of digital grammatization, technology analyses and synthesizes the entire world – and in this synthetic world, the rational has effectively become rationalization, as the general spread of systemic stupidity and madness, as universal unreason. Such is our 'effective reality'.

Furthermore, the speculative proposition, because it cannot neutralize the literality of language in which it holds and pro-poses itself, in the necessity of its inscription in letters, can and must be re-read from an organological perspective. That is, it must be re-read by taking seriously the question of the *inorganicity (the technicity)* of the organs of reading of the objective spirit.

This *other way of reading Hegel* shows that the question of the difference we must make between scanning and passing is not a matter of recording technology that would fall outside anamnesis defined as an 'a-technical or a-technological' passing, as Lyotard argues.[5] Rather, it is a question of a way of reading (and therefore of writing) on the basis of the possibilities opened up by the technicity of reading. Lyotard's problem is that he remains here *too Hegelian* (too idealist) to take this supplementarity truly seriously. Hegel himself undoubtedly does take it seriously, since it is the condition of the objective spirit, but he ultimately dissolves it into his uni-total synthesis: this condition is temporary, merely a 'moment'. It is this sense of synthesis that Lyotard repeats.

It is because this moment is the condition of rational objective spirit that, in *Philosophy of History*, Hegel posits that exteriority is not just that which spatializes time (after the fact), but that which *constitutes* it as *historical* time, making clear that a proper consideration of exteriorization in general is necessary[6] (even if this exteriority is asked to dissolve into absolute knowledge, that is, knowledge absolutely free of any heteronomy).

History must be written because, as *Geschichte*, that is, as a new modality of psychic and collective individuation producing what Hegel described as the phenomenology of spirit (which is the history of philosophy), and not just as *Historie* (that is, as historical science and academic knowledge), history is a *modality* of time – that is, of individuation – such that it is reconfigured (in a way that comes close to Paul Ricoeur) by literal tertiary retention as the specific temporal ecstasy[7] that opens the epoch of ways of reading.

Within this *Geschichte*, ways of reading (and therefore of writing) are pharmacologically conditioned by literal mnemotechnics, that is, by tertiary retentions produced in lettered form. This is the question of attention (A – including the suspended attention in which working through, *Durcharbeitung*, occurs), such that it is constituted by a relation between primary retentions (R1), secondary retentions (R2) and tertiary retentions (R3), and where, as we saw in the preceding chapter,[8]

$$A = R3 \, (R2/R1 = S1),^9$$

S1 being a primary *selection* (there is no retention that is not a selection – and here, we must pass through Nietzsche).

Therefore, the problem of the capacity to produce practices and pragmatics that preserve and cultivate the possibility of anamnesis – which is Lyotard's basic concern in 1979 (at the end of *The Postmodern Condition*),[10] and to which he returns in 1986 (at the end of 'Logos and *Techne*, or Telegraphy'), except that he *no longer believes in* this possibility – involves a politics of tertiary retention, and not just 'witnesses to the differend'. It may well be that this is what Lyotard was saying to Max Gallo. But, thirty years later, it is no doubt quite easy to say[11] – yet it remains to be done.

If Lyotard no longer believes in it, therefore, this is because he perpetuates a profound misunderstanding of the concepts of proletariat and proletarianization – a misunderstanding that persists in

Marx himself. This misunderstanding is also a profound contradiction. For to inherit the Hegelian dialectic is, for Marx, firstly to inherit the dialectic of master and slave – itself founded on the dialectic of the desire for recognition. Now, what leads to the dialectical inversion of the master by the slave, the latter having become 'consciousness in itself and for itself', is, in Hegel, the slave's pursuit of knowledge. That is, the slave achieves this inversion by conquering determinations of the understanding, and through work, by putting technics to work – the worker (who is the slave) gives himself an art, that is, a form of knowledge and individuation, and ultimately a property, which *is* his individuation, that is, his existence recognized:

> Work [...] is desire held in check, fleetingness staved off; in other words, work forms [...]. This [...] formative *activity* is at the same time the singularity [*die Einzelnheit*] or pure being-for-self of consciousness which now, in the work outside of it, acquires an element of permanence.[12]

Work is exteriorization par excellence, that is, as individuation. As such, it is also the exteriorization of the for-itself of consciousness: it is the *retaining* of consciousness outside of itself, and the element of its permanence – retention is permanent only because it has become tertiary.

Through this conquest of self in the exteriorization of self, and for the master, slave consciousness achieves consciousness in itself and for itself, that is, beyond the master. And through the moments of this dialectic:

> In the master, being-for-self is an 'other' for the slave, or is only *for* him [i.e. is not his own]; in fear [that of the slave who has become the slave through his recoil in the face of death, which the master does not fear, who as a result of this becomes the master], being-for-self is present in the slave himself; in fashioning the thing [in the work imposed by slavery as the stage of a *Bildung*], he becomes aware that being-for-self belongs to *him*, that he himself exists essentially and actually in his own right. The shape does not become something other than himself through being made external [*hinausgesetzt*, placed outside, as Hyppolite puts it, *pros-thetized* in some way] to him; for it is precisely this shape that is his pure being-for-self, which in this externality is seen by him to be the truth. Through this rediscovery of himself by himself, the slave realizes that it is precisely in his work wherein he seemed to have only an alienated existence that he acquires a mind of his own.[13]

This dialectic of work and workers, which is obviously the foundation of Marxism, is in Hegel not a question of the *worker becoming proletarian* as much as it is about the *artisan becoming an entrepreneur*, that is, bourgeois. In other words, the reappropriation of this dialectic by Marxism is based on a misunderstanding.

What Hegel nevertheless does not think here – when he analyses the becoming of objective spirit by and in work, and as a stage of the 'work of the concept' – is the *machine's* work, which deprives the worker of his singularity, that is, of his work. Work is for the worker then reduced to a job (a salary), a negativity that turns it into a pure force of labour that is no longer work properly speaking, given that work, as Hegel explains, is an individuation process in which the worker is individuated at the same time as the object, which is thereby individuated technically (this is what I have tried to describe as work in an associated milieu).[14]

It is for this reason that, in Marxist economico-political theory, the dictatorship of the proletariat, supposedly grounded in this dialectic, is in fact based on a profound misinterpretation. For Marx himself showed in the *Grundrisse* that the determination carried out by exteriorization in machines, and as grammatization, is what structurally and materially deprives the slave of all knowledge – the slave who becomes the worker, the wage labourer, a status destined to be extended to 'all layers of the population' via wage labour, as Marx and Engels would write in the *Communist Manifesto*.[15]

It is precisely because materialism, inheriting the 'speculative narrative', is unaware of this question – and what necessarily accompanies it, namely, the question of desire (of recognition, that is, of work as the delay and différance of desire and beyond, desire of the Other and of the 'Thing' absent from the Lyotardian theory of anamnesis) – that materialism fails in building not only an 'emancipatory narrative' (as if materialism and dialectics were only stories told to children, such as Plato considers in Book III of the *Republic*, a bit like the tale told by Lyotard in *The Postmodern Explained to Children*),[16] but a horizon of political struggle capable of opening up alternatives.

To the extent that Lyotard cannot see this problem, he too fails, as does the Marxism that was his provenance and of which he ultimately fails to offer a critique: he prefers to bury it. For to give a critique means *to re-read* – and to re-read in detail and against the dominant clichés. But to do so it would be necessary to believe in it, and, in the end, Lyotard 'no longer believes' – at the risk of sounding cynical. This non-belief, which I also call disbelief [*mécréance*], stems

from the general Marxist confusion about the meaning of the proletariat. And the fact that Lyotard does not see this Marxist confusion
(which is also Marx's own confusion, given that *Capital* tends to
identify the proletariat and the working class, contrary to the *Communist Manifesto*) is all the more strange given that he refers explicitly to Marx and to the *Grundrisse* in his analysis of the so-called
postmodern condition of knowledge.

Lyotard repeats the gesture of Marx that he precisely failed to
critique (to have taken seriously *on this point*). This gesture consists,
on the one hand, in making the concept of the proletariat synonymous with the concept of the working class, and, on the other hand,
in taking the negativity of the proletarian condition as an unsurpass-
able horizon and in never posing the question or the hypothesis
of de-proletarianization – a Marxist drift that extends Hegelian
metaphysics.

What Hegel never thinks is technics as that which bypasses and
short-circuits the knowledge of the slave. Marx attempts to think
machine technology, but without drawing any consequences for the
master–slave dialectic. This is why (because he 'forgets' to think
the positive and negative pharmacology of this organology) he turns
the negativity of the universal subject of history (that would be the
proletariat) into the revolutionary principle, whereas it is in fact the
curative positivity of the pharmacological supplement deriving from
work that inverts the logic of disindividuation, and as technique of
the self, and that must make possible a new age of individuation,
that is, of knowledge. And it must do so as a new history of the love
of knowledge, its savours, as knowing how to do and to live, and
also how to theorize – of which I am here in a way fashioning a
narrative.

As for *The Postmodern Condition*, the issue there is the 'exteriorization of knowledge with respect to the "knower"',[17] an exteriorization that makes possible 'performance' and makes inaccessible the
experience of the 'differend'. This placement into exteriority is,
however, what Plato had already denounced with respect to writing
insofar as it is a *pharmakon*. I have previously argued that this denun-
ciation was the first time that proletarianization was thought as
such[18] – and that this is how Derrida must be read, with or without
him, if not against him.

The process of proletarianization was described by Marx in the
Communist Manifesto (1848) as a loss of knowledge resulting from
exteriorization, and this was further elaborated in the *Grundrisse*
(1857). This then constituted the material basis for what Althusser

and his students Étienne Balibar, Roger Establet, Pierre Macherey and Jacques Rancière would urge their generation to read and re-read, namely, *Capital* (1867) – in so doing differentiating themselves from what they refer to as 'structuralist ideology'.[19] Between the *Manifesto* and *Capital*, however, the question of knowledge, and of its loss, is lost. And this will be a blow to Marxism – including Lyotard.

When in *The Postmodern Condition* Lyotard discusses 'placing into exteriority' [*mise en extériorité*], he refers explicitly to the *Grundrisse*.[20] But strangely, Lyotard does not think this in terms of proletarianization. Like all Marxists, Lyotard fails to see that the proletariat is not the working class, but the *non-working* class [*la classe des désoeuvres*], that is, the downgraded, the class of those who are *de-class-ified*. They are those who no longer know, but serve, systems that exteriorize knowledge: this includes those technicians to whom he refers in *The Postmodern Condition*, those he argues are unable to 'bear witness to the differend', but many others as well, subservient to the retentional systems of consumption (that is, the whole world),[21] not production, and who would nevertheless like to find a *job*, in default of finding *work*.

Here, however, it is not a matter of 'bearing witness to the differend', except in order to reconstitute anamnesic circuits – that is, to think and practise the differend as an experience of the default that leads to a pharmacological struggle against proletarianization. And in this context, *to think* is *to say*, but also *to do*, besides the fact that saying becomes doing in being exteriorized, such that a differend between the subject of the statement and that of the enunciation is constituted via a *third, the factor of proletarianization*: that which constitutes tertiary retention, including as machines and apparatus, and not just through the performativity of speech acts or 'managerial dogma',[22] but which is also a curative third or knowing-third – *organological knowledge*.

We should not conclude, therefore, that legitimation is no longer possible thanks to the computerization or informatization of language.[23] Instead, we must posit performatively (but in a sense other than that which Lyotard grants to performativity) that grammatization – of which computerization is the development that was contemporary with *The Postmodern Condition*, and which has today become digitalization, wherein computing is now available to everyone and no longer restricted to 'computer engineers' and other 'technicians' of 'machine language', and where this extends far beyond language – that this *digital grammatization completely transforms public and private space and time* (which Lyotard feels coming, but which he does not manage to think), just as writing did for the *polis*, according to Hegel. And through this transformational upheaval, digital grammatization opens the possibility of a positive pharmacology as generalized de-proletarianization.

This grand narrative of grammatization as experience of the *pharmakon* tells the story of an idea of that which is great in the non-inhuman being, and which is possible only as the experience of that which is small, that is, of what Deleuze called *baseness* – which may sometimes cause shame, that is, provoke thought.

As for the curative possibility of the digital *pharmakon*, it will not rise up thanks to some illumination coming from who knows where, but because digital tertiary retention, which constitutes a completely original stage of the exteriorization that is grammatization, makes it possible and necessary *at the very moment when the industrial model imposed by consumerist capitalism is collapsing*. Such a collapse represents a *generalization of baseness*, spreading it far and wide, and it requires a *generalized de-proletarianization*, as a task of thought and action in all their forms. And while the irrationality of rationalization that generates this baseness is becoming transparent and obvious, other, de-proletarianizing operations are already under way.

If the negative side of the Hegelian dialectic, however, is not toxic (and this is why it is 'sublatable', that is, reducible and soluble into a spirit become ab-solute knowledge), pharmacological negativity is on the contrary *in-soluble*, that is, it cannot find the definitive solution within which it could be dissolved. It is at all times the object of a struggle. Its toxicity, which appears firstly as disindividuation and loss of savour, that is, as absolute non-knowledge, must form part of a therapeutic, and as dependence, that is, as irreducible heteronomy: the individual individuates only insofar as it knows what to do with, or can make do with, the irreducible toxicity of the *pharmakon*.

This means that toxicity itself, like a practice of voluntary intoxication, can be curative: the curative is not the opposite of the toxic.[24] This is why Bateson posits that, for the alcoholic, there must be something 'right' about alcoholic intoxication, and why he argues that the alcoholic must recognize this at the moment of disintoxication.[25] What Alcoholics Anonymous say to those wanting to detox is that they must firstly understand why alcohol worked for them, what was good about it. And they must do so in order to be able to choose something other than alcohol, to continue their individuation, and to struggle against the disindividuation that is alcoholic dependence. And this also means that, from the pharmacological point of view, there is no final synthesis, but a *savoir-vivre-with-its-dependencies* (what Nietzsche called chains, and which are those of Prometheus bound): a savoir-vivre each time singular, that is, individuating.[26]

Lyotard posits on the contrary that the exteriorization of knowledge, without any return to knowing, and without an alternative horizon, is an inescapable fact: it is precisely the impossibility of such a return that constitutes the postmodern in the strict sense – where 'there is no alternative'. Now, this seems highly questionable, in relation, for example, to the free software movement as an industrial organization of work founded on de-proletarianization, that is, on sharing knowledge and responsibility, and, through that, on the reconstitution of associated industrial milieus – whereas earlier forms of industrialization always led to the dissociation of milieus, that is, to disindividuation.[27]

That this situation can become pharmacologically positive does not mean, therefore, that this tendency to dissociation can be *overcome*, that is, 'sublated', in the sense of the Hegelian *Aufhebung*. It means:

- that it can and must be fought against, and contained, and that this should be the principle of industrial politics and economics in the twenty-first century, through which priorities and lines of flight will be organized, and goals projected;
- that *it is in this that the responsibility of the university lies*, as we shall see in the second part of this book.

45   Re-reading IV – The *Grundrisse*

The Hegelian and 'idealist' definition of the understanding was inverted by Marx when he proposed that exteriorization, in which understanding essentially consists, is first and foremost that of the means of production: such is his 'materialism'. But in so dismissing idealism Marx lost sight of the question of ideality, that is, idealization as that which is at work in all investment and in all knowledge of the object of desire. And poststructuralism, too, leaves this in the shadows by tending to confound desire and drive: the misunderstanding in relation to the proletariat is at the same time a misunderstanding of desire.

In *The German Ideology* (1845), Marx's materialism initially consists in identifying the first 'historical act' of noetic beings with their technical capacity. Non-inhuman beings 'begin to distinguish themselves from animals as soon as they begin to *produce* their means of subsistence, a step which is conditioned by their physical organisation'.[28] The Hegelian question of exteriorization is thus 'put back on its feet', to some extent as a question of general organology, where the materialist dialectic assigns *being* (and its becoming) to *doing*, that is, to *production*:

> As individuals express their life, so they are. What they are, therefore, coincides with their production, both with *what* they produce and with *how* they produce. Hence what individuals are depends on the material conditions of their production.[29]

That this exteriorization can lead to the proletarianization of workers is explained in the *Grundrisse* in terms of the passage from the tool to the machine, that is, to a new stage of exteriorization:

> The means of labour passes through different metamorphoses, whose culmination is the *machine*, or rather, an *automatic system of machinery* (system of machinery: the *automatic* one is merely its most complete, most adequate form, and alone transforms machinery into a system) [...]; this automaton consisting of numerous mechanical and intellectual organs, so that the workers themselves are cast merely as its conscious linkages.[30]

And Marx continues:

> In no way does the machine appear as the individual worker's means of labour. Its distinguishing characteristic is not in the least, as with the means of labour, to transmit the worker's activity to the object; this activity, rather, is posited in such a way that it merely transmits the machine's work, the machine's action, on to the raw material – supervises it and guards against interruptions. Not as with the instrument, which the worker animates and makes into his organ with his skill and strength, and whose handling therefore depends on his virtuosity. Rather, it is the machine which possesses skill and strength in place of the worker, is itself the virtuoso, with a soul of its own in the mechanical laws acting through it.[31]

This analysis forms the basis of Simondon's argument in *Du mode d'existence des objets techniques*. The process of disindividuation that he describes paraphrases these statements by Marx:

> The technical individual becomes at a certain point man's adversary, his competitor, because man had, when there were only tools,

centralized all technical individuality within himself; the machine then takes the place of man because man grants to the machine the function of tool-bearer.[32]

Marx does indeed emphasize that this industrial division of labour, and the replacement of workers and tools by machines, is also a change in the status of knowledge and of the science that it brings. Scientific knowledge is placed at the service of the process of exteriorization, whereby it is knowledge itself, and in general, that is exteriorized:

> The science which compels the inanimate limbs of the machinery, by their construction, to act purposefully, as an automaton, does not exist in the worker's consciousness, but rather acts upon him through the machine as an alien power, as the power of the machine itself.[33]

Hence there occurs, if one here follows Marx to the letter, a *disembraining* [*décervelage*] – as *King Ubu* puts it in 1896. It is thus both scientific knowledge (that is, intellectual labour) and savoir-faire (that is, manual labour) that mutate.

Intellectual labour is used in the service of the reduction of the role of manual labour in the production process:

> The production process has ceased to be a labour process [...] individual living workers [are] only a link of the system, whose unity exists not in the living workers, but rather in the living (active) machinery [...]. The increase of the productive force of labour and the greatest possible negation of necessary labour is the necessary tendency of capital.[34]

And it is placed in the service of capital, and of the appropriation of labour by capital, in the form of fixed capital:

> The accumulation of knowledge and of skill, of the general productive forces of the social brain, is thus absorbed into capital, as opposed to labour, and hence appears as an attribute of capital, and more specifically of *fixed capital*, in so far as it enters into the production process as a means of production proper.[35]

It is in this sense that, for Simondon, a machine is a crystallization of repeatable gestures that become 'functional structures': 'What machines contain is human reality, the human gesture set and crystallized into functional structures.'[36] The subordination of labour (of servitude) to capital (to mastery) operates via the materialization of this knowledge, that is, its grammatization, which eventually enables the elimination of the worker in favour of an *autonomization* of technics, in the form of its *automatization*:

> The productive force of society is measured in *fixed capital*, exists there in its objective form; [...] living labour [as] subsumed under self-activating objectified labour. The worker appears as superfluous.[37]

This grammatization appears with machine technology, which replaces instrumental technics, via the application of science and the loss of empirical savoir-faire resulting from a shift in the end (or purpose) of formal and theoretical knowledge:

> The entire production process appears as not subsumed under the direct skillfulness of the worker, but rather as the technological appli-cation of science. [It is,] hence, the tendency of capital to give produc-tion a scientific character.[38]

Hence knowledge has changed status, both in terms of savoir-faire, which has been replaced by the materialized knowledge of automated machines, and in terms of theoretical knowledge, which could under-take this replacement only by itself becoming technological – that is, as we shall see, by losing its theoretical aspect, and thus itself becom-ing a proletarianized pseudo-knowledge, that is, a rationalization[39] that produces systemic stupidity.

This becoming or this development leads to a capitalist contradic-tion that would later be described by Marx as the tendency of the rate of profit to fall.

> To the degree that labour time – the mere quantity of labour – is posited by capital as the sole determinant element, to that degree does direct labour and its quantity disappear as the determinant principle of production – of the creation of use values – and is reduced both quantitatively, to a smaller proportion, and qualitatively, as an, of course, indispensable but subordinate moment, compared to general scientific labour, technological application of natural sciences, on one side, and to the general productive force arising from social combina-tion [*Gliederung*] in total production on the other side [...]. *Capital thus works towards its own dissolution as the form dominating production.*[40]

A contradiction exists between the fact that labour is the sole source of profit possible for capitalism, and the fact that there is nevertheless a tendency to reduce it so as to transform it into fixed capital, which leads to what in *Capital* Marx called the tendency of the rate of profit to fall.[41]

Here, *invention* becomes the crux of capitalism: 'Invention then becomes a business, and the application of science to direct production itself becomes a prospect which determines and solicits it.'[42] This invention is above all the advance of the process of grammatization as spatialization, reproduction and repetition of gestural time. Gestures are thus turned into the automatic movements of the machine, just as speech became text at the time history began to take the form of *Geschichte* (and just as today, with digitalization and vocal synthesis, speech is automatically 'written' and 'read'):

> But this [...] road along which machinery [...] progresses [...] is, rather, dissection [*Analyse*] – through the division of labour, which gradually transforms the workers' operations into more and more mechanical ones, so that at a certain point a mechanism can step into their places.[43]

It is this process of grammatization, which exceeds the opposition of language and technics (and thus also goes beyond 'logocentrism'), that constitutes the fundamental stakes of différance, and thus of writing in the sense invoked by Lyotard in his theory of anamnesis. To place these two forms of exteriorization in opposition, an opposition that organizes the reasoning and arguments of both *The Postmodern Condition* and *The Inhuman*, would therefore be profoundly metaphysical: it is a philosophical regression.

For Althusser, 'the text of history is [...] the inaudible and illegible notation of the effects of a structure of structures',[44] and the issue for Marxism is to exceed the *logos* and logocentrism of teleological and idealist history by thinking, reading and writing this text *as* this 'notation of the effects of a structure of structures'.

But the *Grundrisse* shows that such an approach requires us to think in terms of grammatization[45] – and in passing through not only Derrida, but also Leroi-Gourhan, himself a structuralist,[46] but one who does not reduce the structural question to language and combinatorial analysis: on the contrary, he thinks structures in terms of what Althusser called the 'combination' of Marx, and closer to what Deleuze and Guattari think as an 'arrangement'. Balibar cites, in relation to this point, Book II of *Capital*:

> Whatever the social form of production, labourers and means of production always remain *factors* (*Faktoren*) of it. But in a state of

separation from each other either of these factors can be such only potentially (*der Möglichkeit nach*). For production to go on at all they must combine (*Verbindung*). The specific manner in which this combination is accomplished distinguishes the different epochs of the structure of society one from another.[47]

The analysis that Marx proposes in the *Grundrisse* leads to organology, and more particularly to an organology of knowledge – a question to which I will return in the second part. Without such an organology of knowledge it is not possible to think economic epochs in terms of such combinations:

> Nature builds no machines, no locomotives, railways, electric telegraphs, self-acting mules etc. These are products of human industry; natural material transformed into organs of the human will over nature, or of human participation in nature. They are *organs of the human brain, created by the human hand*; the power of knowledge, objectified. The development of fixed capital indicates to what degree general social knowledge has become a *direct force of production*, and to what degree, hence, the conditions of the process of social life itself have come under the control of the general intellect and been transformed in accordance with it. To what degree the powers of social production have been produced, not only in the form of knowledge, but also as immediate organs of social practice, of the real life process.[48]

It is, however, not savoir-faire alone that is destroyed by industrial grammatization – and to the service of which theoretical knowledge is submitted. Savoir-vivre, too, is liquidated, through processes that capture attention and reconfigure it by standardizing behavioural patterns.

It is then consumers who are deprived of any inventive role, and who no longer transmit any savoir-vivre to their descendants, nor receive any from their ascendants, since they are on the contrary forced to abandon it in the name of adapting to whatever marketing devises. And, today, all this occurs with the help of the social and cognitive sciences – neuromarketing being the most advanced stage of this aspect of proletarianization.

In addition, fundamental theoretical knowledge is proletarianized, that is, decoupled from theoretical activity – and it is this development that is analysed in *The Postmodern Condition* in terms of 'performativity'. The destruction of the theoretical dimension of formal knowledge consists in transforming *formalisms* into *automatisms*. These are implemented so as to increase the analytical performance of these formalisms, which leads to the automatization of scientific understanding itself. Reason is thereby autonomized – and as such becomes rationalization, that is, material, formal and efficient causality without final causality.

What is taught today, therefore, is increasingly a purely procedural technological knowledge, including in the faculty of sciences, at the expense of the historical and critical knowledge of the theories lying at the origin of these formalisms. Scientific instruments have become machines to which scientists, who are more and more technologists and less and less scientists, must adapt themselves without having time to go back to the axioms and synthetic judgements that govern the mechanisms through which they formulate analytic judgements.[49]

In the economic field, one result of this abolition of theory has been the proletarianization of Alan Greenspan himself.[50]

46 Alternatives, reform and revolution

The political dogma of the dictatorship of the proletariat postulates that there is nothing beyond proletarianization. In other words, this dogma posits a priori that there is nothing beyond the liquidation of knowledge, that proletarianization is insurmountable and that labour or work cannot be reinvented through a new relation to the *pharma-kon* and to the generalized grammatization that makes possible generalized proletarianization. This is the point of view of dialectical materialism inasmuch as it puts to work the Hegelian concept of negativity.

This dogma is the true problem of Marxism – which will then be translated into the errancies and inversions of Lenin in relation to Frederick Taylor.[51] The major question of materialism becomes blurred as a result, namely, the materiality of knowledge, and the problems associated with its mechanized grammatization in the industrial age, the determinations of the understanding (in the Hegelian sense and as faculty of the *res cogitans*) being concretized through a process of automatization via the writing of formalisms in matter (the highest degree of automatization being achieved when this matter becomes silicon). In matter: that is, in space (*res extensa*).

Overcoming this Marxian dogma means inverting the negativity of toxicity into a curative positivity through the creation of a new age of work founded on a new industrial model that would also constitute a new libidinal economy of the industrial age, that is, *a new kingdom of industrial ends.*

In the process of proletarianization, the techno-logical determinations of the understanding and the formalisms in which they consist – formalisms that are designed to serve efficiency (which Lyotard calls performance) through their materialization – are cut off from the time of final causality (which is temporality as the reason of matter, of form and of efficiency) without which there can be no theory, that is, anamnesis.[52] But final causality, after Freud, is constituted as the object of desire, that is, as libidinal economy (in a sense very different from the way this is understood by Lyotard).

Marx (like Althusser after him) commits a fundamental error in assuming that the way the proletariat can escape their condition is by becoming conscious of their proletarianized situation, rather than through the elaboration of a new kind of knowledge. This new type of knowledge would not be the Marxist 'science' sought by Althusser, but the invention of a new process of psychic, collective and technical individuation constituting a new relation to technics. This is the horizon of the following statement by Simondon:

> These structures [functional machines] must be maintained in the course of functioning, and perfecting them coincides with increasing their openness, increasing the freedom of their functioning.[53]

This proposition provides a particularly clear perspective on positive pharmacology. Through it, we can understand how and why machine-based tertiary retention, written and read in silicon by the reading and writing machines that are contributory digital systems and networks, opens the possibility of de-proletarianization, not in some 'post-industrial' age, but in a new industrial age.

Despite his extreme foresight in the *Grundrisse*, Marx did not think technics as this memory it would always have been (constituting as such an organology of the unconscious), something that becomes patently obvious in the stage of digital grammatization, when industrial *hypomnēmata* (called software, hardware, data, netware, web, metadata, and so on) become the primary economic element. Marx continues to think technics under the category of means for the collective subject that is the proletariat, as class and as class-consciousness. He does tend, however, to identify the proletariat with the working class-become-inactive [*désoeuvrée*], that is, no longer working in the sense of opening the world. They are proletarianized: those to whom the world is closed by dissociation.[54]

Unaware that the technical 'element' is a *supplement* putting to work a logic of the supplement through a history of the supplement, and not a means in the service of ends,[55] Marx failed to think the trio of psychic, collective and technical individuations. Even if he suggests that all wage labour leads to the proletarianization of labourers, he postulates that it is the *manual* working class that is the bearer of the contradictions of capital, and that can overthrow them – which is an error in every way that has led Marxists in general in the direction of what is wrongly called 'workerism'.

The proletariat is in no way what Lyotard, Althusser or Marxist thought in general believed it to be: the proletariat is constituted not by the working class or labour in general, but by the 'exteriorization of knowledge with respect to the "knower"'. The great significance of *The Postmodern Condition*, despite everything for which it can be reproached (for a start, by Lyotard himself, who later declared that this text was no more than a product of circumstance), lies in making clear that the fate of knowledge consists in its exteriorization, which is both its condition and the possibility of its loss.

The problem is that, even if Lyotard refers to the text of the *Grundrisse* in order to show that Marx is the first to think and to posit in principle this becoming,

- on the one hand, he does not see that proletarianization is a fate common to both manual labour and intellectual labour (and this is something that Marx himself did not conceptualize in clear terms, even though he posited from the outset that proletarianization affects 'all layers of the population');
- on the other hand, he does not see that this was already Plato's subject, in relation to the pharmacological dimension of writing – which becomes 'telegraphic' only in the absence of a therapeutic as *epimēleia* practised in order to access anamnesis.

In effacing the fact that knowledge and its loss is the principal factor associated with proletarianization, Marx himself could not see that the fundamental contradiction of capital is less that the rate of profit tends to fall – as counter to which Schumpeter will devise an answer (albeit temporary)[56] in the form of 'Creative Destruction' – than that libidinal energy tends to fall. In other words, Marx did not see that capital brings about the destruction of knowledge *in all its forms*, which is also the destruction of tastes [*saveurs*] and, with them, of desire, as that which engenders them through sublimation. And if he cannot see this, it is because he is no longer able to see that the main problem that the Hegelian dialectic poses lies in the fact that it induces the end of desire – and that it anticipates an actual, effective becoming that in fact describes the world we inhabit today. And, through a ruse of history, the installation of this world is due in no small part to the contribution of poststructuralist anti-Hegelianism.

Lyotard in fact shared with poststructuralism in general, as with Marxism in general, this erroneous perspective on the proletariat, a perspective *that stems from an error concerning the question of desire*. This error consists in failing to take into account the evolution of Freud's ideas in relation to his theory of the drives – indicated, for example, in Freud's statement in 1920 that 'the immediate aims of psycho-analytic technique are quite other to-day than they were at the outset'.[57] By largely leaving in the shadows this new question that Freud opened up,[58] the poststructuralist perspective on desire remains confused about how desire and the drives are to be distinguished and articulated.

The proletariat must be thought otherwise: it must be thought via re-readings of Plato, Hegel and Marx (and also Adam Smith) *with* Freud, precisely because *desire and its economy are destroyed by capital*, something that is implicitly foreshadowed in *Phenomenology of Spirit*. Grasping this, however, depends on being able to distinguish desire and drive clearly, which is obviously not the case for that 'Great Ephemeral skin' through which Lyotard aims to think the affects in what he imagines to be the libidinal economy of capital: in *Libidinal Economy*,[59] published in 1974, one year after *Dérive à partir de Marx et Freud*[60] and two years after Deleuze and Guattari's *Anti-Oedipus*, desire is *explicitly not* this economy – the issue there is not desire, but the drives.[61] And this is to a large extent true of poststructuralist thought in general – which claims to define its place by breaking with Marcuse but on this point largely repeats him.[62]

Two misunderstandings are therefore established during the twentieth century: one concerning the proletariat; the other concerning desire. Together, these misunderstandings have resulted in great confusion about how these two concepts relate to work (which is the principal modality of *différance* – this is what must be retained from Hegel, but in passing through *The German Ideology*, the *Grundrisse*, and the *Introductory Lectures on Psycho-Analysis*).

Moreover, these two misunderstandings have not ceased to mutually reinforce each other – at the same time as they have inhibited understanding of what would be the historical specificity of the twentieth century, namely consumerism. And this severely flawed theoretical situation was to lead progressive movements into errant oscillations between reform and revolution:

- *Reform* is what proposes no alternative: it aims to improve a finite system, assuming that it can manage the contradictions-without-alternative implied by its finitude.[63] Lyotard's systemic turn is from this perspective a return to reformism.
- *Revolution* is what posits that a finite system has reached or will reach a limit, at which point the system must be changed. A strict Marxist materialism argues that this system-change becomes necessary when the material of the system leads it to its limits – inducing a passage to the limit in the sense of René Passet.[64] But, because he misunderstood his own theory of exteriorization as leading to proletarianization, Marx himself was ultimately incapable of thinking this hyper-material materiality that is knowledge as fixed capital, and he failed to think and to critique the technicity of capitalism as pharmacological revolution as well as therapeutic revolution: he failed to theorize technological *shock* and its transformation by psychosocial individuation and by a state of philosophical shock.

The twenty-first century begins, however, by establishing a *revolutionary situation*, for two reasons:

- on the one hand, a mutation of industrial material, produced by an industrial world now dominated by this industry of the supplement that is digitalization (by the digital tertiary retention industry, firstly as hardware and software, then as dataware and metadataware),[65] resulting in a systemic industrial mutation both by accelerating the obsolescence of the consumerist system founded on centralist organizations, and by opening new, undetermined possibilities in the field of machines, which amount to new possibilities of psychic and collective individuation;
- on the other hand, the 'technicians' of 'language machines', technicians assumed by Lyotard to be incapable of 'bearing witness to differends', have for almost thirty years (that is, since shortly after the publication of *The Postmodern Condition*: firstly at MIT,[66] then in California, in particular at Berkeley) been engaged in a revolutionary struggle, a struggle concerned with the production and sharing of knowledge, with a new industrial organization of work, and with intellectual property, and the goal of this struggle has been to constitute an industrial organization founded on de-proletarianization.

Here, 'revolution' does not necessarily imply barricades or the seizure of power: it refers to the process through which an epoch that has run its course [*une époche révolue*] gives way to a new epoch. A revolution is as such an exceptional modality of what Simondon called 'quantum leaps' in individuation, in which it is the very conditions of individuation that are transformed. The question is thus to define what makes an epoch – and we shall return to this question in the following part.

47   The decline of progressivism, the twin fictions of the 'working class' and the 'middle class', and the reconquering of knowledge

A revolutionary process is under way. It is both technological and economic. It is not yet political: it is yet to reach the second moment of the doubly epokhal redoubling in which the revolutionary socialization of technological shock always consists, this being what, for example, the bourgeoisie accomplished in the nineteenth century, according to Marx and Engels.[67]

It has not reached this second moment because those in the twentieth century have failed to grasp this dual misunderstanding (including André Gorz, who in some respects caught glimpses of it).[68] The movements and parties that in the twentieth century called themselves 'progressive' continue, in the twenty-first century, to suffer more than ever from this dual misunderstanding – having learned strictly nothing capable of bringing us into the twenty-first century, and this is yet one more aspect of the reign of stupidity.

Progressive movements and parties are at the same time blind to what is being played out on this new revolutionary scene, and they have proven incapable of playing their role as laboratories of alternative perspectives. Furthermore, these movements and parties are also cut off from the 'popular' classes and the 'middle' classes, thereby reinforcing the extreme rightward drift of government, and contributing to the possibility that forces of the extreme right will succeed in taking power.

During the twentieth century, progressive movements and parties addressed the 'popular' classes and the 'middle' classes in discourse that did not speak to them: the *popular* classes[69] may have been those who bore the brunt of proletarianization, but no illumination of the meaning or significance of this proletarianization (as loss of knowledge) was received from these so-called progressive movements and parties. Hence the struggle was essentially aimed at 'defending buying power', that is, at reinforcing consumerism, and this in turn contributed to the liquidation not only of the skills (savoir-faire) required for work, but also of the knowledge of how to live (savoir-vivre) outside of work.

The same logic was at work among the so-called *middle* classes: the same liquidation of savoir-vivre, to which was added the liquidation of theoretical knowledge (that which is taught in secondary schools and universities), which became obsolete thanks to the proletarianization of processes of design and decision-making by automated understanding.[70] Furthermore, their pauperization and downgrading [*déclassement*] pushed them towards the popular classes, given that the general degradation of wage labour was the inevitable result of speculative financialization (which became, from the 1970s, the new response to the tendency of the rate of profit to fall, at the moment when Schumpeterian entrepreneurial capitalism reached its limits with the postcolonial situation).

Comprehending next to nothing of these developments, progressive parties and movements, or those historically deemed to have been such, have proven incapable of deriving any political advantage from them. The struggle against 'downgrading' in all its forms, by emphasizing the solidarity of the 'middle classes' with 'manual labourers' and 'employees', should thus also have consisted in positing the reconstruction of knowledge as a main objective. Instead, the opposition between the 'blue-collar' (who have become) employees and 'white-collar' (who have become) managers (or '*bobos*') can lead only to populisms of all kinds.

It is understandable, however, that until the 1980s, such an objective could not be adopted or even imagined: the material and technological reality of knowledge exteriorized in fixed capital simply did not allow for it. What is not understandable, on the contrary, is that this is *still* the case today: the therapeutic specificities of the new digital pharmacology – brought about by the evolution of grammatization in which consists not only industrial machinery, but also and above all, now, the apparatus of digital cultural and cognitive technology that typifies the 'technical reproducibility' of the twenty-first century – make it obvious that such prospects are already developing. Parties and movements are, however, nearly wholly ignorant of these developments, and for this reason they can rightly be referred to as 'progressive' only between inverted commas.

Having forgotten that the extension of wage labour was also the extension of proletarianization, unaware that the latter proceeded essentially from the exteriorization of knowledge, through a grammatization that with the rise of financialization affects even the ruling classes (in relation to which it is necessary to read Paul Jorion), the 'progressive' parties and movements, in the twentieth century, ultimately made common cause with consumerism. And they did so by maintaining the fiction (since the proletariat are no longer workers) of a 'working class' whose purchasing power it was necessary to defend, as well as the fiction of a separation between the 'popular classes' and the 'middle classes'.

The 'working class' have been transformed into a reserve army, that is, into a pure force of deskilled labour. They are a class who for quite some time have not been workers, and who for a very long time have been 'downgraded' and 'de-*class*-ified' under the constant and threatening pressure of unemployment. This transformation has created an electorate that is increasingly difficult to convince, because to talk to them about 'buying power' is to address them with messages that are incomprehensible – because they are incoherent.

Failing to understand the problem common to the 'popular' and 'middle classes', namely their loss of knowledge, one constantly 'betrays' these 'popular segments' by turning towards the 'middle class', preferring a safer and more understanding electorate, thereby ignoring the fact that the 'middle class' is itself just as much a fiction and a fantasy as the 'popular segments' or the 'working class', and is so because it is equally entangled with and affected by proletarianization – as, even more, are its children. One thus at the same time 'betrays' the 'middle class' itself.

These issues are now emerging as such, and they should lead to the abandonment of the discourse that defends purchasing power, in favour of the goal of developing a *purchasing knowledge*, founded on a new *producing knowledge* and a new *conceiving and designing knowledge* in the age of digital grammatization and of the contributory economy that it makes possible. The contributory industrial economy must be founded on shared knowledge, on conceptual processes (that is, processes of the individuation of knowledge) that are elaborated collectively, and on processes of critical decision-making – all of which are made possible by the transindividuation technologies that disseminate 'netware'.[71]

The alternative, then, is to de-proletarianize the middle classes also – who are undergoing downgrading and de-classifying just as much as the popular classes – an alternative the possibility of which clearly lies in the reticular reorganization of knowledge.

48   Beliefs and disbelief, credit and discredit

> I had to seriously undertake, once in my life, to rid myself of all the
> opinions I had received into my set of beliefs [*créance*] up until that
> moment, and to begin afresh from the foundations.[72]

So writes René Descartes at the beginning of his *Meditations on First
Philosophy*. 'Créance', here, refers to that in which one believes, to
which one gives credit.[73]

Three hundred and thirty eight years later, Lyotard declares at the
beginning of *The Postmodern Condition*: 'I define *postmodern* as
incredulity toward metanarratives.'[74] And in *The Inhuman*, he posits
that 'capital is grounded in the principle that money is nothing other
than time placed in reserve, available'.[75]

Now, such 'time placed in reserve', that is, exteriorized through a
supplement, which Marx called the general equivalent, can function
only through being invested, that is, through being re-temporalized,
that is, given credit: in re-constituting belief [*créances*]. Money is
indeed, as element of grammatization and as tertiary protention, that
which allows time (the time of the protentions in which belief essentially consists) to be trans-formed into an exchangeable and storable
quantity.[76]

In the middle of a desert a billion dollars may be spent (but not
invested) on a little water or some bread, by someone who, in absolute desperation, is no longer capable of believing – that is, of projecting themselves beyond their situation, and, as such, of ex-sisting
– because what must be assured before anything else is their immediate subsistence. He or she suddenly realizes that his or her capital has
lost its entire value, that is, its capacity to crystallize belief and to
give credit: in a desert, objects of credit in this sense no longer exist.

The consumerist system has become such a desert in which one can
no longer believe, that is, give credit. Consumerism is the reality of
nihilism as the destruction of all values, and it is where the desert
grows by destroying the libidinal economy, giving way to drive-based
capitalism and industrial populism. Consumerism, after the conservative revolution, has become totally speculative and is systemically
destroying all credit and bringing with it the reign of stupidity and
madness – which are the ineluctable consequences of 'disembraining'.

Since the crisis of 2008, which caused this situation of planetary
discredit to become general, hyper-financialized consumerism has
turned to the immediate necessity of its own self-reproduction. It has
tried to do so by fighting to defend its 'positions', but by struggling

in this way it is succeeding only in digging its own grave and preparing its self-collapse – induced by the logic of disinvestment that it establishes in every domain. It generates discredit in a mechanical way by making 'credits' circulate that no longer maintain any belief. By circulating this 'funny money' it prepares the increasingly likely ruin of the whole system – of which the failure of states is only the second stage (after the bankruptcy of Lehman Brothers and the first series of systemic consequences that followed from that initial collapse).

Incredulity – or rather, miscreance and disbelief [*mécréance*] – ruins all economy. Can a claim or a belief [*créance*] be constituted outside of all metanarrative, to put it in Lyotard's terms? Further analysis would be necessary of the meanings of 'meta' and 'narrative'. I will not undertake these analyses here (but this question is the horizon of the question of metadata).[77] And I will close this first part[78] by asking whether the crisis of public debt has been the result of the incredulity and disbelief that has led to the general spread of a loss of credit, which can benefit speculators only in the very short term – while leading all of them, and all of us, to the very brink of the abyss.

The problem of public debt was caused by a global economic war of unprecedented destructiveness, which is creating greater ruin than the first two world wars combined. Since the implementation of the conservative revolution by Margaret Thatcher and Ronald Reagan and continued by Tony Blair, Silvio Berlusconi and Nicolas Sarkozy, there have been countless victims as a result of this extremely destructive war.

A billion people currently suffer from hunger, populations migrate from the South to the North in search of work, urban zones have been destroyed or lost their 'urbanity', rural regions have been turned into deserts, the younger generation is confronting economic despair, illiteracy grows, there is widespread regression in terms of health, the apparatus of production is being destroyed by speculation, both familial education and public education are being annihilated, and on it goes. This situation has been systematically cultivated by the financialization of the economy, which has initiated a struggle to the death – and a suicidal struggle – against all forms of human collectivity, and in particular against public powers, which have been forced into public impotence. Hence have been ruined and destroyed those states formerly considered sovereign.

Certainly, towns are not being razed, factories are not being bombed, agricultural regions are not being mined, or battered by shelling. But what Joseph Schumpeter called 'Creative Destruction', having become, with financialization, exclusively speculative, has indeed led to generalized disinvestment. A logic of disposability and destruction has been imposed, with the result that 'globalization' has become a faithless and lawless battle by speculators against all values. This war is blind: those conducting it are themselves blind to the fact that they are destroying the objects of their speculation, that soon there will no longer be any economic combatants. And that it is then that military combatants will emerge.

Faced with the extreme effects of global economic war, and with the imminence of a global military war, it is imperative that an alternative to this global war be proposed. This imperative imposes itself on political organizations and on universities. An alternative to war: we call this peace. For this reason the second part of this work is devoted to the need for universities throughout the world to constitute an *'internation'*, to elaborate an *economic peace treaty between nations*, founded on a new idea of public power (national and international).

We are told that the reason public powers and governments have become impotent is because they are in debt. But the problem of public debt, which is certainly not a false problem, is not the *cause* of this impotence. A debt is generated by a credit that itself has a rate. This rate is tied to a *belief* that creates the credit: one extends credit to the degree that one has belief in the beneficiary. Since it has become clear that the economy is now a war without limits of all against all, and because everyone, beginning with the speculators, now knows that the road ahead promises widespread ruin, speculators speculate more than ever – until there is no longer anything left to pillage – including by lowering credit ratings (Greece, Ireland, Portugal, America, Spain) and by speculating 'downwards', as they say, by making use of the system of 'credit default swaps'.[79]

The 'financialization' of credit has engendered generalized discredit – and, in Europe, it has led to the liquidation of all public sovereignty, the Treaty of Maastricht and then the Treaty of Lisbon submitting the European Central Bank, and thus the European currency, exclusively and as nowhere else in the world, to the law of financial markets, themselves having become purely speculative.[80] In order to oppose this mortifying logic, it will not suffice to propose new regulatory mechanisms. These may be indispensable, but they are not capable of reconstituting the horizon of belief without which there can be no credit. Public debt has become unsustainable only because the 'financial industry' is based on a generalization of discredit that inevitably engenders disinvestment.

The reason for such discredit, the reason that belief in the future has been lost, and that confidence has been lost between banks, economic actors, public actors, political institutions, between the generations and, finally, between citizens themselves and in relation to themselves, is because the consumerist model that appeared at the beginning of the twentieth century has become toxic and destructive for the planet (as foreshadowed in the 1972 Meadows report),[81] and did so at the moment 'Creative Destruction' combined with financialization, the logic of which was imposed in the form of 'globalization'.

Consumerism then became the bearer of addictions, maladies, malaises, the depletion of natural resources, environmental disequilibrium, the systematic flouting of fiscal laws and regulations, attention deficit disorder, the destruction of educational models, the looting and liquidation of systems of production via leveraged buyouts, and on and on.

Regulations must obviously be introduced in relation to global finance. But the real issue lies elsewhere: we must massively invest in the new industrial model that is emerging with digital tertiary retention, and we must implement totally new public industrial policies, and rethink all other policies (educational, fiscal, familial and intergenerational, that is, social policies, health policies, regional planning policies, and so on) according to this imperative, which alone will enable humanity to regain confidence and avoid a new global military war.

This model, which is that of the economy of contribution, and which was first developed by computer science with the advent of free software, is valid for almost all sectors that hold promise for the future, and in particular in the energy sector – the centralist organization of which must, after the Fukushima nuclear accident, be abandoned. But this model is also being extended into the sphere of material production – with the development of 'fab labs',[82] for example, which should be analysed in terms of the ideas developed by Marx in the *Grundrisse*, and on the basis of which the *Grundrisse* itself must in turn be reassessed.

These propositions, which will be developed in greater detail in the following three chapters and then in a forthcoming book,[83] are a way of responding to the final two pages of *The Postmodern Condition*, where Lyotard explores, 'pharmacologically', the effects of the 'computerization of society' (the report published with this title by Simon Nora and Alain Minc having obviously struck a chord with the author of the *Report on Knowledge*):

The computerization of society [...] could become the 'dream' instrument for controlling and regulating the market system, extended to
include knowledge itself [...]. In that case, it would inevitably involve
the use of terror. But it could also aid groups discussing metaprescrip-
tives by supplying them with the information they usually lack for
knowledgeable decisions.[84]

Lyotard refers at this point to what he calls *paralogy*, which he
had developed in the preceding pages, and, from this point of view,
he anticipates in a surprising way what, starting in 1992, will be put
into place with the specific stage of digital grammatization that is the
constitution of the world wide web. In his singularly lucid conclusion,
Lyotard advocates a true politics of digital tertiary retention: 'The
line to follow [is to grant] the public free access to the memory and
data banks.'[85] One can see here that in 1979 Lyotard still believed
what by 1986 (in *The Inhuman*) he will hold in profound doubt.

Perhaps he moves in this direction because *The Postmodern Condition* and paralogy closed off all critical access to Hegel and Marx
– seeming at the time and afterwards to have constituted a legitimation of delegitimation, that is, of the destruction of sovereignty,
reason and responsibility, and to have done so by suggesting there is
no alternative to the systemic dilution of responsibility – in a context
where the metaprescriptions of the focus groups evoked by Lyotard
are incapable of opening any prospect for de-proletarianization, the
proletariat having not been thought beyond Marxist dogma. Thus,
seven years later, Lyotard's viewpoint has become more sceptical.

The proposals contained in *The Postmodern Condition* therefore
seem compatible with those which, especially in the universities of
Columbia, Berkeley, Brown and Harvard (but there are a thousand
other examples), have led to academic malfeasance in relation to the
industrialized speculation of the 'financial industry'. The latter has
become so pervasive that it could with reason be referred to as a
suicidal industry (whether financial or otherwise), given that it
submits to the imperatives of global economic war (wherein, for
example, it becomes possible for a seismologist warning of the
extreme dangers associated with the Fukushima nuclear power plant
to be dismissed by the shareholders who are its operators).

'Grand narratives' have in the meantime given way to the little
narratives of 'storytelling', and the postmodern condition, as a narrative of the end of narratives and fables (which could only be one
more vast fable), has emerged as a confabulation in the service of a
base narrativity – not minor, but in the service of baseness, and constituting a key element of systemic stupidity.

Part II

The University with Conditions

Negotia in otio gerimus bene.
Inscription found in Amsterdam by Patrick Crogan

7

The New Responsibilities of the University: In the Global Economic War

49 Formations and deformations of reason

It is in the context of the current, ongoing retentional revolution (which was just getting under way at the time of *The Postmodern Condition*, and which is the real issue in terms of the commodified exteriorization of knowledge) that the question of the school, with which we opened the first chapter, must be posed anew. But the knowledge that schools are required to transmit to their students is generated in universities, and it is only if universities can be thought in a new way, on the basis of this new context, that it will be possible to find answers to the questions raised by Lyotard at the end of *The Postmodern Condition* and then in *The Inhuman*.

The vocation of the education system as a whole (in the sense of the *skholē* in its totality: from primary school to graduate schools)[1] is to form (and, in graduate schools, to trans-form) a type of attention that – from ancient Greece until today, and passing through the Reformation, the Counter-Reformation, the French Revolution and, in France, the Restoration and the Third Republic, that is, laicism – was initially called *logos*, and then reason.

Reason is formed. Every human being is reason-able, but their capacity to reason must be formed.[2] The formation or training [*formation*] of reason (*Bildung*) passes through disciplines.[3] The disciplines through which reason is formed are themselves schools of thought. They emerge from a process of transindividuation[4] in which the experiences of thinking of the individual researchers who have left their mark in the history of these disciplines constitute a body of knowledge shared and criticized by a community of peers, and recognized as such.

Reason is the attentional form emerging from those processes of transindividuation that result in rational disciplines. In general terms, an attentional form is a way of articulating retentions and protentions.[5] The forms of knowledge deriving from the heritage in which a discipline of *logos* consists – such that this *logos* is formed in those potentially rational minds that schools address, from the elementary level to the doctoral level where it is trans-formed – are composed of such retentions. And the new forms of knowledge that a discipline seeks and aims at through its researchers (in graduate schools) are its protentions – those protentions that it is possible to project on the basis of these retentions.

Attention is always both psychic and collective: 'to be attentive to' means both 'to focus on' and 'to attend to'. As such, the formation by schools of attention also consists in educating and elevating pupils [*élèves*]; in the sense of making them civil, that is, able to consider others and capable of taking care – of oneself and of that which is *in oneself*, as of that which *is not oneself* and of that which is *not in oneself*.

We live, however, in an age of what is now known, paradoxically, as the *attention economy* – paradoxically, because this is also and above all an age of the dissipation and destruction of attention: it is the epoch of an *attention dis-economy*.

50   Attention and thought: the war against school and the task of the university

As a result of this diseconomy of attention, it becomes increasingly difficult for schools to solicit attention from students – attention seems to be exclusively captured and depleted by an industrial apparatus designed essentially for this purpose, which is the very reason it has been named the 'attention economy'.

Any question concerning the university, its past, its present or its future, is bound to go back over and pose in a new way, and in this new context, the question of knowing what it means to think. To think is to participate in the production of an attentional form, and to transmit or even invent an attentional form. What must be thought today, however, and this is a trait specific to our age, is the fact that attention has become the major stake of a global economic war of unprecedented violence (I will return to this), and the fact that this war is taking place in schools. And it is a war against school itself insofar as schooling is first and foremost a struggle against the destruction of attention, and in general a struggle with minds insofar as they are capable of reasoning.

The question of the attention that schools must form, however, also and firstly concerns the university. It is not just a question of pedagogy or educational psychopathology in hyper-industrial societies: it is in a general way the question of rational thinking as specific attentional form. And today, the issue is the transformation of knowledge by analogue and digital technologies – which are the *pharmaka*[6] and *hypomnēmata* of our time.

Before going any further, I must add that we cannot pose the question of the future of the university in a credible way without first posing the question of the future of the children and the youth of tomorrow. While it may seem obvious that for 'academics', for university professors – the 'functionaries of humankind', as Husserl said[7] – the function of the university and of its professors is above all to 'profess the truth', as Derrida wrote,[8] for mere mortals, for those who are not 'professionals of the profession', those who are not professors, the first function of the university is *to form and train young people*.

I myself posit in principle and from the outset that the function of 'professing the truth'[9] defines the university, but I posit at the same time that today, the question of truth cannot *not* be conditioned through and through by the question of knowing how and why it may still be possible to save youth. The latter is clearly possible, or so I believe: I am one of those who says and thinks that it is never too late for something, and I believe in the performativity[10] of this assertion, an assertion that must confront the question of will[11] – and, more precisely, how and why it is still possible to save childhood, and even infancy.

51   Salvation and pharmacology of the generations: on decadence

If philosophy *always comes too late*, it is, nevertheless, *never too late*. The question of delay and advance (that is, of retention and protention) must be addressed from the perspective of the doubly epokhal redoubling mentioned previously in reference to the shock doctrine, and to which I will return in more detail in chapter 8.

I use this loaded term 'to save' (childhood and even infancy) – and I assert the urgency of this salvation – in a deliberate and reflective way, although no doubt in a way that is still not reflective enough, in order to emphasize this absolutely dramatic context that amounts to an extreme threat hanging over childhood, youth and, more generally, over intergenerational relationships.

The development or becoming of the contemporary *pharmakon* has been placed at the service of the systematic, industrial exploitation of attention. This has occurred through the use of attention-capturing psycho-technologies, the advent of which has literally ruined the very possibility of any *formation* of attention whatsoever. This is a situation of unprecedented gravity, and it is global. And it may well be feared that it is the beginning of a process that we should not hesitate to refer to as decadent. History has seen numerous periods that have turned decadent, in various ways and each time singular: the fall of empires, the destruction of Christianity by itself – which lay at the origin of the Reformation and the religious wars – the French Revolution that put an end to the Ancien Régime that had generated both the salons of Louis XV and the Enlightenment, and so on.

There have, then, always been such processes: they punctuate what we call history. And the declared goal of Polanyi in *The Great Transformation* is to 'trace the institutional mechanism of the downfall of a civilization'.[12] To deny decadence or the possibility of decadence is to deny the very possibility of history and time. There have always been processes of decline and decadence, and there will be again – at least I hope so, assuming that decadence may bring something other than just the monsters and refuse that it always also begets, and of which it is necessary on occasion to burst the abscess.

But until now, the decadent processes of a society were usually related to external factors, to differences from external regimes that greatly facilitated internal transformations. This can be seen, for instance, in the role that England and its parliamentary system no doubt played in the genesis of the French Revolution. Many other examples could be found.

Decadence expresses itself in the first place as corruption – in Aristotle's sense, whereby the corruptible exists wherever there is generation and where, all of us being what we are, we are all *inherently* corruptible. The corruption of the attentional capacities of youth and childhood by colossal industrial means is the fundamental question in relation to which the imperative to 'profess the truth' must be totally re-elaborated. And this must be done, in particular, in relation to the conditions of formation of an experience of truth, that is, the conditions of formation of rational attention, as that 'deep attention'[13] formed according to the academic canons that Plato was to elaborate.

52 Retention and the conditions of the university

Contemporary attentional forms are radically transformed by contemporary tertiary retentions, that is, in this instance, by analogue and digital technologies.

This *trans*-formation of attentional forms raises the question of a radical transformation of the university, itself capable of reconstituting the field in which the future of the university could again open itself up, that is, be projected. This presupposes, however, undertaking an examination of the pharmacological condition of the university in general – and, through it, of the pharmacological condition of the universal.

More generally still, what I am here referring to as the pharmacological condition conditions the *technical form of life* that Canguilhem tried to think, that of the 'being that we ourselves are'.[14] At the end of the First World War, the pharmacological condition of the life of the spirit was thought, *as such*, in Paul Valéry's 'The Crisis of the Mind', and it was thought in terms of a crisis of universalizing thought, that is, as a crisis of the very idea of the university. Allow me to recall from this text two famous sentences, but sentences that are yet to be truly read, analysed and pondered:[15]

We later civilizations ... we too now know that we are mortal.[16]

So many horrors could not have been possible without so many virtues. Doubtless, much science was needed to kill so many, to waste so much property, annihilate so many cities in so short a time; but moral qualities in like number were also needed. Knowledge and Duty, then, are suspect.[17]

Valéry was to return to this discourse in 1939, in terms of the question of 'spirit value',[18] of the fall of this value and of its political economy. It is a discourse that inaugurates an entirely new question of the university, that is, a new question of the universal, breaking with that which, in Bologna, the Sorbonne, Oxford, Cambridge and Berlin, and passing through the royal academies of France and England and through Harvard, had hitherto configured academic axioms.[19]

It nevertheless took almost a century for this new question of the universal (about which Deleuze said that it has been socialized above all through the universalization of the market) and of the university (including 1968, which, a mere twenty-nine years after Valéry's second warning, may have just been a tremor between two cataclysms) to reveal itself finally through what perhaps constitutes the greatest calamity of our time.

That the retentional question emerges as such in the university is, I believe, a fact that is reflected in the *Manifesto for the Digital Humanities* written in May 2010 during a 'non-conference' organized by nineteen laboratories, the École des hautes études en sciences sociales and the University of Provence. This document begins as follows: 'Society's digital turn changes and calls into question the conditions of knowledge production and distribution.'[20] Note should also be taken of a seminar on this subject held at the Collège international de philosophie, hosted by Éric Guichard.

53   The pharmacological condition of possibility of apodictic reasoning

The university can *work* only under the pharmacological condition – and we must briefly examine the relation between academic ergology and pharmacology, between work and instruments of work, that is, between these *pharmaka* that are, on the one hand, technical systems in general, and, on the other hand, the therapies or therapeutics that are the trades and professions in general, and that work should be in general, and academic work in particular.

The university can work only under pharmacological conditions because the process of elaborating and transmitting rational knowledge – that is, knowledge forged in the experience and the possibility of apodictic reasoning, formed according to the geometrical canon or model[21] – is over-determined by tertiary retention.

The process of the elaboration and transmission of rational knowledge is always and firstly that of a consciousness – for example: that of the protogeometer. This consciousness is constituted and woven above all by retentions, memories – for example, those referred to by Diotima in the *Symposium*:

> Our knowledge arises within us and passes away, and we are never identical to ourselves even in this respect. And even each single piece of knowledge is subject to this change. [...] Reflection [*melētē*, which could and perhaps should be translated as *discipline*], generating a new memory in place of that which has departed, thereby preserves knowledge, in such a way that it seems to always remain the same.[22]

In 1901, in the sixth paragraph of the fifth investigation of the *Logical Investigations*, Husserl explicitly and crucially thematized such memory by positing that consciousness is a stream that continuously links retentions together.[23] In 1904, in the course on time that was published in 1928, he examined the phenomenological conditions of this linkage.[24] What he showed there is that what he calls *primary* retention must be distinguished from *secondary* retention, that is, from memory properly speaking.

Primary retention is what constitutes the temporal fabric of all perception insofar as it lasts: insofar as, retaining in itself its own duration, it thus enriches its perceptual content (in aiming at the eidetic kernel that organizes a projection of protentions on the basis of these retentions). Secondary retention is what is produced by memory (on the basis of primary retentions), and as the fruit of the imagination.

I have introduced the concept of *tertiary* retention in order to designate artificial retentions – mnemotechnics in general. And, whether these tertiary retentions are fashioned by tools from marble, or from instruments for measuring cultivated surfaces or buildings,[25] or in writing that grammatizes the dianoetic and temporal stream of consciousness,[26] thereby passing from ideation to idealization, they constitute for Husserl the *condition* of geometry[27] – which is also to say, of rational thought.

Such a condition is pharmacological, if it is true that writing – but also any technics or technique – is a *pharmakon*.

Husserl's introduction of mnemotechnics into the heart of geometric rationality, and as its meta-empirical condition,[28] if not its transcendental or 'quasi-transcendental' condition, occurs in 1936, during the period when he wrote *The Crisis of European Sciences*. This was, in fact, a truly dramatic turn of events: thirty-five years after the *Logical Investigations*, two years before his death, Husserl accords 'phenomenological' status to tertiary retention, which had hitherto been relegated to the sphere of the constituted world (constituted by consciousness defined as transcendental, that is, constituting) and of the empiricism that typified what he referred to as the natural attitude.

We must, however, place the term 'phenomenological' in inverted commas, to describe this new status accorded to tertiary retention: for along with giving tertiary retention this new status, which makes it here constitutive *of reason*, it is the fundamental principles of phenomenology that are thereby called into question.

54   The contemporary revolution of analogue and digital tertiary retention

Tertiary retention, of which alphabetic writing is an instance, has a long and complex history, over-determined by a process of grammatization[29] that thoroughly traverses the history of the university and that, at the beginning of the twenty-first century, not only enters into the foreground but constitutes the fundamental question of the artefact as meta-empirically conditioning all other academic questions.

For twenty years we have been living through an intense revolution of tertiary retention of a previously unknown magnitude. This revolution has undoubtedly been more transformational than that which led, with the advent of printing, to the Renaissance, the Reformation and the Republic of Letters: it changes our entire everyday environment, as well as the conditions in which knowledge is elaborated and transmitted. It changes the ways that life reproduces itself and brings about the possibility that quantum mechanics may be applied to the development of nanomachines.[30] Digital humanities, software studies, web science, digital studies, philosophical engineering, and so on are all attempts to understand this situation.

The university exists under pharmacological conditions to the extent and the excess [*dans cette mesure qui est aussi la démesure*] that struck not only Valéry but also Freud and Husserl, during the very period when the latter delivered his lecture on the origin of geometry. Today, however, all this must be rethought by the university itself, taking into consideration a specific pharmacological context of which neither Valéry nor Freud nor Husserl could have imagined the consequences we are aware of today, and which has brought about the appearance:

- on the one hand, of *analogue technologies* that, on the basis of instruments devised for scientific observation such as the phonautograph (which preceded the phonograph) and chronophotography (from which was derived both the cinema and the scientific organization of labour outlined by Frederick Taylor, which in turn led to the assembly line), have radically transformed the space and time of industrial society;
- on the other hand, of *digital technologies* that, from the 1890 census that brought about the mechanography industry in the United States, up until the definition of the TCP-IP and HTTP protocols and then HTML language, all of which enabled the web to come into existence, via scientific computing and computerized

management, have completely overturned economic life, political life and social life in general.

Digital technologies are the most recent stage of alphabetic writing, augmented by the signs of the decimal system. Electronic, transcoded according to the ASCII standard into binary data, alphanumeric writing can be subjected to the rules and algorithms of Boolean algebra, and thereby calculated and processed at the speed of light.

All this stems from a becoming of tertiary retention that enables, with the analogical, an exteriorization of the mental functions of perception and imagination, and then, with the digital, an exteriorization of the mental functions of intellection and logical operations of all kinds. This raises the question of the proletarianization of the mind or spirit that for Plato, at the beginning of the fourth century BCE, will have been the crucial issue of philosophy – it was in confronting this challenge that he was to found the Academy.

55   Learning to live and teach within technical exteriorization

Education is the first question posed by philosophy – first of all in Plato's earliest known dialogue, *Hippias Minor*, then in *Meno*, as the question of knowing whether virtue can or cannot be taught.[31] This is not just a theoretical question: it is practical, political and institutional.

Philosophy has been based on a repression and a process of denial affecting not only literal tertiary retention but technics in general:[32] nascent philosophy wanted to hear nothing about the technicity of *logos* other than in a pejorative tone, in particular as rhetoric, even while practising the latter. This denial also extends to the technicity of the modes of noetic life, to this *learning to live* that is noetic existence and that requires *epimēleia*, *tekhnē tou biou*, *melētē* and techniques of the self in Foucault's sense that inspired Pierre Hadot.[33]

If we must learn how to live, it is because noetic life, which must be formed, is technical through and through.[34]

The question of teaching and education lies at the very origin of philosophy and leads to the foundation of the Academy. On this basis – today in ruins – of which these denials were intended to constitute a foundation, and that came to be called 'metaphysics', it was a matter, in and through this question, of establishing a therapeutics in order to try and struggle against the poisonous effects of the

pharmakon that is writing. But it was a matter of doing so by practising literal tertiary retention in a curative way, that is, under the
authority of a discipline (*melētē*) that would in some way be a therapeutic prescription.

Hence philosophy is defined as 'medicine for the soul'. It prescribes
noetic modes and methods that prefigure the academic disciplines
that we ourselves have inherited. In its inaugural character, the philosophical question of education presents itself as a crisis of education.
The context of this crisis was the use and misuse by the sophists (who
in those days were teachers) of the *pharmakon* that is literal tertiary
retention – writing. The misuse of writing proletarianizes the soul,
according to Socrates. This was the interpretation of the *Phaedrus*
that I proposed in *For a New Critique of Political Economy*.[35]

Writing, by exteriorizing memory, shapes the life of the noetic soul
(this is what Husserl reiterates in 1901). As an anamnesic and dialogical capacity in this sense, it connects the *psyche* to its origin *before*
the fall into the body – anamnesis allowing the soul to regain its
wings[36] in dialogue when, in being true, it 'grants wings' to speakers
(to their soul) and enables them to rise up, therefore, before their fall
into mortality.[37] But writing, by exteriorizing memory as technical
hypomnēsis, threatens to bypass or short-circuit the living memory
that is *anamnēsis*: it threatens to atrophy this anamnesis that the mind
constitutes so long as it lives (and that we can name *esprit de mémoire*,
just as we say *esprit de vin* to refer to alcohol, or *esprit de sel* to refer
to hydrochloric acid).

But psychic memory is originally struck by *retentional finitude* (a
phrase that comes from Derrida), because it is the memory of a body
that is mortal and that is continuously dying (that is, getting old)
from the first moments of life. And thus writing, if it is a threat to
memory, is nevertheless also what makes it possible for psychic
memory to fill in this default of origin, in relation to which writing
is as such a supplement.

And if this supplement supplementing finitude is also an increase
of finitude, an augmentation or overgrowth of finitude, a kind of
hyper-finitude – which we realize when a library burns down, or
when we accidentally delete a digital file that we had stored on our
computer – this hyper-finitude itself enables us to experience the
inestimable value of this exteriorization, as well as its cost, equally
inestimable, a value and a cost that exceed its price.

All this confronts us with the obvious fact that we must take care
of this pharmacology: we must protect it at the same time as we
protect ourselves from it, writing being a crutch of understanding

that is at the same time constitutive of understanding itself.[38] For if this retentional supplement constitutes, notably as alphabetic writing, a supplement of finitude, it is also and especially an *infinitizing supplement*: it opens the possibility of infinitizing; it is the condition of the power to infinitize and to know infinitely that lies at the basis of all noetic knowledge. It thus makes possible the opening of that *infinite we* of geometers that properly constitutes and founds the universal – that lies at the origin of geometry, and that does so as its default, a default in some way infinite, but a default that *must be*.

56 Knowledge and disindividuation: pharmacological fate

This pharmacological question is also a question for Marx and Engels in the *Communist Manifesto*, where, already, they posited that the exteriorization of the gestures of work in the machine-tool leads to the proletarianization of workers because it bypasses and short-circuits their knowledge. And this then receives deeper analysis in the *Grundrisse*.

It is a question here of the circuit on which all knowledge is inscribed, traced, woven or pursued, insofar as it is always, in one way or another, the cumulative retention of experience, whether 'manual' or 'intellectual' – and I, like Galileo, or as Brecht interprets Galileo, believe that this distinction is highly debatable.[39]

Whatever its forms, this short-circuit proletarianizes 'knowing'[40] through the exteriorization of knowledge. Simondon analysed this as a process of disindividuation, yet individuation *presupposes* this pharmacology, if it is true that technicity in general is pharmacological, and if it is true that the transindividual, that is, meaning and significance in all their forms, is the outcome of this technical exteriorization of the traces of individuation – that is, if it is made possible by tertiary retention in general.

Such is pharmacological fate: insofar as it pursues a process of hominization as exteriorization,[41] it can always disindividuate and as such unweave what it had allowed to individuate and weave as the motives of reason (*reasons* for reason). This state *of fact*, which constitutes the pharmacological condition in general, nevertheless opens the possibility of a state *of law*, via the various therapeutics of this condition in which the disciplines, in all their forms, consist. This passage from pharmacological fact to pharmacological law must be made the subject of a *positive pharmacology* – and not just a deconstruction of the logic of the supplement, the denial of the latter having constituted 'metaphysics'.

Positive pharmacology – which presupposes the pharmacological deconstruction of the oppositions lying at the foundations of the institution of reason – must become the primary task of the university of tomorrow and of the new academic context of scholarly life.

A process of disintoxication, however, is also required. We must struggle against the dis-apprenticeship and disindividuation generated by the hegemonic appropriation of analogue and digital tertiary retention by an economic and industrial sphere that has lost all restraint. The result has been the generation of an apocalyptic feeling throughout the planet, and the pharmacological character of all technics and all science has become, for everyone, *evident*.[42]

57   Truth as criterion of social individuation

What Simondon referred to as the transindividual is the outcome of a process of transindividuation: such a process occurs when psychic individuals not only co-individuate (for example, by discussing things, as we do every day) but metastabilize[43] the transindividual that founds a collective individuation (for example, that of geometry, forming the infinite *we* of geometers). They thus implement criteria for retentional selection, and therefore for the production of protentions, which, in the case of the attentional form that is *logos*, provide criteria for truth (always specified through disciplinary rules).

A psychic individual is that which is engendered by a continuous process of individuation, that is, constant trans-formation – as Diotima says. This psychic and somatic flow individuates itself, however, only by participating in collective individuation: psychic individuation occurs only insofar as it is inscribed on or in the circuits of an individuation that creates a world and holds together [*fait monde et fait corps*], given that the world forms – it 'worlds' – only if it forms a social body [*un faire-corps social*].

Plato suggests that a true co-individuation is a dialectical (or dialogical) process wherein those who co-individuate succeed in individuating *together* only insofar as each of them *themselves* individuates – not in a purely autonomous way, since they need interlocutors in order to individuate themselves (thinking being a dianoetic dialogue that is derived from this initial situation), but anamnesically. And where the latter means: by retracing the entire circuit on which one's individuation is inscribed, and *continuing* this individuation, *pursuing* it – as when Socrates helps the slave Meno 'give birth'.[44]

Hence is framed or woven the knowledge that is taught on the basis of the geometric experience of the universal. And this is why geometric experience is the foundation of all forms of academic knowledge: one cannot enter the Academy without having undergone this *experience*, which is as such a propaedeutic. Ideally, the knowledge that can be taught at university – and on this basis form and train schoolteachers – is universalizable knowledge, because it more or less constantly appeals to this anamnesic experience.[45] That is, those who are learning it do so by reconstituting within themselves, and as subjects capable of being affected by the geometric experience of the universal, the entire circuit that has been successfully elaborated in the history of knowledge. In so doing it becomes *their* history insofar as it is 'universal history'. Knowledge that does not require this exhumation of its history is not academic knowledge (this does not mean that it is not knowledge, but that it cannot be taught by academic institutions).

Academic knowledge has no end: there is no final word, either in geometry, philosophy, literature or history, and so on. Organized into disciplines, this knowledge is woven as the facilitation – and writing – of circuits: aiming at this end that will never be reached, this infinite protention, it is always in some way returning to the forgotten origin of the series of retentions in which it consists as the accumulation and formalization of experiences. It always tries to *go back over the entire journey* and to refound by re-journeying as the necessity of establishing it as the transindividuation of knowledge, whereby the psychic individuation of each scholar or scientist is trans-formed by the ideal individuation of their discipline.

58 Pharmacology of ideas

The never-attained end of universal knowledge is its mover or its motor, which remains always to come – a 'motricity' that is less Plato's subject than Aristotle's, and which concerns that object of every contemplation (*theoria*) that is *theos* (which also means god – which in Aristotle means no more nor less than what is universally desirable and as such the object of every contemplation, every theory, that is, all rational attention).

This 'prime mover' (that is, the hidden object lying behind every object of desire, which Freud and then Lacan called *das Ding*)[46] opens up the question of the infinitely protentional character of such circuits founded on *eidē*. The *eidē* aim to found ideal objects that every university houses through its disciplines and faculties, which they protect and maintain as objects of the desire for knowledge itself universal – the academic horror being the moment of dis-idealization in which knowledge becomes insipid, that is, dangerous.

Tertiary retentions are technical realities that evolve, and thus psychic individuation constantly de-functionalizes and re-functionalizes itself on the hypomnesic plane[47] – and trans-forms itself through the resulting new mnesic arrangements. It is in such arrangements that consist the consciousness and unconscious of this psychic individuation, given that the synaptic connections within which learning is metastabilized are interiorizations of the diverse hypomnesic connections[48] with which the intellect and the affects operate insofar as they manipulate symbols of all kinds, and always in passing through the hand (and this is why I describe it as Galilean/Brechtian).[49]

Confronted with tensions generated by this retentional becoming, Socrates argued that those teachers who were the sophists were abusing the *pharmakon* that is literal tertiary retention, and that they were doing so by ceasing to make the transmission of knowledge the moment of its re-elaboration: they were not *recreating* the experience of what Husserl was to call the originary intuitions. And hence they were proletarianizing those they claimed to be forming – and this means they were de-forming them.

A trans-formational use of literal tertiary retention – that is, individuating a circuit of rational transindividuation – is a tertiary retentional practice that on the contrary aims to plasticize the secondary retentions of the learner, and through that make accessible those primary retentions that bring before us that which presents itself as the experience of the universal itself (of the infinite protention in which it consists).

A discipline such as the geometry of the protogeometer imagined by Husserl would be one such practice – which leads in Husserl's language to the release of an *eidetic correlate*,[50] or *noema*,[51] but which, on the basis of 'The Origin of Geometry', we know can present itself only in a noetico-retentional experience involving the three, inseparable layers of primary, secondary and tertiary retention.

What consequences should be drawn from these analyses with regard to the condition of the university, and its basis or its extension, in relation to education at all levels, including outside the academic sphere?

59   Organology of knowledge

Hence I have argued, relying on Léon Robin, that Plato's Academy was a 'writing machine':[52] a machine for producing tertiary retentions and for inscribing in the psychic apparatus and the memories of academicians the consequences of their dialogues, in the form of long circuits of transindividuation that inevitably pass through writing – and which have provided us with the *Dialogues* and with the *Letters to Lucilius*. Plato practises writing, and this practice is essential to life in the Academy.

Knowledge of any kind, regardless of the discipline in which it consists, and through which it constitutes itself as a body of rules, is always a pharmacology. It is always implemented through a therapeutic that takes care of the *pharmakon* that is tertiary retention, and that can short-circuit knowledge or on the contrary intensify it, producing infinitely long circuits of transindividuation – this is the meaning of the infinite *we* of Husserlian geometry.

A long circuit of transindividuation is not just *long*: it is *absolutely* long. I must be inclined to return (like a salmon)[53] to the originary intuitions and to project myself into the infinity of scientific protentions, so as to ensure that the discipline constitutes an academic discipline, that is, a discipline that is universal, and scientific in this sense. I must do so, even though this rational epistemic inclination, this attentional form – which is rational only in that it tries to unify the diversity of experience accumulated by the discipline through the concepts of a theory that theorizes its necessity – never reaches the point of pure satisfaction: knowledge is infinite and rational only insofar as it is flawed, deficient, *makes* faults [*fait défaut*]; it is infinite and rational only insofar as it is knowledge of the necessity of this fault (through the faultiness that always affects it as the limit of this or that scientific or philosophical theory).

The history of knowledge is inscribed, written, exteriorized and tertiarized – including in those various technical devices that arose along with Galileo's telescope, but which begins long before, with tattoos, the abacus, counting frames, and so on. These last examples take the place of fingers, which had been used to count and were thus material for a bodily technique that in this sense was already digital, as well as also and immediately a technique of the mind. And this history of inscribing, writing, exteriorizing and tertiarizing knowledge also sets up the evolution of tertiary, and also secondary and primary, retentional processes, and this opens up the question of an *organology of knowledge*.

This organology is composed of sets of instruments equipping and improving upon the organs of perception – such as microscopes and telescopes – as well as instrumental augmentations of the capacities for understanding. These artificial organs are arranged together, and thus participate conjointly in the grammatization of the nervous system.

Understanding is today grammatized to such an extent that its functions can be delegated to instruments, devices and machines without any longer having the ability to govern reason, that is, without the power to idealize or to theorize. This is what led Derrida to refer to the 'absolute *pharmakon*',[54] which I have tried to show leads to the proletarianization of the political function itself – or in other words, to its outright destruction.

60   Phenomenotechnics of rationalization

Reason itself cannot be exteriorized. Rather, reason is and always has been the *interiorizing of exteriorization*. And it is so as a desire capable of infinitizing its objects, which are those of sublimation.

Exteriorization that (lacking interiorization) sterilizes the understanding is what Adorno and Horkheimer, then Marcuse, and eventually Habermas, forty years after Weber, all described as a process of rationalizing irrationality. But they did not have, in my view, a correct analysis of the historico-pharmacological causality at work in this process.

We will need to examine the appearance of the new type of retentional system that lay at the origin of the rationalization described by Weber, which is first of all printed writing. And we will need to analyse the new regimes through which knowledge is elaborated and transmitted that arose with the Reformation and Counter-Reformation. We will conduct this examination and analysis when we turn to the work dedicated to these questions by Elizabeth Eisenstein.[55]

Analogue and digital technologies – like printing and, we should add, machine-tools, which alter and grammatize the motor-behaviour and the sensorimotor loops of producers – are tertiary retentions. They form tertiary retentional layers that, as the spatialization of the duration and time of life, fundamentally affect all forms of the life of the body and mind – that is, the life of the social body and, notably, the life of the scientific mind and spirit.

Here we must pass through Bachelard and Canguilhem, and remind ourselves that these questions are not new – five years before 'The Origin of Geometry', Bachelard posed the question of phenomenotechnics.[56] To what extent does a dialogue between Bachelard and phenomenology remain possible, necessary and relevant, in this light? It would also be necessary to turn back to Valéry and to Foucault (on the questions of *epistēmē*, documentation, economics, and so on).

Today, a phase transition[57] is occurring, within which a critical, or even hyper-critical – but I do not say 'more than critical',[58] since I have never understood what Derrida meant by this phrase – threshold is being crossed, after which the question of the pharmacological character of the academy becomes irreducible and inevitable. And this question thus lies at the very heart of the question of the university, its organization, goals and research programs, its relations with the world beyond the university, in particular the economic and industrial world, its relation to its own history, especially in terms of grammatization and its organological and pharmacological stakes, its configurations of the retentional materials on which the university has always relied, and that have always underpinned its universal construction, and its new protentions, which open up as the very projection of its future, erupting in and through the kaleidoscope of its disciplines.

61   Extreme disenchantment, anti-knowledge and spiritual peace

All this has occurred at a time when the global mnemotechnical system has become the heart of the techno-industrial system.

Throughout academic history from Plato to Jules Ferry, by way of the University of Berlin and up until Napoleon, the technical system on the one hand, and the mnemotechnical system on the other hand, were structurally, functionally and canonically separated. This separation meant that everything falling under the banner of mnemotechnics belonged to the symbolic power of the clerics and was not part of the economy, the *oikonomia* of the Trinity notwithstanding, the economy being, as *negotium*,[59] inherently secular, and the power of reading and writing being exclusively accessible to *otium*. The essential displacements wrought by the Reformation, however, fully reveal themselves only much, much later. They do so as total secularization, and in the context of an extreme disenchantment that is not established until the advent of the digital industrial mnemotechnical system: this is precisely what has befallen us today.

The creation of this 'industrial mnemotechnical system' is the result of work that companies such as Google have undertaken to implement publication systems. In the context of this mnemotechnical development, knowledge becomes fundamental to the industrial economy. And today, the extension of the global mnemotechnical system via analogue and digital technologies has led to an unprecedented functional integration of knowledge into the apparatus of production and consumption.

This *total integration* of knowledge into the functions of conception, design, production, consumption and speculation – which is a kind of *dis-integration* of knowledge itself – has occurred during a global economic war in which knowledge has become a commodity, both for those in the economic world who buy and sell knowledge and who are the players conducting this war, and for those who want to 'learn' so that they may be *enlisted in this war against themselves*.

Education thus finds itself reduced to these strictly miserable 'war aims', which destroy *otium* and knowledge itself, which produce an essentially proletarianized knowledge,[60] that is, disindividuated knowledge. This is ultimately *anti-knowledge*: it exudes an academic hyper-sophism, approved and evaluated in these terms,[61] and mostly blind to the human, social, ecological and psychic ruins that this war brings.

The university, moreover, can place itself at the service of the universal (that is, of the singular, which transindividuates itself as its very necessity) only on the condition that it is understood to be the promise of a peace indispensable to the life of the mind and spirit, and provided by the spirituality of life itself.

Logos, which is not merely an intellectual faculty but a psychosocial order, as rational attentional form, is this civil peace: in the *agora* of the *polis*, through which it is civilized [*policée*], weapons are replaced and war between the clans is brought to an end by making *polemos*, 'father of all things', the dynamic principle no longer of war but of dialogue, and as the diachrony of the transindividuation that is thinking 'in the making' (which thinks only if it is constantly in the making *anew*).

62 Neoliberal jihad and positive pharmacology

These truths have been destroyed by the neoliberal jihad, which has brought about the reign of its ideology with great force. Hence we learn in the documentary *Inside Job*, for example, that the Columbia University business school has been criticized for contributing to the legitimation of almost Mafia-like practices undertaken by the 'financial industry'.

How and why has the neoliberal jihad been able to carry on this war, which is clearly being conducted not by one corporation against another, but by shareholders against companies (who can, after the 'financialization' resulting from the 'conservative revolution', remove their boards whenever it suits them), and, through these companies, against the people? And how has all this been carried out in the name of 'democracy', understood above all as free enterprise, and in the name of human rights, understood above all as having abandoned the question of economic rights?

This could happen only because academics have given up thinking the *pharmakon* in its positivity – and hence have given up any critique of the legacy of idealist and materialist dialectics. Only capitalist industry, and especially, more recently, the financial industry, has succeeded in taking advantage of the positivity of the *pharmakon* that is tertiary retention, that is, technics in all its forms, and digital technology in particular.

Positivity must be thought on the foundation of an analysis of the irreducible negativity of the *pharmakon*, that is, on the basis of the recognition of the *pharmacological condition of the university itself*. Only if positivity is thought in this way will it be capable, ultimately, of inventing the conditions of a peace treaty that could be imposed on the horsemen of the financial industry, and on the other horsemen of that apocalypse to which the neoliberal jihad inevitably leads.

The effect of the commodification of knowledge – and what, in the now global competition between universities, establishes a logic of supply and demand such that, increasingly, the academic world is faced with the threat of finding itself *prescribed* by 'demand', in terms of the demand for employment, not the demand for knowledge – is that the retentional criteria that form a discipline are subjected to extra-academic criteria:

- in the field of research, where, under the pressure of shareholders, industrial criteria are subjected to the shortest-term efficiency possible, even though this kind of efficiency is condemned to inefficiency in the long term;[62]
- in the field of education, where it is a matter of subjecting the formation of attention to the criteria of so-called employability, which has nothing whatsoever to do with professionalization – given that the latter depends on supplying knowledge, not adaptability to the battlefield that is flexibility – and which is contrary

to the formation of rational attention, and therefore contributes to irrationality and the de-formation of minds.

Faced with this, the academic world 'resists',[63] arguing that the university is in the first place the freedom to think without constraint and without condition: such is, for example, the discourse of Jacques Derrida in 'The University Without Condition'. In fact, this unconditionality relies on a blind spot that threatens to collapse at any moment: *there is no university without condition* – academic freedom is *always* a *conditional* freedom.

This freedom is conditional because it is subject to pharmacological conditions that have themselves always been, and always will be, radically extra-academic. This very general statement calls for detailed commentary on the work of Derrida.[64] To contribute to this struggle for a spiritual peace treaty necessitated by the extreme toxicity of our pharmacological situation, we must elaborate therapeutic inventions rather than piling up one resistance strategy after another. The latter can lead only to the insularity [*entre-soi*] that threatens from all sides (between academics, between bankers, between scientists, between digital natives, between the aged, between the French, and so on): such is our academic responsibility.

63   Seven proposals for the intergenerational

Only by reflecting on research is it possible to rethink education, not the reverse: it is not pedagogy that should be the starting point for this thinking, but *hermeneia*.[65] The fact remains that pedagogy is intrinsic to the passage to the act of knowledge: hence Socrates opposes the sophist precisely by referring to 'thinking for oneself'. Consequently, we must place the pedagogical question – and the observation of experiences and empirical approaches that accumulate in the context of digital pharmacology – at the heart of new epistemological research. The digital humanities, digital studies and the web sciences should consist in just such research.

A society is first and foremost a way of organizing the formation of attention of those who must live together in civil peace, and the enactment of reason as academic life is the attentional modality specific to the *polis*. Attention articulates retentions and protentions, and what is referred to as *logos* is the rational form of attention that is woven in and by absolutely long, that is, *infinite*, intergenerational circuits of transindividuation. These circuits are founded on an infinitizing power and an infinitizing knowledge[66] that we must cultivate, which is also to say, on an an-amnesic capacity, which is the condition of what Katherine Hayles calls 'deep attention'.

If in the twentieth century, and even more in the twenty-first century, attention is a commodity that has become scarce, as Jeremy Rifkin says, and ultimately the key resource for the economic war and hyper-industrial economy of reticular societies, and if the tertiary retention that conditions the formation of attention always has two sides, then the mission of universities is to *reconstruct deep attention*. It is to reconstruct deep attention in an age in which a global mnemotechnical system is placing psycho-technologies under the hegemonic control of marketing, the effects of which are highly toxic (effects that the manifesto on the digital humanities referred to previously does not seem to take sufficiently into account), even if some curative effects also occur.

We must rethink the university project on the basis of the pharmacological question, and in the context of industrial and digital tertiary retention, with the goal of constructing new therapies and therapeutics. Philosophy itself is not a therapeutic, but a critical pharmacology within a general pharmacology that itself presupposes a general organology. The latter constitutes a paradigm for the humanities in the age of digital humanities, posing, theorizing and experimenting in transdisciplinary ways the question of how therapeutic knowledge might be capable of specifying both the toxic and the curative aspects of *pharmaka*.

There is no 'post-industrial' future. Nor is there any future in 'resistance' to the new industrial age. The future lies in re-founding the industrial model. This new foundation of the industrial future of humanity in turn requires the university to be re-founded: industry is the conjugation of science and technics as technology, and no industrial future is possible without a university that has learned to think in terms of the inherently pharmacological nature of the technological knowledge deriving from the industrial enterprise.

The university of such a future will be an academic institution (inheriting what was produced on the basis of Plato) that will:

1 put organological and pharmacological questions at the heart of its work, general organology constituting the paradigm of a *transdisciplinary heuristic*;
2 make tertiary retention not only an object of study, but an object of *practice*;
3 set up around these two objectives a *new integrated system of primary, secondary and tertiary education*;

4 be tightly articulated with the new publication system generated by digitalization, transforming public space, public time and the public thing, the *publishing and audiovisual industries having been accordingly reoriented by national and international public powers in the course of negotiations conducted at the instigation of academic authorities*;

5 take up the question of cosmopolitanism in this new context, which will also be that of a post-consumerist globality, organizing *within university networks the relation of the universal to diversality;*[67]

6 initiate a new critique of knowledge, become techno-scientific knowledge, that is, a *critique* (in the Kantian sense) *of industrial power as such*;

7 implement, in order to accomplish this, new protocols for contributory research,[68] *tightly connecting new scholarly and scientific associations to the academic world as a whole.*

8

Internation and Interscience

64 Speed and thought

The programme of the future university must, as a priority, serve a politics of de-proletarianization, and struggle against the process of dis-apprenticeship, of unlearning. It must fight against the destruction of cognitive functions and the short-circuiting of reason in which rationalization has consisted, as a toxic becoming induced by the pharmacological character of reason in the industrial context.

This programme must be applied at every academic level and it must expand into the whole economic sphere: this is the challenge of what Ars Industrialis has described as an *economy of contribution*, which is the concrete expression of de-proletarianization in a society in which knowledge of every kind must once again become the basis for the production of value.[1]

We are living through a period in which the technical system is mutating, involving a doubly epokhal redoubling[2] wherein, in a general way, the *pharmakon* that is tertiary retention:

- is inscribed in a technical system that, when it changes, engenders a new retentional stage (and a new stage of grammatization) and interrupts the existing socio-ethnic and socio-political programmes, producing a suspension, and in this sense an *epokhē*, which destroys the long circuits of transindividuation that are the foundations of these programmes, and in this way disorients, and places in a state of shock and into question,[3] both individuals and social groups;
- becomes, in a second moment, not just poisonous due to the short-circuits that it initially brings about, but on the contrary curative and therapeutic, that is, it reconstitutes long circuits and thus

forms a *new process of psychic and collective individuation*: retentional finitude then gives rise to the anamnesic projection of new infinite protentions, and the becoming of tertiary retention is adopted as an increase in the power to infinitize and to infinitize knowledge (infinitization being the condition of action for any 'power to act': itself *enacting* the conatus).[4]

This analysis interprets anew the lateness constitutive of philosophy in the 'phenomenology of spirit', which is here thought as genealogy and from an organological and thus materialist perspective (in a mode that is not dialectical but, precisely, pharmacological – there is no pharmacological synthesis because the poisonous character of the *pharmakon* cannot be dissolved in any therapeutic). According to this analysis, we would currently be occupying a moment of in-betweenness.

The epokhal redoubling that we, non-inhuman beings of the twenty-first century, have been confronted with for the last twenty years, however, has installed a very specific situation, without historical precedent: the extreme speed of technological development seems to short-circuit in advance the very possibility of the second moment, and in a way to strike it down. It is for precisely this reason that we must refer to *generalized* proletarianization, that is, to the destruction not only of savoir-faire and savoir-vivre, but also and especially of theoretical knowledge. And it is in this context – in which this global economic war arises – that there has emerged what the Slow Science movement refers to as fast science.

This short-circuiting of the very possibility of a therapeutic moment now *seems* inevitable. But this appearance results essentially from an anti-critical internalization of the ultra-liberal dogma proclaiming 'there is no alternative' – which in this case means no alternative to generalized proletarianization or to the permanent establishment of systemic stupidity. We must, however, relate this question to that of war and peace. This is indeed the question of a time and an art of peace – whereas speed is the fundamental question in any art of war.

> The first goal [of war] is to defeat the adversary, and thus render them no longer capable of resistance. War [...] is an act of violence intended to compel our opponent to fulfill our will.[5]

So writes Clausewitz. Naomi Klein's 'shock doctrine' is clearly a description of one such strategy of war, one that consists in *outpacing* the adversary – which is the goal in every war.

Technics and technology are always systems and devices of acceleration – and thus are always, and for this very reason, also weapons. Civilization consists in placing these weapons *in the service of care* – in the service of these systems of care that are social systems.[6] In this regard, digital technologies are exceptional: their speed constitutes an 'absolute *pharmakon*' capable of absolute short-circuits, that is, absolute shocks.

And yet – and this is the central hypothesis of this book – they also constitute a new associated, dialogical and retentional milieu, which interrupts the process of dissociation that analogue technologies and industrial grammatization processes in general have imposed in both the world of wage labour and the symbolic field.

Digital technologies constitute 'light-time',[7] whereby the tertiary retentions from the data centres of the whole world can be scanned in a way that seems almost instantaneous, radically modifying the conditions of the work of thought (its ergology) and opening totally unprecedented prospects – provided that the struggle for deproletarianization is engaged explicitly and concretely.

If the university and the academic world in general are therapeutic institutions charged with bringing about the emergence of the second moment of the epokhal redoubling in which the systemic evolution of technics always consists, and, through it, an evolution of tertiary retention, then in the epoch of digital pharmacology the university must place the speed of the *pharmakon* in the service of peace – that is, in the service of a new type of suspense (of *epokhē*, that is, of *absolute slowness*) and a new type of civil conflictuality: in the service of those logical disputations that alone make it possible to avoid military conflict.[8]

If the university is confronted with the impossibility of operating the doubly epokhal redoubling in the ultra-liberal technoscientific context, this impossibility is a state of fact, and not a state of law.[9] The 'conservative revolution', which got under way at just the moment *The Postmodern Condition* was being published, essentially consisted in liquidating those public systems that attempt to absorb the technological shocks between, on the one hand, the evolution of the technical system that has become industrial – that is, techno-logical, and not just technical, and that is now a mnemo-techno-logical system – and, on the other hand, the social systems.[10]

The *modern public thing* emerged in the nineteenth century in the form of the nation-state: Bertrand Gille has shown[11] that its first purpose was to reduce the disadjustment between the technical system and the social systems by preserving the latter – that is, by absorbing shocks. The conservative revolution, however, having decided that 'government is the problem, not the solution', has been committed to liquidating all public authority, to be replaced with marketing as the secular arm of private financial power, and just as committed to orchestrating constant shocks, but 'soft' and psychological shocks, centred on commodities. This has enabled large-scale (global) processes of 'co-linearization'[12] to be established, through which psychic aims are submitted to the requirements of the economic sphere and social aims are short-circuited ('bypassed', in Franglais managerial jargon).

After the 'conservative revolution', it is marketing that defines the conditions under which technological innovation is socialized – replacing public political systems. These systems had hitherto allowed a period of time for social systems to adopt the technical system, trans-forming and trans-individuating a *becoming* into a *future* [*le devenir en avenir*], thereby opening up the possibility of a second moment of the epokhal redoubling, through which the short-circuits in transindividuation make way for long circuits.

The global economic war we call financialization has been first and foremost a war against public systems, and against everything they make it possible to preserve as a process of collective individuation through which specific attentional forms are produced. The outcome is extremely weak social structures, and a dangerous fragility of the psychic apparatus – that is, of reason.

65   The rationalization of impotence and the time of positive pharmacology

The Athenian academic sphere (and that which preceded it, Presocratic thought and the tragic age), in its first moment (and as an age of the second epokhal redoubling caused by the literal *pharmakon*), imposed itself as a symbolic power *containing* technical and hypomnesic becoming: circumscribing, circumventing, limiting, as *hubris*, and doing so, beginning with Plato, in the name of an opposition of *being* (of science founded as ontology) and *becoming* (of technics emerging from blind empiricism, that is, uncritical empiricism). This was at the same time an opposition of science and technics, and hence a denial of the intrinsic technicity of science itself.

Such a denial, however, became impossible once technics and science were combined into technology. It was then the opposition between *otium* and *negotium* that found itself dissolved, the idea of progress having brought about a convergence of symbolic and noetic benefits with an abundance of subsistence provisions and a revaluation of their economy. It then seemed possible to believe in a progressive, general spread of existences prosperous enough to be capable of individuating themselves freely (which we call individualism),[13] that is, capable of accessing *otium*.

This general, relative spread of prosperity (in the industrialized world) for noetic souls, however, is not leading these souls to that passage into actuality that would characterize them *as* noetic by, precisely, keeping subsistence concerns at a distance, that is, submission to *negotium* (to business). The economic system that made this relative prosperity possible on the contrary requires that *otium* itself be placed in the service of *negotium* – that is, of growth ('growth', which is how we should translate the Greek *phusis*, from the verb *phusein*, 'to grow'). And the latter is defined solely by the consumption and destruction of raw materials of all kinds supplying subsistences of all kinds. And the 'needs' of subsistence are constantly increasing thanks to the exploitation of social mimetism, through which one person's subsistence is being constantly imposed on the other.[14]

The dissolution of the opposition between spirit, which acquires its freedom only in *otium*, and business, which thwarts it as *negotium*, or in other words the dissolution of the opposition between 'the Academy' and what we now call 'the Market', occurred in the wake of the Reformation[15] (we shall return to this) and led to what Weber thus described as a process of rationalization, secularization and disenchantment. This eventually reached, with the conservative revolution, the extreme disenchantment within which we are currently trying to survive and to which we more or less submit, overwhelmed by the feeling of fatal impotence. It is a new Dark Ages where the *diktat* is impunity – in this case, for ratings agencies, for the financial system that they serve, and for the uses that their experts make (but without knowledge, and in this sense they are unknowing because they have been proletarianized) of contemporary pharmacological systems.

So long as the modern, progressive state (whether of the right or the left) retained control of the socialization of technology (which is also to say, of economic management, that is, of its credit and debt), the time required for socialization remained relatively compatible with that of a thought that could only ever occur in the therapeutic aftermath of pharmacological toxicity, as the second moment of the doubly epokhal redoubling. The age of structuralism was probably the final instance of an epoch of this type.

Since the implementation of the TINA programme ('there is no alternative'), with virtually no resistance, despite calls for 'resistance',[16] this time has been strictly eliminated: TINA was the declaration of economic war, a declaration made by the international financial powers to the entire planet, but also and firstly to thought and to reason, discharging them in favour of an automated understanding – which has led us to our present madness.

Universities were then charged by psycho-power with the task of rationalizing the need for these acts of war, not just in Weber's or Habermas's sense of rationalization, but in Freud's. 'Rationalization' means here the fabulated internalization of a state of fact. This fabulation consists in denying even the possibility of rediscovering, after this state of fact, that is, after its pharmacological critique, a state of law, that is, the possibility of the second moment of the *epokhē*: the moment of positive pharmacology.

66   Global crisis and the internation

The global economic collapse of 2008 changed the course of events: the irrationality of the Market (or 'markets') has become clear, systemic stupidity has patently led to global unreason, and speculative madness has reached intolerable levels, even though it is not only still tolerated, but more dominant than ever – expressed publicly through ratings agencies, but operating through many other systems of which the public is still largely unaware, agencies and agents that render manifestly impossible any sovereign initiative, that is, any democratic decision or action. And yet, with the exception of Paul Jorion, very few academics are working towards a critical analysis of this situation.[17]

Speculative madness has become intolerable because:

- since 2008 capitalism seems to have become manifestly mafia-like, anti-economic and massively destructive because it is guided exclusively by the war aims pursued by speculative hedge funds against the apparatus of production, against populations, and against natural resources, cultural resources and thought – the latter finding itself reduced, by systemic proletarianization that now constitutes the very principle of those projects that aim to 'modernize' the school and higher education, to the capacity to implement automated models of calculation, and to the acquisition of 'competences' at the service of adapting to the fatal

inevitability of TINA, rather than any acquisition of non-adaptational knowledge;[18]
- the pace of technological innovation, made possible by the dramatic reduction in the time it takes for technologies to be transferred to society – transfers that are themselves subject to the conditions of socialization dictated and orchestrated by marketing – has become unsustainable: this is the true question of sustainability.

In this context, universities around the world, and academics around the world – from schoolteachers (in France called *professeurs des écoles*) to professors of the Collège de France, and including education inspectors – should unite under a framework that we should no longer define as an international organization but rather as an 'internation': via processes of co-individuation and transindividuation wherein the nation gives way to the internation, the concept of which was outlined by Marcel Mauss in 1920:

> An internationalism worthy of the name [...] is not a denial of the nation. It situates it. The internation would be the opposite of such a-nationism. It is also, therefore, the opposite of nationalism, which isolates the nation.[19]

The internation would not refer to what has now been around for several hundred years: agreements, treaties and conventions of international law. These seem in any case to have increasingly facilitated the disindividuation of national individuation processes, by giving rise to situations that, precisely, escape all public law (*public international law*, which governs the international relations between states, has abandoned the juridical management of the now-established global economic war, and it has abandoned it to *private international law*, which governs the international relations between private, legal persons or entities).

The internation should be developed, on the contrary, as a process of the juridical co-individuation and transindividuation of nations and of continental associations of nations, and, through these, as a global framework for the peaceful collective individuation of the psychic individuals who are the citizens of these nations – who have already entered into the internation *in fact*, but who should now enter it *in law*.

National citizens (that is, psychic individuals co-individuating and transindividuating themselves under the framework of the rules of national law) are already profoundly disaffected from their citizenship, as consumers of an internation 'in fact' shaped by international marketing campaigns, which now almost always extend beyond national borders on the basis of originally deterritorialized strategies. These strategies and campaigns functionally and systemically combine with an international economic law that is itself constantly being renegotiated in expansionary ways, and through which the service economy tends to replace public powers. This capturing and harnessing of the attention of psychic individuals, however, involves processes of disindividuation – which short-circuit the processes of collective individuation forged in the national and other frameworks – more than it does processes of transindividuation.

The current opportunity that exists to constitute an internation 'in law' is the outcome, almost a century after Mauss, of a new state of fact. Nations are now suffused with reticularity, thanks to the circulation of forms of tertiary retention that are completely new to national law, which has failed to conceptualize these tertiary retentional forms correctly. This new reticular situation disindividuates nations and every form of collective individuation of which these nations were the territorialized synthesis. At the same time, it radically changes the relations between the inside and the outside that over-determine the difference between private and public – *private* in this context being less and less a matter of intimacy and more and more a matter of submitting to the imperative to obtain profit, that is, to become calculable and therefore 'commensurable', as Lyotard says.

Original processes of transindividuation are now tending to form, processes that surpass national frameworks. And these processes are occurring in the context of digital reticularity, via the global circulation of these new forms of tertiary retention. At the core of these processes, the academic internation should furnish the *internation 'of fact'* – which the *economic internation* shamelessly exploits, supported by the non-law that it has set up – with elements and principles through which a state of law can be defined. And this new state of law should establish, on the basis of these new retentional specificities themselves, synthetic criteria for transindividuation that go far beyond both the public international law that governs the relations between nations and the private international law that applies in the economic sphere.

The *academic internation* could and should, therefore, become the catalyst for a new process of collective individuation at the global level, enabling negotiations to be conducted towards a global civil peace treaty. As a global process of collective individuation founded on the new public space that it should form in and through the digital system of publication that has already been installed 'in fact', it will tend to constitute (in the juridical sense) the global public and political space that it should claim and represent, by opposing the reduction of the public interest to the private interest of global oligarchs – if necessary by, for example, engaging in international academic strikes.

It is only within such a framework that it will be possible to pose new juridical questions in new ways, including – in both economics and politics – questions of global common goods and intellectual property.[20] And here, the struggles undertaken for de-proletarianization and for a new relation between, on the one hand, the university and research, and, on the other hand, industry and the economy, in the fields of computer science and information technology (and now in the field of what we are calling 'web science'), have exemplary value for the whole academic community.

67   The internation against disindividuation

This political constitution of global digital and retentional space, conceived as the political constitution of the internation – that is, as a process of rational transindividuation initiated at the instigation of the academic sphere, which will form the kernel and the germ of this internation, and will do so by posing, in the context of industrial technoscience, the question of the universal under pharmacological conditions – is both urgent and necessary. It is all the more urgent and necessary given that, with the emergence and development of international economic organizations, private international law tends to impose the criteria for these organizations in relation to those transindividuation processes that do indeed develop in international space, and that as a result become processes of disindividuation: the criteria for these processes, which are those of global economic war, are destructive rather than peaceful, that is, contrary to the interests of the logical disputation required for the exercise of reason.

A peaceful internation capable of countering global economic unreason: criteria for this can be defined only if the international academic sphere supplies the internation's political individuation process with proposals in law (that are curative) *on the basis* of processes of transindividuation in fact (that are toxic). Deploying such proposals in the new global public space will lead to the formation of absolutely long circuits of transindividuation generating and transindividuating – in these states of fact and on the basis of the

foundations of the academic disciplines that are themselves such
circuits – *criteria of truth*. Criteria such as these are what replace
criteria of force, that is, of violence, and are those without which
there can be no constitution of political law.

As such, the academic sphere of the internation must nourish the
process of individuation of reference in the absence of which no collective individuation is possible – and a nation is one such process of
collective individuation, metastabilized as one such process of the
individuation of reference.

A nation is composed of citizens who are also psychic individuals.
A nation's citizens and psychic individuals psychically individuate
only insofar as they participate in processes of collective individuation in reference to a national law, publicly and explicitly expressed
in literal form, à la lettre, and internalized à la lettre. As such, this
law governs the conflicts between the various collective individuation
processes going on *within a single individual*, even before it governs
the conflicts between those psychic individuations that are citizens.
In so doing, public law is intimately tied to the superego, and symbol-
ized through the ego ideal that constitutes the private individual
insofar as they are capable of participating in collective individuation
– that is, precisely, in the symbolic.

A psychic individual can in fact individuate themselves (only)
by participating in collective individuation processes that *contradict*
each other: the diachrony that constitutes the individual as a
singularity is the result of these phase differences (this is how
Simondon formulates the basic principle of the dynamic of
individuation).

In *La Télécratie contre la démocratie*[21] I attempt to show that, just
as the primary identification process that forms in early childhood is
indispensable for the various and often competing secondary identi-
fications that then allow psychic individuals to pass into adulthood
(to go through adolescence) without destroying their ability to project
their own unity (which is their desire as the power to bind), so too
processes of the collective individuation of reference are indispensable
to human groups – without which they will be unable to maintain
their unity (that is, their civility) while preserving their 'diversality'
(that is, the individuation of their singularity).

A process of the individuation of reference is founded on circuits
of the transindividuation of reference that enable the unification of
psychic individuals and of the various spheres to which they belong.
In the course of history, the individuation of reference has evolved
along with the retentional and pharmacological conditions of the

production of circuits of transindividuation, and in particular of *intergenerational and absolutely long* circuits of transindividuation.

Absolutely long circuits are those allowing the production of the infinitizing power and infinitizing knowledge in which the noeticity (spirituality and intellectivity) of the noetic soul consists. On the basis of the anamnesic experience of geometry, that is, on the basis of the experience of *alētheia* constituted in geometric perspective (*more geometrico*), such circuits are called 'rational' – the meaning of rationality being transformed as the history of reason unfolds, up until the stage of rationalization, which reveals the pharmacological character of the rational spirit, that is, its limitations and its irreducible *duplicity*.

The onto-theological path taken by philosophy meant that it arranged the conjunction between circuits of rational transindividuation and circuits of theological transindividuation. This led to the establishment of a process of the individuation of reference founded on the spiritual power of the church as postulating a revealed higher reason. To this spiritual power, which formed canonical power, the nation-state, traversed by the process of secularization and rationalization described by Weber, opposed an intellectual, spiritual and rational power, founded on secular public education (what Valéry called the Mind or Spirit). This amounted to a new process of the individuation of reference, a new transmission and adoption of the noetic embodied in the nation, including in its letters, its history and its geography.

During the twentieth century, the 'Market' has replaced trade[22] and has facilitated the global organization of a consumerist industrial economy. National processes of the individuation of reference have been emptied of their substance, as the transindividuation processes on which they were founded have been short-circuited. This evacuation of substance has affected not only the academic sphere and therefore schools, but also all those processes that are carriers of intergenerational relations in general,[23] occurring within this or that cultural and political sphere, and such that these generations are always forged through territorial anchorings[24] wherein, precisely, they form and adopt processes of the individuation of reference.

Such processes always *exceed* these territorial anchorings: this is shown, for example, by the fact that national law can be imposed on regional particularities, or that Western feudal systems and then monarchies more or less submit to ecclesiastical and spiritual authority based on canonical Christianity. And the University of Bologna, that is, the oldest academic university, is itself already precisely such an enlargement:

> At the request of four doctors from the university, in 1158 Emperor Frederick Barbarossa promulgated the *Constitutio Habita* with which the university became, by law, a place where research would develop independent of any other power. This is the beginning of the independence of universities vis-à-vis power.[25]

One might be tempted to believe that the 'market', unfolding at a global level, and exceeding local modes of life as the consumerist 'way of life', therefore constitutes a new process of the individuation of reference. And this is exactly what marketing would have us believe, as would advertising,[26] brands, and everything that, by capturing and deforming attention, short-circuits the attentional forms that typify the various collective individuation processes forming and cultivating cultures and nations.

The 'market', however, cannot be a new process for the individuation of reference because, unlike trade, it is founded on generalized proletarianization. For this reason, it can replace those systems of the transindividuation of reference within which it develops only by short-circuiting these systems, rather than by re-individuating them in a new context.

Short-circuiting those long circuits of transindividuation and processes of identification through which the knowledge of how to do, live and theorize are formed, the 'market' dissolves social structures and psychic apparatus, and subjects the evolution of the global technological system to the exclusively adaptive and speculative imperatives of an economy of carelessness and neglect. This leads to generalized disinvestment and renders impossible the curative adoption of contemporary *pharmaka*.

The 'Market', based on this destruction of knowledge, has become hegemonic, and the name for its worldwide expansion is globalization. This 'market' is inherently a process of disindividuation, that is, a process that destroys all institutions and discredits every form of authority – recognizing the violence of the law but not its symbolic force, which one calls its authority. Global unreason hence becomes patently obvious and mimetically terrifying, as credit systems are ruined and, with them, all trust, confidence, surety, all belief in a future, and therefore all investment, in the widest sense of the term.

This obviously does not mean that it would be possible or even desirable to restore a *national* individuation of reference – which would immediately become a national individuation of *preference*. It means that the constitution of a global individuation of reference, in a context now recognized as irreducibly pharmacological, is the task and the responsibility of universities united within the internation. And it is in *this* way that the internation will be formed, by bringing about a real globalization, that is, as worlding [*mondanéisation*], as a world-making that will re-found individuation, unifying itself in and by the formation of new absolutely long circuits of transindividuation, constituting a *new critique* and a *new reason* – to act.

(Globalization, rethought in these terms, might well be able to reconstitute conditional customs restrictions against the barbarous practices that the market imposes on social systems – which ruined them from the moment financialization turned the market into the enemy of trade and commerce as much as of the entrepreneurial economy – but this is another question.)

This new reason, combatting the new unreason, is a pharmacological reason to act, and this means above all that it is *impure*, that is, both:

- constituted by a tertiary retention that is a *pharmakon* and that can always be turned (like a glove)[27] into a rationalization that leads inevitably to unreason, that is, to demotivation and disinvestment;
- thought first and foremost as motive, that is, as a reason to act in the service of a potential to act, and thought as such on the basis of a re-evaluation of the question of desire in the course of *noēsis*, a re-evaluation that requires a re-reading, in particular, of Aristotle, Spinoza, Kant, Hegel and Nietzsche, in relation to Freud's 'Copernican revolution', whereby consciousness is no longer just a dimension of reason and the unconscious constitutes the preindividual funds of all motives to act – whether they are reason-able (projected *more geometrico* in reference to the geometric canon of anamnesis) or unreason-able – 'of all motives to act', that is, of the passage into action, acting out.

68   Internation and interscience

The need to constitute the internation, in an absolutely political and *as such rational* sense, is all the more keenly felt now that the Fukushima disaster has revealed the immediately global nature of the effects of the carelessness and neglect of the 'conservative revolution'. The need to establish a new public power[28] – that of the internation – has become obvious and it has nothing to do with the motives that govern international institutions such as the World Trade Organization, the International Monetary Fund, or even the United Nations.

A new public power, founded on the new *public thing* (*res publica*) constituted by the retentional publication systems of digital pharmacology, must establish a new relation to knowledge, explicitly conceived as the struggle against proletarianization, and it must articulate forms of knowledge with one another and according to new modalities.

The individuation of reference that the internation must develop for nations and continental regions must be founded on pharmacological reason, that is, on a reason that may always become unreasoning, but which knows this, and which constitutes as such and above all a new *vigilance*, that is, a new critique that is also in some way a pharmaco-vigilance. This impure reason would by no means be a new figure of mastery. But it always remains a figure of *reason* as the claim that thought passes through apodictic experience and never renounces the canon of geometric truth that constitutes the purest form of rational idealization.[29]

Only reason and its universality – projected locally and utopically as a consistence that, not existing, infinitizes itself in the irreducible diversality of singularities, and makes reason, as a noetic modality of desire that can itself desire only singularities[30] that exceed the universal, a power of singularities – only this universal reason can re-found an individuation of reference beyond nations and beyond continentalizations, and as horizon of a peace treaty between continental blocs. Everyone knows that the ruin of international institutions by the 'Market', of which the United Nations is the fig leaf, and which organizes the global economic war, makes this peace treaty essential, failing which the outcome will be global *military* war.

Only by passing through this intercontinental and therefore global horizon will it be possible to revive a European project worthy of the name – European meaning firstly: specific to the continent that has disseminated, over the entire planet, literal tertiary retention, and then industrialization and rationalization, on the basis of its experience of a reason it always believed pure. Europe, stunned by the discovery of the impurity of 'its' reason, has become stupid – which is also to say, impotent. Only its projection onto the horizon of an extra-continental collective individuation of reference can give it the reason and the power to act.

Impure reason must today critique a pharmacology itself founded on a general organology. General organology, which will be explained in the coming pages,[31] constitutes the paradigm of transdisciplinarity without which no critique of pharmacological reason, and no positive pharmacology, are conceivable.

To take up a term from a 1998 issue of the *Revue du Mauss*, itself borrowing from a text co-signed in 1982 by François Châtelet, Jacques Derrida, Jean-Pierre Faye and Dominique Lecourt in order to found the Collège international de philosophie,[32] an *'interscience' for the twenty-first century* must take shape within universities worldwide, united by an internation of law.

This interscience, which is inseparable from techno-logical becoming, must undertake and critique the genealogy of the acceleration of the transfer time of technologies, in order to effect a bifurcation. This task is all the more urgent and necessary given that this acceleration has now combined with a radical evolution of publication systems in light-time.[33] The latter has increased the ease with which these intellectual technologies (*pharmaka*) have been placed in the service of toxic processes that no longer invent any therapeutic practices, let alone potential antidotes.

This absolute acceleration short-circuits governments and public powers, that is, it literally disintegrates the political sphere as such. If it is not a matter of returning to the national public sphere, which is in any event manifestly impossible, we must nevertheless invent, individuate and transindividuate the new public power that is the internation. And we must do so by re-posing the question of sovereignty on the basis of the pharmacological critique of autonomy. Autonomy: which is named sovereignty when it is the collective individual that requires a pharmacological history, from *raison d'état* to the social contract. And which, beyond that, refers to the submission of sovereignty to economics that occurs in the age of globalization, destroying national law and, ultimately, installing political lawlessness.

National laws, which are at present the only authentically political laws, and which have defined the economic rights of ordinary people (and 'people's rights'), are now subject to the economic law of corporate actors, dictated by the World Trade Organization.

The internation should not short-circuit states, but allow them to reinvent themselves (to re-individuate themselves) by involving them in the constitution of a new process of the transindividuation of reference that neither evacuates them of their substance nor deprives them of their sovereignty. Rather, it should re-pose the question of

sovereignty and of its territorialization (including economic territorialization) in the epoch of the public thing as internation (collective
individuation within digital systems of publication). This requires
territoriality to be thought anew in an epoch of re-territorialization,
which would be the end neither of de-territorialization nor of globalization, but rather a new regime of both.[34]

69   'Creative Destruction', efficiency and disindividuation – on the aims of innovation

Schumpeter elevated innovation to the rank of being a fundamental
principle of industrial economics. But the reduction of the transfer
time of technologies and the resulting acceleration of innovation –
now unbridled – has led to a generalized disindividuation of social
systems and to an increasing disruption of natural systems. Whereas
Schumpeter presented innovation as the fundamental condition of the
production of value, today it is seen merely as that which accelerates
the individuation of the technical system without regard to the conditions of psychosocial individuation.

Defined as 'Creative Destruction', industrial innovation leads inevitably to the short-circuiting of the adoption of technical individuation by psychosocial individuation, generating massive, systemic and
ruinous disindividuation of psychic apparatuses and social systems.
To conceive innovation in this way is to overlook the question of
transindividuation, which alone produces the transindividual, that is,
meaning [*signification*], which is also to say, adoption, and not adaptation. Given that meaning is what remains always to be interpreted
by psychic individuals and social individuals, this interpretation is
what gives meaning its sense [*sens*].

Rather than contributing to an *intensification* of the individuation
of social systems (which should be understood here also in Niklas
Luhmann's sense), conceiving innovation in this way makes such an
intensification simply impossible, because it robs social systems of the
knowledge in which they essentially consist, taking hold of this individuation and thereby taking control of it – for example, today, via
the grammatization of social relations.[35]

What Ars Industrialis refers to as the economy of contribution is
founded on a different conception of innovation[36] – which passes
through a re-evaluation of territorial innovation in the context of an
internation, through which academic authorities must implement
contributory research, and rethink in new terms the questions of

industrial policy and of the economy of investment and taxation, in order to encourage processes of capacitation.[37]

The political form of psychosocial individuation arose, as the *polis*, almost three thousand years ago, when civil peace became possible because logical disputation replaced war between the clans, of which the current mafia-like oligarchs are the resurgence. The noetic milieu in which the *polis* arose was based on those tertiary retentions that made possible the production of *scholarly secondary retention*. The school – the *skholeion* – and the academy, and then the university, are institutions of the trans-formative transmission of these scholarly retentions, through which the latter become collective, that is, trans-individuate themselves.

Secondary retentions become collective for an academic community when they endorse them, make them their own, that is, adopt them by themselves individuating. To know a theorem, and recognize it *as such*, consists in making it one's own, that is, in making what at some point was retained and thought by one scholar into something that *I* retain and *I* think, so that I can now rightly call it *my* knowledge (this sharing of secondary retentions in the course of a process of metastable transindividuation – that is, composed of a multitude of singular individuations – is what all academic life aims to do).[38] As this becoming-collective of secondary retentions plays out for an academic community, scholarly secondary retentions then constitute the criteria enabling the selection of primary retentions[39] in the experience that is thinking as such.

As the role of digital tertiary retention in innovation becomes increasingly important, the speed with which knowledge circulates accelerates, transforming knowledge into information, which in turn becomes calculable data, and hence allows this selection to be automated. The anamnesic process is thereby short-circuited, and this leads, seemingly inevitably, to the destruction of the après-coup and the elimination of delay, without which there can be no time for reflection.

The production of the criteria by which retentions are selected (selections that always consist in projecting protentions) thereby becomes industrial. Noetic life then becomes subject almost exclusively to the internalization of efficiency-based criteria, ignoring the other three criteriologies described by the theory of the four causes.[40] When knowledge has become a function of the industrial economy, what is true for the economy proves true for academic activity as well: the criterion of efficiency governs everything in these 'free-market societies'.

Nevertheless:

> The dethroning of efficiency as sole guiding principle is inevitable in a
> free society. It is only through being in competition with other aims,
> values and ideals that the concept of efficiency can be accepted.[41]

This is so because society cannot endure without continuously
replenishing its circuits of transindividuation, which are always
inscribed in intergenerational relations. As these circuits are transmitted through these intergenerational relations, they are re-interpreted,
and in this way pursued further.

Efficiency may lead to technological innovation, but it comes at
the expense of social innovation, that is, at the expense of knowledge
in general, because it is in direct conflict with the task of teachers
and professors at every scholarly and academic level, given that every
generation of teachers is subject to questions from those of the
younger generation – questions which, at the current pace of innovation, and of the resulting evolution of knowledge, can no longer be
given answers *from an academic perspective*, since teachers cannot
have been trained to do so.

70   Knowledge time and generational time

The speed with which knowledge is evolving can be seen, for instance,
in the ways that biology has been affected by the achievements of
biotechnology. But from the beginning, these transformations have
been accompanied by promotional discourse in the 'marketplace of
ideas', through which these biotechnologies are *sold* to society: the
'ideas' are placed on the media market as soon as they have been
published in scholarly journals, and sometimes even prior to appearing in such publications, or even without any scientific publication
whatsoever, that is, without any critique. This speed, which in the
eyes of the public increasingly often seems inordinately hasty, and
which now generates public distrust, also means that schoolteachers
and college professors find themselves having a deficit of knowledge[42]
in relation to their pupils and students.

In a situation where the transindividuation time of knowledge is
disconnected from the transindividuation time of the generations –
since the axioms, theorems, experimental facts and other apparatus
of the establishment of proof or of the basis of a thesis are now
produced at a far greater pace than generational renewal – it becomes

necessary to teach in a different way, which must be founded on a different relation to knowledge.

This means that teachers must receive epistemological training (firstly, during their university studies) in relation to a chronic state of non-knowledge, that is, a state of knowledge that is not transindividuated in a homogeneous way, above all because the time for this transindividuation is no longer available. Questions raised by students,[43] students who have not had time to mature into an academic community of peers, require answers from professors who are ill-equipped to teach what has changed in knowledge in the last two centuries, let alone, a fortiori, in the last fifty years.

To invent academic responses, faced with this totally unprecedented and truly revolutionary situation – wherein everything in every field seems to be in permanent revolution – requires returning to the history of the industrial transformation that radically disrupted the way in which Kant, in *The Conflict of the Faculties*, grasped the question of the relations between the inside and the outside of the university.

71   The thirst for knowledge and the stakes of power

The digital public mind and spirit opens up an era of new forms of scholarly or scientific society – of which Wikipedia is one contributory international organ in the internation that is forming – in the Kantian sense, wherein *scientific societies* are the interlocutors of academic authorities:

> In addition to these *incorporated* scholars [that are the professors], there can also be scholars *at large*, who do not belong to the *university* [...], either forming independent organizations, like various workshops (called *academies* or *scientific societies*), or living, so to speak, in a state of nature so far as learning is concerned, each working by himself, as an *amateur* and without public precepts or rules, at extending and propagating [his field of] learning.[44]

The scholarly or scientific societies[45] and academies of the classical age were formed on the basis of the Republic of Letters, during the noetic turn that the dissemination of printing constituted for Christianity. Elizabeth Eisenstein has analysed the huge transformations wrought by the mechanical printing of alphabetic tertiary retentions (of which Sylvain Auroux analysed the innumerable effects on thought and the sciences of language, that is, on modern philosophy)[46] on

Renaissance society. Eisenstein quotes Johann Sleidan: 'Each man became eager for knowledge, not without feeling a sense of amazement at his former blindness.'[47]

This knowledge, for which all were eager, became not just a spiritual issue, but a political one: 'The art of Printing will so spread knowledge, that the common people, knowing their own rights and liberties will not be governed by way of oppression.'[48] Knowledge shows itself to be a political issue in the struggle against the spiritual power exerted by the papacy on the interpretation of Scripture. In this way, knowledge begins to define itself in opposition to spiritual authority: 'either the pope must abolish knowledge and printing or printing must at length root him out'.[49]

Through these epistemic and spiritual struggles (that are in a broad sense noetic),[50] a new order is set up. This new order challenges the authority of the clergy and gives rise to secular scholars, while at the same time supplying Scripture with a new readership, that is, a new public space and a new public time of Christianity:

> For Bible printing subjected the authority of the medieval clergy to a two-pronged attack. It was threatened by lay erudition on the party of a scholarly elite and by lay Bible reading among the public at large. On the elite level, laymen became more erudite than churchmen; grammar and philology challenged the reign of theology; Greek and Hebrew studies forced their way into the schools.[51]

The knowledge emerging from the old universities (Bologna, the Sorbonne, Oxford, Cambridge) thus comes to be contested by new scholars who begin (as will Kant, after being reprimanded by the king of Prussia)[52] to dispute the place of the faculty of theology in the academic hierarchy, that is, by 'independent scholars' who will later form those 'academies or scientific societies' to which Kant refers as lying *outside the university*. As this occurs, the influence of the clergy on those who could speak only the common language begins to fade, and there rises what is referred to as the vernacular and the vulgar, extending well beyond the peasants and the poor:

> On the popular level, ordinary men and women begin to know their Scripture as well as most parish priests; markets for vernacular catechisms and prayer books expanded; church Latin no longer served as a sacred language veiling sacred mysteries.[53]

And these tensions between secular and religious knowledge and power brought with them changes in law, such as the order promulgated by Henry VIII in 1543, 'prohibiting the use of annotated English Bibles, forbidding unlicensed persons to read or expound Scripture, and placing Bible reading out of bounds for "women, artificers, apprentices, journeymen, yeomen, husbandmen and laborers" '.[54]

72 The requalification of scientific societies and the new division of intellectual labour

It has frequently been observed in recent years that this struggle to take control of these new forms of tertiary retention, to shape their pharmacology (between the toxic and the curative) and to prescribe a therapeutics (the best ways of dealing with the *pharmakon*), seems to be occurring again, and with some similar features, with the advent of digital retention.

Electronic *hypomnēmata* are today transforming the entire world, and this involves issues resembling those that marked the Renaissance, Humanism, the Reformation and the Counter-Reformation. This has resulted in a new grammatization of idioms[55] – today's challenges are the repetition of a familiar scene that happened also to be the starting point for the Platonic academy, and the questions they raise lie at the very heart of the fate of schools, universities and academies of all kinds.

With those new types of *hypomnēmata* that are hypermedia (of which HTTP, HTML and XML are protocols and languages), forms of electronic writing are imprinted into silicon-based memory, where symbols circulate at the speed of light on digital networks, passing through circuits printed at the microelectronic level (at the micrometric scale), through which radically new processes of writing, editing, distribution and reading have been implemented.[56] The change to which all this has given rise is obviously comparable to those great moments of grammatization that profoundly shaped – and in a way that has been largely ignored by philosophy[57] – the content of modernity.

It is not just archival *data* – libraries, media libraries and documentation centres of all kinds – that has become generally accessible, thanks, for example, to the digitalization processes carried out by both major public institutions and private operators. What has now become accessible is not just data but *functions*: in previous times these were reserved for the exclusive use of clerics, whether religious or secular, but for the past century they have been kept in the hands of professionals working in the information industries (information and documentation technologies) and the communication industries (audiovisual technologies). Today, in the epoch of digital networks, these functions are being passed into the hands of the public themselves.

Apprehended during the last three quarters of the twentieth century as consumers and audiences of the mass media, the public is now de-massifying and forming into communities of contributors. This is what produces the bulk of the data and metadata that circulates on networks, where it generates 'network effects' capable of exploitation by marketing strategies – particularly via 'social networks'. The latter may, however, also constitute *new public spaces* where, for example, shared retentions are aggregated, retentions that are also collective secondary retentions, and that could thus become scholarly or scientific secondary retentions.

But under what conditions? There is no doubt about the answer: on the condition that schools and academic institutions play their part – which remains entirely to be invented. Failing which, these collective secondary retentions will remain those of industrially organized stupidity and viciousness.

New public spaces aggregate retentions that are shared, for example, by the anonymous, innumerable and mostly totally disinterested contributors who are building Wikipedia, thereby creating an immense work of transindividuation (15 million articles as of February 2010), produced within an internation (in 281 languages) and at the speed of light, according to rules that are not orders but guidelines that have been widely followed for ten years by a global collectivity whose sense of responsibility is surprisingly impressive, in an era in which carelessness and neglect seem globally dominant.[58] This programme was to a large extent inspired by principles arising from the free software community: communities of shared professional knowledge struggling against their own proletarianization by making technology serve the individuation of those who are its practitioners.[59]

Within these publics who are no longer audiences, who have passed from being a mass of consumers to associations of contributors, the figure of the 'amateur' emerges in various ways, in the sense of this term that Kant used to describe the scientific societies of the Republic of Letters, forming at the time of Erasmus, Luther and Henry VIII. These publics are communities of amateurs of all kinds: artistic, encyclopedic, scientific, medical, technological, and so on. Such amateurs are not just practitioners of so-called collaborative technologies of Web 2.0; they also make use of electronic equipment through which the ability to record, post-produce, broadcast and index audiovisual tertiary retentions becomes widely accessible, as well as highly advanced digital forms of research and of the processing and dissemination of data.

This is a new division of noetic labour (intellectual, poetic, artistic), occurring in a new retentional milieu, and one that comes to disrupt greatly the understanding of this division that derives from Kant himself,[60] who highlighted the fact that literal tertiary retention – sacred or profane – was the condition of the faculties ('all three higher faculties base the teachings which the government entrusts to them on *writings*'),[61] as well as of *Öffentlichkeit*, which is itself the condition of rational knowledge,[62] academic institutions being in many respects 'artificial' (*künstliche*).

But here, for us, *artificial* also and firstly means *pharmacological*, because what is constituted by this artifice is precisely tertiary retention insofar as it extends beyond the campuses of the academy or the university, and it is on this point (which Habermas completely ignores) that we must now insist.

73 Autonomy and heteronomy of the university: the condition of the unconditional

In Kant's thinking, rational noetic work is responsible not only for the division into faculties, but for what distinguishes the inside of the university from its outside, which, depending on its porosity, makes it more or less autonomous or heteronomous. What is at stake in *The Conflict of the Faculties* is clearly and simply the conditions that guarantee the autonomy of the university – the conditions of an autonomy that always tends to be defined as unconditional. What are the *conditions* of the unconditional? Such would seem to be the formally and irreducibly aporetic question that conditions any reflection on the unconditional – or on 'autonomy'.

The conditions of the unconditional are *pharmacological*, and they constitute the *pharmacological condition of the noetic*. This condition can come to pass (and pass into action) as rational only via those tertiary retentions that I have elsewhere called orthothetic.[63] Such tertiary retentions are themselves highly heteronomous, subject to social, historical, economic and political logics, among others, each of which is highly accidental.[64]

These social logics are themselves subject to irreducibly technical conditions that extend beyond the hypomnesic field. Inscribed into a process of rational transindividuation, that is, governed by transindividuation criteria respecting the principles of reason that are constantly being redefined as the process unfolds – notably as a result of the test that they constitute for retentional history itself insofar as it is pharmacological – these logics enable the projection of law, that is, of the 'therapeutic principle' (in the sense intended by Freud when he refers, for example, to the 'pleasure principle'), on the basis of that *fact* that is the 'pharmacological principle' (which here becomes the principle behind the 'reality principle').

The question of the inside and the outside of the academic sphere, therefore, becomes that of the way in which these *hypomnēmata* that are tertiary retentions constantly redistribute the process of psychic and collective individuation that is the noetic community in totality (the internation). And this redistribution of the effective conditions of individuation is not confined to the academic sphere, which is central to all those idealizations that presuppose this rational attentional form that is *logos*, but extends to extra-academic processes of collective individuation. The latter include all those collective individuation processes with which the academic collective individuation processes that are the disciplines must compose, and with which they must work, while forming as well their objects, beginning with the process of collective individuation that is language.[65]

This *hypomnesic overflow* both frames academic life at its most intimate levels (if tertiary retention is indeed the condition of reason, for example, 'addressing the entire reading public') and at the same time constitutes its heteronomy, because this also frames its outside, which can in any case appear as such *only* on this condition. This overflow, this heteronomy and autonomy in which it trans-forms itself – by the therapeutic work of the academic disciplines – is today constituted by a global industrial landscape (that of the internation), so that the inside work of academic transindividuation is thoroughly transfixed and framed by digital *hypomnēmata*.

These digital *hypomnēmata* have become the framework through which all extra-academic social relations are grammatized (familial relations, friends, work relations, commercial, financial, political and diplomatic relations, and so on), rearranging the fabric and the retentional material of psychic life at its most intimate, as well as the systems of retentional (and protentional) selection in which consist the most institutionalized forms of social life, and of which the academic disciplines are in principle the referents.

This is the basis on which we must analyse the semantic displacement that, in relation to the question of the autonomy of the university, occurs between Kant's day and our own, the latter being the time of the Law on the Liberties and Responsibilities of Universities[66] – which would doubtless appear to Kant's eyes to amount to an unrestrained and fatal submission of the university to the greatest possible irrationality.

The autonomy that this law accords to university presidents would in Kant's eyes undoubtedly amount to a deprivation of the autonomy of 'incorporated scholars',[67] to be conferred instead upon those '*businessmen* or technicians of learning [...] who are instruments of the government',[68] and who in some way 'co-linearize' (to use an expression of Frédéric Lordon's) their interests with those of the government.

74   The industrial condition of the university

Behind all of this lies the question of knowing what relations the university can and must maintain with its external milieu when that milieu becomes industrial, that is, techno-logical. Technology here means the integration of rational knowledge into the process of technical individuation, but also the intervention of technology itself into the becoming of reason, via those tertiary retentions that arise from industrial development, both as instruments of observation and as global retentional milieu. In such circumstances it is impossible *not* to question the *industrial conditionality* of technology.

At least two attitudes are possible here:

- either to ignore this becoming, and to deny its effectiveness, all the while claiming to be 'resisting', condemning oneself to irrelevance like the pope, that is, like Benedict XVI, who chatters away in a secularized landscape in which the religious has become a mere caricature;
- or to move from resistance to invention, that is, to critique: to turn this situation into an object of idealization, that is, capable of projecting a new state of law, no longer opposing pharmacological heteronomy to therapeutic autonomy, and taking performatively[69] the positive promise of the *pharmakon* – as this *profession of faith* that is the honour of everyone granted the title *professor*.

The second attitude is possible only on the condition that an inextricably heuristic and educational programme is implemented, for which the considerations of the previous chapter constitute guidelines.

This programme asserts before anything else that knowledge is pharmacological, in the sense argued by Paul Valéry, and that this pharmacology is irreducible, which means that there is no knowledge incapable of leading to the opposite of what was aimed at when it was conceived: there is no conceptual and rational knowledge that may not result in the irrational or rationalization – which is always a way of proletarianizing the rational via the mediation of tertiary retention. And this is so in default of producing an appropriate critique within the university, a critique (in the Kantian sense) that must be disseminated through practice at every level of the academic institution (in passing through Hume's moment of experience, *empeiria*).

75   Knowledge and experience: the generalized proletarianization implemented by 'elites' themselves proletarianized

The rapid spread of digital technologies (since 1992) produced a techno-logical *'epokhē'*, that is, a suspension of processes of transindividuation that were hitherto in force, and that concretized social systems. This digital *epokhē* is connected to a prior *epokhē*, induced by analogue media, and in particular by the very rapid growth of television,[70] the suspensive character of which was not felt as clearly or as immediately as that of the digital *epokhē* – even though the shock was at least as violent. (This difference lies in the fact that the first was the completion of the consumerist system, whereas the second, the web, put this into question.)

These two processes – which short-circuited the transindividuation processes lying at the basis of the various components of the education system (in particular the disciplines) or the systems that interact with the education system (virtually all the social systems) – are today combining, via the convergence of the digital and the analogue, in ways that are all the more complex given the many respects in which they are contradictory. The resultant toxic epokhal redoubling is less curatively redoubling – 'epoch-making' – than it is contributing to the accelerating decomposition of the consumerist industrial model within which it developed.

In terms of academic and university life, this blockage generates effects comparable to those that played out in the age of Luther: as protest against clerics, the erudite, scholars. Equivalent roles are played, in our age, by 'experts' – that is, *proletarianized elites*. Today, also, these protests crystallize or catalyse tensions arising from a situation that is far older than the revolution itself, which is in this case the digital revolution: scholars become experts when they yield to rationalization in the Weberian sense, resulting in a situation that was described by Valéry as well as Husserl, Adorno, Marcuse and Habermas.

James Watt's steam engine concretely expressed, in the eighteenth century, the encounter between science and technics, through an object that would become the fundamental element in the transformation of society by the industrial revolution. Beginning with the machine-tool (1760), then with Watt's machine (1775) and eventually with the Jacquard loom (1801), a process of the grammatization of gesture was unfurled. This process would be Marx's focus in the *Grundrisse*, and through it the very nature of labour and work would change – including, in the twentieth century, intellectual labour and the work of the teacher or professor. Watt thus radically transformed not only the status of knowledge but the methods by which it individuates: this now occurs only in a constant, bound relationship (albeit often unconsciously) with the industrial world.

From this point, knowledge begins to evolve ever more rapidly according to the demands of industry, in relation to the new aims characteristic of a society dominated by the idea of progress. But these progressive aims will themselves eventually be dissolved as financialized capitalism becomes entirely speculative and is reduced to a single aim: that of speculative profit, which no longer possesses any efficient causality, since it imposes the reign of carelessness, neglect and, ultimately, paralysis, that is, industrial inefficiency (if not venality).

Transindividuation processes weave non-academic forms of knowledge (savoir-faire and savoir-vivre) into every social system. Short-circuits in these processes have induced the destruction of citizenship and its replacement by consumerism, while television has in addition short-circuited the primary identification processes between child and parent[71] and the relation to the transitional object occurring between mother and child.[72] Consequently, secondary identification processes are also modified, as is identification in general (which is also to say, the countless dimensions of idealization and sublimation, especially in terms of the life of the mind or spirit).

Furthermore, the epistemic short-circuits occurring in the academic and university fields also have consequences for society in general. The system through which knowledge was hitherto transformed – by opening critical spaces between peers within the university, and which also spreads outside the university and trans-forms society, opening prospects for idealization projected and individuated at the collective level as *social knowledge* (as *culture*) – all this too finds itself short-circuited by the fact that the transfer time from research to industrial development, to the marketing and distribution of products, tends to reduce, if not quite to zero, at least to insignificance with respect to social time.

In this way *desocialized time* is established, wherein, from top to bottom of the 'social ladder', there prevails both incivility and attention deficit disorder. But this situation – the contemporary causes of which lie in the acceleration of Creative Destruction by a 'conservative revolution' that took the 'self-regulating market' to extremes, or purified it of its social slag – has its roots, as Derrida explained, in a shift that took place in the seventeenth century, between Descartes and Leibniz.

76   Deconstruction after the *ars inveniendi*

In *Psyche: Inventions of the Other*, Derrida examined the concept of invention and its modern history. And he emphasized both the centrality of the imperative to invent in modernity and in contemporary society, and the aporia that consists in having to programme what essentially disrupts any programme, what the programme cannot foresee, like a fantasy of 'reinventing invention' itself:

> If the word 'invention' is going through a rebirth, on a ground of anguished exhaustion but also out of a desire to reinvent invention itself, including its very status, this is perhaps because, on a scale incommensurable with that of the past, what is called a patentable 'invention' is now programmed, that is, subjected to powerful movements of authoritarian prescription and anticipation of the widest variety.[73]

Obviously this relates first and foremost to the university, but not exclusively:

> And that is as true in the domains of art or the fine arts as in the technoscientific domain. Everywhere the enterprise of knowledge and research is first of all a programmatics of inventions. We could evoke the politics of publishing, the orders of booksellers or art merchants, studies of the market, cultural policies, whether state-promoted or not, and the politics of research and, as we say these days, the 'orientations' that this politics imposes throughout our institutions of higher education; we could also evoke all the institutions, private or public,

capitalist or not, that declare themselves to be organs for producing and orienting invention.[74]

All governmental policies on modern science and culture attempt [...] to program invention.[75]

This assumes, however, that a change in the meaning of invention, the concept of *inventio*, occurred during the seventeenth century, and that this somehow technicized invention and its very concept:

According to a displacement already under way that, it seems to me, was stabilized in the seventeenth century, perhaps between Descartes and Leibniz, invention is almost never regarded as an unveiling discovery of what was already there (an existence or truth), but is more and more, if not solely the productive discovery of an apparatus that we can call technical in the broad sense, technoscientific or technopoetic.[76]

This shift, however, is what led to the Leibnizian project of a new *ars inveniendi* that trans-forms the function of the imagination, in some way short-circuiting it:

Leibniz, as we know, elaborated the fundamental concept of a new kind of writing that constituted a new *ars inveniendi* that both liberates the imagination and liberates *from* the imagination. It passes beyond the imagination and passes through it. Such is the case of the *characteristic universalis*.[77]

And here Derrida cites Leibniz:

That is the principal aim of this great science that I have come to call *Characteristics* [...] that teaches us the secret of determining rational argument, and compelling it to leave something like a modest amount of visible traces on paper to be examined at leisure; and it is finally this science that causes us to reason at little cost, by putting written characters in place of things, so as to disencumber the imagination.[78]

What point does Derrida want to make? Before allowing him to express it in his own words, we should note that what Leibniz seems here to be programming is a new form of tertiary retention, based on a conceptual and mathematical machine, which both stimulates and amplifies the imagination, and short-circuits it, that is, sterilizes it, by condemning it to being programmed, that is, to programming its fantasies that are essentially unprogrammable. It would be necessary to dwell at length on these questions, which is not possible here. I will thus come to the point:

> The invention of the other, the incoming of the other, is certainly not *constructed* as a subjective genitive, and just as assuredly not as an objective genitive either, even if the invention comes from the other – for this other is thenceforth neither subject nor object, neither a self nor a consciousness nor an unconscious. To get ready for this coming of the other is what can be called deconstruction.[79]

9

Interscience, Intergeneration and University Autonomy

77 Contributory research beyond the inside and the outside of the university

What, then, is the other? This is a question that, taken in its original philosophical breadth, and up until everything that deconstruction will bring to this tremendous case, would require us to re-read Plato's *Parmenides* – but I will not do so here. I will simply say: the other is always *who*. That is to say, it is always the question of who the other is. Even if it is neither a mere subject nor an object, nor that on which the subject or object are predicated, to put it in the terms of an old language, the other always carries with it the question *who?* And it is also, and at the same stroke, the question not of the object but of the Thing: *das Ding*.[1]

Who, then, is the other? This question, vertiginous as it may be, is above all political, economic and technological, and yet: the other is that of which and those of whom we must *take care* (and Derrida knew this better than any other – he who took care of me and of so many of those who needed it, and in the first place those immigrants persecuted by Charles Pasqua, who was himself recently convicted in relation to the Angolagate scandal).

Back, then, to our path. In the global economic war, universities and research organizations are mobilized in the service of an unlimited acceleration of innovation (the effects of which on the programming of invention were described by Derrida), which is presented as the very condition of survival – a survival that itself seems, however, no longer possible except in the short term: at the expense of future life.

That research has been brought to this point raises enormous questions concerning noetic becoming and the noetic future. Faced with these questions, the university in its current state:

- either allows to be instrumentalized, and transformed into various specialisms, those who are no longer scholars but 'experts', thanks to which the academic function increasingly often finds itself discredited;
- or takes refuge in a dream with no future, the dream of unconditional autonomy, free from all pharmacology, believing that it is thus possible to dispense with thinking the condition that afflicts everything noetic, that is, every form of psychic and collective individuation – in the university's interior as well as its exterior.

To escape this false alternative, it is essential that the university invent a new relation to its outside (and, through that, to the question of its milieu, and not just of the 'environment',[2] whether physical, economic, political or mental), via the theory and practice of *hypomnēmata* and in relation to the community of amateurs, that is, through the development of contributory research.

Communities of amateurs – forming what might be called in some cases *digital academies* – are already involved in various fields of research, for example in epidemiology, entomology, astrophysics, computing (in relation to the open source model of industrial production), economics, and so on.[3] Such communities obviously exist in the artistic field and the political field, and more generally in the nonprofit and activist worlds. Robin Renucci, who currently heads Tréteaux de France, made this the heart of his project.[4] It is also one of the stakes of the urbanization of the Île de Nantes.

The curative transformation of digital pharmacology (and, through it, of analogue pharmacology) passes through a new arrangement between the university and this outside, where collective de-proletarianizing initiatives of all kinds proliferate, and this constitutes an entirely new process of *social innovation*. This must be the subject of academic research, from which it must nourish itself and learn, just as it should invite the inscription of such initiatives onto the absolutely long circuits of transindividuation that are the academic disciplines, to which teaching establishments at all levels are, above all, the introductory pathways.

It is this programme that we refer to as contributory research: action research[5] that redefines the division of intellectual labour by making performativity[6] work in an age where speech acts and symbolic productions in general profoundly transform this performativity, in the highly specific context of light-time, that is, of digital organology.

Biotechnologies and nanotechnologies are referred to as transformational sciences and technologies,[7] but we must conceive the human and social sciences as likewise transformational, that is, performative. In this case, performativity and transformativity, which result from the formation of an attentional form, and as such a kind of *Bildung*, are obviously conditioned by the tertiary retentional horizon – that is, the pharmacological horizon. And we should re-read Bachelard from this perspective:

> Physics is thus no longer a science of *facts* but a technique of *effects* (the Zeeman effect, the Stark effect ...) [...] a phenomenotechnique through which new phenomena are not simply found but invented, constructed and built from all parts.[8]

> By following contemporary physics, we leave nature behind to enter a factory of phenomena [...]. Two societies, theoretical society and technical society, touch, cooperate. To achieve this, it is not enough to deepen a native spiritual clarity or to undergo again, with greater precision, a common objective experience. We must resolutely adhere to the science of our time. We should first read books, many of them difficult, and gradually settle into the perspective of these difficulties. We have tasks. On the axis that is not scientific work, on the technical side, we must handle, as a team, apparatus that is often, paradoxically, delicate and powerful. *This convergence of exactitude and force does not correspond, in the sublunary world, to any natural necessity. By following contemporary physics, we leave nature behind, to enter a factory of phenomena.*

> Rational objectivity, technical objectivity, social objectivity are now three strongly connected characters. If we forget just one of these characters of modern scientific culture, we enter the domain of utopia.[9]

One of the key aspects of the contemporary context, which adds another layer of complexity to the Bachelardian analysis, is that the rational therapeutic prescription that the social systems need in order to adopt tertiary retention – in particular in the context of the extreme speed of innovation, and where social innovation is what must make this speed serve social (and rapidly socialized) thought – cannot simply come from the academic world. It must be produced by society, and by the social systems in dialogue with the academic world – including in terms of what Ars Industrialis understands as techniques of the self and the we,[10] relational technologies of societal innovation and an economy of contribution. Hence arises the question of a *new maieutic*.[11]

General organology is a theoretical approach that constitutes a methodological element for contributory research, that is, for social innovation in hyper-industrial societies. In such societies, the primary task is the reconstitution of a social projection of final causes (and as economy of archi-protentions):[12] this is what is meant by the 'deproletarianization of savoir-vivre', and this equally entails the re-politicization of the industrial economy, that is, a new public thing and a new public power. But this also and at the same stroke implies a new intergenerational contract.

78   The life of the spirit as new intergenerational contract

Conditional autonomy is an autonomy of aims, of finalities, such that it may constitute itself as a doubly epokhal redoubling, that is, as a curative inversion of the poisonous factors that are always firstly introduced in the name of efficient causes, which, in becoming hegemonic, always end up establishing highly toxic situations.

In a world where *logos* has become a *technologos* and is incapable of functioning outside of the industrial system, in a society where the economy occupies a position that demands incessant critique, but where its primacy is irreducible, in particular insofar as the inscription of the mnemotechnological system of digital tertiary retention into the economy is irreversible, the reconstitution of final causes – which passes fundamentally through digital associated milieus as supports (media) and laboratories (workplaces) of contributory research, and which ultimately constitutes the key issue for digital studies and the digital humanities – all this presupposes a new critique of political economy.

It is in this context that the so-called LRU law claims to restore 'autonomy' to universities, but this is an autonomy that has nothing to do with the university, but rather applies to that 'technician'[13] and manager whose mission is, unlike our proposals here, to optimize the heteronomy of efficient causality at the expense of final causes. This law is as such profoundly archaic: it sends the understanding of the situation backwards, it proceeds entirely on the basis of the regression that Adorno and Horkheimer referred to, because it is harmful to an academic understanding of industrial knowledge – in the epoch of the hyper-industrial societies into which 'digital natives' are born.

This technological nativity,[14] however, requires a resetting and rearming of the intergenerational contract in terms of the projection of final causes. And it must confer on new generations a place and a role they have never hitherto occupied, and in relation to which the industrial approaches deriving from consumerism are completely obsolete. This also means that the days when academic research would be forced to surrender unconditionally to an economic power dictating the 'objectives' of that research are over, that is, archaic.

For the pharmacological condition that strikes knowledge and academic institutions also strikes the industrial and economic powers, and therein lies the best chance for university power and knowledge to protect its autonomy under these conditions – that is, in the context of a pharmacological condition that is common to all, constituting as such the inside as well as the outside of the university, including the economic world.

This is also why academic and industrial power and knowledge must negotiate a peace treaty with a view to forming a *peaceful alliance*[15] – failing which there will no longer be any civilized future for anyone – which would be an *intergenerational alliance*, that is, a new contract between the different generations, and with bodies dedicated to the transindividuation of reference on absolutely long time-scales.

In other words, a fundamental condition of civil peace in the service of logical disputation – that is, in the service of a revaluation of spirit and of a struggle against that 'lowering of spirit value' that results in generalized proletarianization – is that, from the perspective of an economy of contribution, and throughout society, which only in this way becomes a society of effective knowledge, the partnership between the university and economic civil society must also pass, contractually and necessarily, through a *partnership of the university with political civil society*. 'Politics' here means: associations of citizens, amateurs, activists and residents who are encouraged to work together with the academic world.

This is also a way of associating the academic world with the world of parenting, where parents today feel totally excluded from these processes of technological innovation, social innovation, academic research and the transmission of knowledge. It has already become clear that such exclusion is highly dangerous at the primary and secondary levels, and could become so at the university level, and in a fairly short space of time, given that, as in Tunisia, many young graduates in France and elsewhere have little prospect of finding employment.

79   Knowing what to do with the *pharmakon* between the generations

This situation does, however, afford new and promising prospects, given that:

- there are multiplying signs of the fact that society wants to know, wants to confront itself through debate, wants to rediscover its 'savours' and, in order to do so, develop practices of all kinds;
- the younger generations know more, technologically, than their elders, and their knowledge is rich and noble in the sense that it is frequently teeming with therapeutic inventiveness.

Academic and university communities can and must take advantage of this reality of our changing epoch, an epoch that has so far failed to be 'epoch-making' – that is, to create or give credit, in particular by cultivating, through knowledge, a relation of intergenerational trust. They must begin to recognize this situation as involving *technological nativity*, that is, pharmacological and retentional nativity, involving know-how [*savoir-faire*] in relation to the *pharmakon* and the retentions (and therefore protentions) that it generates, inscribing the intergenerational contract within a horizon that is to this (immeasurable) extent itself originally and natively temporal and omnitemporal.

Hence we can posit: that the conflict between philosophy and sophistry took place in the context of the emergence of *literal nativity* (Socrates, Meno, his slave[16] and Plato are all 'born of the letter'); that the spiritual war lying at the origin of modern capitalist and industrial society passed through the emergence of *printing nativity*; and that the generation that has for some time dominated in France (and still does so in 2011) and in the academic world (and this would also be the generation of 1968, and of the radio network Europe 1) is composed of *analogue natives* (even if they may not always be aware of it – which explains how Jean-Luc Godard was able to believe that the twentieth century was the century of cinema).

In this regard, we must conclude by insisting on three major issues:

- the question of metadata, and therefore of metalanguage;
- the question of new missions that should be promoted by public powers to encourage the publishing and editorial industries in a knowledge society;
- the question of the integrating role of the school in the republic.

80 The gay science – metadata and metalanguage

With digital technologies, all partners in a network produce metadata (whether consciously or unconsciously). This fact is crucially important and radically new:[17] never before has metadata – which refers to the categories of categories through which a metalanguage forms – been generated by actors other than 'clerics', whether religious or secular. The spontaneous ideation referred to by Husserl is also a spontaneous categorization.[18] But *idealization* presupposes a *meta-categorization* occurring in a formal language, which is the subject of what Husserl himself presented as a 'pure grammar'.[19]

Plato devotes an essential part of his efforts to setting out the conditions of production of such formal languages by submitting them to what Aristotle called the science of being qua being – *ontology*.[20] Now, the so-called 'bottom-up' production of metacategories, that is, of metadata, opens up a new epoch of metalanguage. Here, the question of the relation of the academic sphere to its outside is that of the relation between the 'bottom-up' production of meta-categories, on the horizontal plane that is called 'peer-to-peer', and 'top-down' metalanguages, which are still subject to selection by communities of peers – but by peers *accredited* by the Academy.

From where does this credit derive?

Metadata is in general composed of metacategories that form the access criteria for those retentions through which, in a process of transindividuation, a central authority more or less orders, controls and synchronizes this process.

The appearance of 'bottom-up' metadata breaks with this ordering and constitutes an absolutely fundamental change of knowledge that we must, again, relate back to the figure of Luther and the Reformation: Luther challenged the monopoly on commentary, that is, on the direct or indirect production of metadata. This transformation of public space is comparable to what played out when the Greek gerontocracy protested against the advent of natives of the letter and, through Anytus, accused both Socrates and the sophists of corrupting Athenian youth.[21]

There are, then, conflicts of pharmacological generation, or conflicts of models of transindividuation, in which the preceding ('descendant') generation, accusing the new *pharmakon* of toxicity, is countered by the following one (the 'rising' or 'ascendant' generation), who are projecting their future.

Today, new tertiary retentions displace the retentional field (the space-time) of intergenerationality and call for an internation and an interscience through which the new public thing can transgeneration-ally individuate itself. Derrida is remarkably lucid in this regard, not only in 'The University Without Condition' but also, already, in *Right to Philosophy*.[22] Within this new *res publica*, then, and *only there*, will the public thing of knowledge find its place: a gay science capable of producing the theoretical thing proper to our epoch.

Within the contemporary academic sphere – for example, among those who signed the manifesto for the digital humanities – links are being formed between the inside and the outside that challenge the opposition between them, but that do not ignore what distinguishes the university from the rest of the world. They make these questions work performatively – performing a 'profession of truth' – on the basis of the play of the *pharmakon* that is put at the heart of the epokhal life of the spirit, which is here called digital: it is always the *pharmakon*, that is, the supplement, that challenges the opposi-tion of inside and outside.[23]

This outside, however, is also and firstly intergenerational differ-ence (which is an intergenerational *différance*): the 'outside' *pene-trates* 'inside' through pupils and students, and what is referred to as the 'outside' is therefore firstly those who, as we say, are on the outside, and whom we invite to come inside (too often firstly out of fear that some or other masters or doctoral programme, connected to some or other training and research unit, in some or other faculty, will lose positions).

These generations in formation, who come to elevate themselves and to study with those who are inside – and also their parents, their friends and even their Facebook 'friends' – must indeed, and once and for all, be invited to the 'banquet where all are equal' in the companionship of the techno-logical symposium that is now being woven by digital tertiary retention.

81   The editorial and publishing industries of scholarly and scientific society

Every educational system rests on a system for conserving, editing and transmitting tertiary retentions. Literal tertiary retention makes rational anamnesis possible, to the extent that, enabling the 'ortho-thetic' (that is, without loss) engramming of significations (of the transindividual), it affects readers who can read only insofar as they can write: literal retention is the mnemotechnical milieu of what Husserl called *communalization*,[24] that is, the constitution of a community of peers – namely, the academic community – and as such it forms what we refer to as an associated milieu.

Throughout the twentieth century, analogue retentions were implemented and monopolized by the culture industries. These have, on the contrary, produced an asymmetry and imparity between, on the one hand, those who become industrial producers of images and sounds by complying with the criteria outlined by their financial backers (the whole point of the Nouvelle Vague was to struggle against this constraint), and, on the other hand, the mass of consumers who no longer form publics of a public space and public time, but audiences for publicity. Hence is installed *de-communalization*, that is, a dissociation of symbolic milieus and, ultimately, a disindividuation.

In such circumstances, analogue retentions have proven completely unable to support in-depth academic research: neither for academic teaching, nor for scholarly practice (apart from a few notable exceptions, such as anthropology – Jean Rouch, for example, who is better known as a filmmaker than as an anthropologist).

This situation is, however, profoundly transformed by digitalization, which creates an apparatus of production, post-production and dissemination accessible to all. The consequences of this evolution – which radically changes the conditions of transindividuation – have barely begun to be thought.[25] They undermine the most important structuring components (that are now, rather, destructuring) of the societies that emerged from the second half of the twentieth century: the so-called 'programme' industries imposed their rhythms, their objects, their hierarchies, their conditions of enunciation and their publicity – whereby *Öffentlichkeit* gives way to advertising, and attention becomes a 'scarce resource' to be captured and sold, at the cost of its *de*-formation.

All public life has been subjected to this calamitous fact, which we have all internalized as a virtual inevitability – and the machine for producing so-called *'pensée unique'*[26] is the central tool utilized by the partisans of TINA, through which its 'experts' have conducted their jihad. Inverting this state of affairs seems totally impossible. This at least is what we are led to believe, even though this inversion has already begun – and even though the major private television networks are finding it increasingly difficult to maintain profitability (despite the fact that, in France's case, public broadcasting is kept out of the advertising market) in a world where the digital networks, whose success has been stunning, are siphoning off an ever greater share of advertising revenue, while Google is preparing to launch twenty television channels designed for 'connected' television.

If digital networks are having such success, it is firstly because they reconstitute systems of communalization, whether these are 'peer-to-peer' or otherwise – for example, 'social networks'.[27] That this new pharmacology frequently, mainly and firstly flaunts its own miserable origins, and that it does so shamelessly, is simply a fact: this 'communalization' is often of the most mediocre kind, if not the worst. But this fact ought not blind us to the demands *for law* that it expresses – and which can pass into the noetic act gestating within it only if there is a public policy to guarantee this law, and to do so by making this its duty.[28]

It is the entire model of the audiovisual industry that must here be rethought with the introduction of a new digital public space – of which this industry becomes a sub-category. This requires public authorities to provide television and radio networks with missions that place them in the service of new forms of social utility, and, above all, in the service of the scholarly society that industrial democracies will form through the internation. The publishing industry in general must become a partner of universities and national academies, themselves oriented towards this 'outside', including the universities and academies of other countries.

Audiovisual enterprises will not disappear: they will become network head ends, shop-windows for new types of programmes conceived on the basis of economies of digitalized stock, rather than being based on the calendar and the Hertzian terrestrial network. This will be a very different publishing industry, where the programme becomes a database (in the form of sites, such as 'web docs', or in other forms, such as audiobooks and videobooks[29] and especially multimedia systems of clickable video),[30] which is also to say, an instrument of work. Such programmes will be produced by schools and universities themselves, rather than by 'professionals of the profession'.

Let us recall that Louis Hachette created the Hachette publishing house because, as a teacher, he had started to edit textbooks – for which François Guizot had created a market. And it is because this industrial production of books made these works accessible to rural communities – since mass printing meant reduced prices – that Jules Ferry was able to institute general public education, thereby making the fortunes of Fernand Nathan, Armand Colin and others.

All this depends, however, on the existence of an academic world capable of writing these works. The development of a publishing industry in the service of new scholarly and scientific societies, and of the academy as a whole, depends on having academic works – presentations, theses, scientific publications in general – that take full advantage of digital publishing systems and that do so in every tertiary retentional field, not just à la lettre. Hence *contributory publishing* may develop as a counterpart to contributory research – which presupposes the design and development of systems of contributory editorial production (this is what the Institut de recherche et d'innovation endeavours to do).[31]

If we base this on the economic model that emerged from the terrestrial audiovisual programme industries, the solvency of the new editorial and publishing sector will be zero – not only because advertising, as a source of funds, is being stretched ever thinner, but because the function of the audiovisual is being changed by digital grammatization.

Multimedia editorial productions will consist in audiovisual programmes based on clickable radio and clickable video, making possible the digital delinearization and discretization of the analogue signal.[32] Such productions will become solvent only through public offers, supporting academic editions of reference works and collaborative reference instruments, realized on the basis of detailed tender specifications, and conceived as instruments of work as well as organs for the satisfaction of the *otium* of the people – of its *leisure* in the ancient sense, the Latin here being almost synonymous with *skholē*, the place of which is the *skholeion*, that is, the school.

In other words, an economy of knowledge must valorize the new social utility of media, cast into the service of a scholarly society that remains in potential, but that hopes to become one in actuality[33] – provided we give it the means of doing so. It is not an inevitable fate that the 'audiovisual' submit to the corporations of disembraining and generalized proletarianization. The basic condition required for the reconstitution of political will is to posit anew that the principle of the *politeia* is that it can be constituted only by citizens capable of becoming rational – provided that the republic in charge of the public thing acts as guarantor for this possibility.

It is a question of knowing how public and academic institutions could and should handle the pharmacology of the tertiary retentions of their age – writing on papyrus and in marble in the epoch of Socrates, the printed Bible and account books in the epoch of Luther, newspapers and the textbooks of Louis Hachette, Fernand Nathan and Armand Colin in the epoch of Ferry, and, in our epoch, the digital associated milieu that should henceforth give rise to the epoch of scholarly and scientific society. Educational television's lack of success in the 1960s lay in the fact it was a decommunalizing industrial medium: receivers could not also be senders – and this is what has changed. And it changes everything.

Designing and prescribing these kinds of editorial industries should to a large extent spring from the contributory research previously mentioned. This requires the university to become the principal partner of public power in reviewing audiovisual and digital media policy, and, more generally, it must prescribe new editorial functions, made possible by digital retention. This should be one of the major subjects of inquiry for digital studies.

One could no doubt object that academic institutions remain insufficiently acculturated to these technologies. Our response is that it is precisely a matter of *creating the conditions required for rapid acculturation*: we must recruit, in all disciplines, *young researchers* capable of keeping pace with this editorial mutation.

Such a transformation of the academic world requires the implementation of national and long-term projects, that is, on the timescale of a generation, and it must at the same time allow for the total reinvention of public space itself, and lead to a profound transformation of teacher training. Teachers should become practitioners of the apparatus of production of academic tertiary retentions in each of their disciplines, just as they should be trained in the study of the role of tertiary retention in general (as instruments or technologies of formal and experimental science, as well as of the humanities and the human and social sciences – in the sense that, for example, Sylvain Auroux defines the dictionary as a 'linguistic tool').[34]

82   School, nation, internation

It is in the school and through the school (*skholeion*) that public space and time are formed, that is, a public thing, a *res publica*. There is no school outside of a *polis*, a *civitas*, a republic, and in these societies no form of life is protected from incivility without school. School is as such political: it constitutes the matrix of a process of psychic and collective individuation founding a civility itself founded on and through a specific formation and training of attention, namely, rational attention – the formation of *logos* on the basis of the apodictic experience of geometry.

It might be said that at school – understood as that which constitutes the elementary academic level – we do not yet go through this experience of demonstration, of the evidence of this experience, of its universality. Nevertheless, the teachers who teach at elementary or primary school have themselves had this experience, and it is on the basis of it that they teach: this is what, as matrix of all rational criteria, founds the tone and the attitude through which they can establish their authority. Teachers raise their students so as to project them into a perception of the *necessity* of this experience.

The city, that is, the *polis* that gave birth to this experience, and with it the experience of the universal that gave its name to the university, eventually becomes the nation, which took the name of the *republic*[35] by engaging the process of secularization that Weber described in relation to the whole capitalist world – and, in the French context, in a specific mode, that of laicism, which led to the law of 1905.[36] The historical forms of the city succeed one another throughout the long individuation of Western society, from the *politeia* up until the nation-state, in which school grounds the republic in the sense described by Kant and Condorcet.

This framework has, however, broken down: the *koinē* is no longer a political space – *koinē*, that is, that which is common to all, which in the time of Luther was called the vulgar (in a sense that contemporary vulgarity – which predominates in the highest realms of government and international organizations – has rendered inaudible and inconceivable).

School is the matrix of psychic and collective individuation founded on the experience of the rational and its intergenerational transmission. It is thus a place of integration, where one 'becomes French' – via disciplines that are themselves processes of transindividuation on the basis of which are formed the intergenerational times and spaces that found a city. But the exterior milieu of the contemporary school has become purely and simply incompatible with this function of the school: it is no longer a matter of a political milieu but of a literally *anti-political, economic* milieu, anti-political because it disintegrates[37] and discredits in advance any cosmopolitical[38] desire – that is, for what I have, after Mauss, called the internation.

The exterior milieu of the contemporary school, which dissolves it by disintegrating its political framework, is the economic milieu founded on consumption. The scholarly process of psychic and collective individuation was in the twentieth century replaced by the enterprise of psychic and collective disindividuation to which consumerism has led:

> America started the tradition where the richest consumers buy essentially the same things as the poorest. You can be watching TV and see Coca-Cola, and you know that the President drinks Coca-Cola, Liz Taylor drinks Coca-Cola, and just think, you can drink Coca-Cola,

too. A Coke is a Coke and no amount of money can get you a better Coke than the one the bum on the corner is drinking. All the Cokes are the same and all the Cokes are good. Liz Taylor knows it, the President knows it, the bum knows it, and you know it.[39]

Integration can be understood as the re-tracing and sharing of intergenerational pathways, founded on human experience that re-transmits and re-forms itself from one generation to the next. Integration is the formation of intergenerational attention in a political society founded as a society of rational attention, itself tempered in and by the universal experience of apodictic demonstration, through which the distinction is drawn between knowledge and belief.[40] Given all this, then what Andy Warhol is describing is a situation of inter-generational disintegration, wherein the relation to language that Maurice Blanchot described as a Riemann curvature[41] has been lev-elled out – and, with it, dia-logical experience as such.

Patrick Le Lay was later to explain[42] the consequences of this situ-ation, which for Warhol was still specific to North America: analogue tertiary retentions are exploited in hegemonic fashion by the audio-visual media in order to divert and thus de-form attention from the common objects that found the public thing, namely, objects of knowledge, in favour of the fabrication of a 'community' of consum-ers, which could be called the *vulgarity of the market*, where what 'vulgar' meant in Luther's time, and which in Ferry's became secular, has been dissolved into the 'prosaic' from which Édouard Glissant and Patrick Chamoiseau suffer.[43] As does everyone, from the 'penni-less tramp' to the American president, by way of Elizabeth Taylor, Patrick Le Lay and teachers themselves, who are themselves often great fans of 'TV'.

Fans and lovers of TV – or in other words, analogue natives afflicted with discredit by this disintegrating situation (that of tele-cracy against democracy, of the programme industries against the programme institutions).[44] This situation is centrifugal, and it expels those who 'profess the truth' and, with them, every form of knowl-edge, the authority of which finds itself short-circuited in the eyes of the younger generations who suffer from this escheat – but who do so much more lucidly than might be imagined.

83   For a European school within the internation – against the decadence of Europe

Marketing destroys those identification processes without which there can be no collective individuation. It destroys identification with parents and it destroys identification with the nation founded on its knowledge and its ways of transmitting, of which the school was the apparatus of production, always passing more or less through identifying with teachers and, through them, with disciplines (including in the mode of counter-identification – 'I'm no good at maths', 'I don't like chemistry', 'I hate this teacher').

Europe *ought* to have been the relay in the process of national identification – the new framework of the process of the transindividuation of reference[45] – when the framework of the nation-state found itself inexorably weakened by the global expansion of the technical system.[46] But this did not in any way take place, and what did occur was in fact the direct opposite: the European Commission, completely contrary to what might have enabled the integration of the idea of a European individuation founded on European culture,[47] has instead promoted a society of consumers lagging thirty or forty years behind the United States, and has done so *by eliminating every ambition with regard to knowledge*.[48]

As the formation and training of attention understood as civility, that is, as the sphere not only of instruction but of education, the school became, as a place of integration into the collective individuation process that is the nation, the elementary organ of national education, constituting, by instituting, the body of the nation. This elementary organ of national integration – which was also the bearer of an intergenerational dynamic founded on the authority of rational transindividuation processes that in turn ground the academic disciplines – has disintegrated, thanks to consumerist disindividuation. So too has initiation into adversarial debate between peers, that is, the formation of that critical space and time that is the space of public time, a space and time that must be formed just as attention must be formed. And the former must be formed through the constant formation of the latter, precisely insofar as it is oriented towards reasoning in potential, which, via the public thing, can then pass into action.

Such are the terrible effects of installing a systemic stupidity that is presently destroying all credit – and therefore all economy – and not just all belief, all trust and all authority. Hence grows that desert that for Nietzsche was nihilism.

Before Jules Ferry, schools formed – through the Reformed Church and the Jesuit colleges – in Western Europe and then in America, the body of the faithful, that is, for Christians, the body of Christ that the Church, after Paul, is intended to be.[49] This was a communion-based process of collective individuation, founded on the possibility of the Eucharist. It was this against which Ferry fought: it was for him a matter of disintegrating this apparatus founded on dogmatic faith, in order to constitute a new process of integration, based on the separation of knowledge and belief.[50]

The *skholeion* – and its higher forms, colleges and universities – has always been this system forming and training the politico-noetic (intellective and spiritual) social body. The history of this system is inseparable from that of tertiary retention, without which there can be no noetic activity for psychic individuals or for the civil societies formed by collective individuation. And the theological conflict between Luther and Catholicism, which obviously passes through this, is also the historical condition of the conflict of the university faculties, and of a politics of the relations between the inside and the outside of the academic world and scholarly and scientific societies.

In this regard, however, we today find ourselves confronted with an exceptional situation that has engendered a terrifying problem: dis-integration – which always occurs whenever a new *pharmakon* arises and the first epokhal redoubling is in effect, and which generates a new integrative model when the second epokhal redoubling occurs (sometimes at the cost of heavy conflict, such as the wars of religion) – is in this case occurring completely *outside* the school. Disintegration is being produced by marketing, which, for the sole benefit of its own purposes, short-circuits noetic life in all its forms and, with it, all intergenerational relations. Through a consumerism that now targets the drives, disintegration thereby eliminates the transindividual as such, that is, both credit and meaning.

The problem is that tertiary retentions have become, first and foremost, the means of carrying out the economic function that consists in organizing production and consumption. It is in this context that, having totally abandoned the task of making Europe a scholarly society, the European Commission has committed itself exclusively to constituting the European market and to submitting academic life solely to efficient causality, thereby confusing knowledge and information, and to simply eliminating its historical legacy, of which *The Conflict of the Faculties* was a milestone in the collective individuation of modern Europe.

Through a European Commission as ultra-bureaucratic as it is ultra-liberal, virtually uncontrolled by the European Union and European Parliament, that is, by the representatives of its citizens, Europe has not ceased to intensify rationalization in the sense given to us by Weber, Adorno and Habermas. It has not ceased to subject academic research to the imperative of market efficiency at the expense of other ends – despite the fact that, as the new public power necessitated by the decline of the nation-state, it should on the contrary have sought to contain the violence of efficiency and to ensure, at the level of the European continent, the possibility of a new age of rational collective individuation.

In the new global industrial context, this carelessness and neglect have allowed the abandonment of any politics of the attention of youth *as Europeans*, and hence as heirs to a history that gave birth both to the Greek idea of *logos* and to its transformation by the first industrial societies in England, France and Germany, then the whole of Europe, and passing through Protestantism. The outcome, today, is violently anti-European sentiment: 'European construction' has been experienced by Europeans as the destruction of the processes of collective individuation that had hitherto engendered them as Europeans in a proliferation of forms and types.[51]

In *Taking Care of Youth and the Generations* I attempted to show that this is a matter of abandoning new generations, and that the pharmacology of the mass media has as its main goal the *replacement of the intergenerational transmission of prescriptions*. Such prescriptions, in which the entry into civility always consists, are replaced by the control of behaviour, constantly transformed by marketing – and via its main carriers, the productions of the programme industries.

It is thus *thought itself* that will have been destroyed, a destruction that brings with it generalized proletarianization and systemic stupidity: the hegemony of consumerism has imposed, counter to the formative mission of the school, an enormous system of unlearning and dis-apprenticeship of every kind.

The time of thinking is itself, natively, intergenerational. Such is the horizon of Diotima's statement to Socrates, explaining what it means to gain knowledge, namely, 'to let a younger individual take the place of an older one'.[52] This is why national and continental disintegration, accelerated by European carelessness, has generated an intergenerational disintegration that inevitably leads European culture into decadence.

84 Knowledge and rebirth in contributory teaching

Composed of technological and as such pharmacological nativities, the intergenerational is itself conditioned by the tertiary retentions that make possible the transindividual and the transindividuation processes that are the disciplines. If this condition is today, in general, pharmaco-logical, this pharmacology is felt and suffered first of all through the acceleration of industrial and mnemotechnological innovation, which produces short-circuits between generational nativities, destroying the intergenerational itself – that is, the relation to knowledge, and the 'Riemann curvature' that all knowledge presupposes, and through which it imposes its authority.

There is, however, nothing fatal about this situation.

Reconstituting an academic project, renewing, between interscience and its outside, which is the internation, an intergenerational relation re-founded on, by and in the retentional field of contemporary *noetic nativity* (and knowing is born, that is, individuates itself, as is well known – that is, reborn in and through the generation to which one wants to give a place), reactivating through this the hypotheses and questions of action-research in the epoch of digital media, of the associated milieus that they form, of the collaborative technologies and contributory economy that emerges, initiating a critique (in the Kantian sense) of knowledge in the industrial epoch, putting the issues of digital studies at the heart of a long-term research policy – and only as such is it worthy of the name 'heuristic' – all this is also to provide the means of *creating truly contributory teaching practices*.

For contributory research must obviously result in contributory teaching, in higher education as in primary and secondary education – which in no way implies the disappearance of lecture courses, but their arrangement with the private works and collective works that the contemporary retentional field alone makes possible.

This doubtless means that contributory research should begin with the pedagogical construction itself, and that it should do so as a project of intergenerational research of a new type, involving every academic level. Here, the analysis by Philippe Meirieu of the policy implemented by Ferdinand Buisson on the basis of the Protestant pedagogical tradition should form the heart of a debate in which it is a matter of rethinking the conditions of the transindividuation of rational disciplines through retentional practices, and at every level of the formation of this attentional form that we call reason.

Notes

Introduction

1 See Claude Lelièvre, 'L'éducation, sujet majeur des présidentielles?', *Mediapart*, 18 July 2011, available at http://blogs.mediapart.fr/blog/claude-lelievre/180711/leducation-sujet-majeur-des-presidentielles. And see Denis Kambouchner, Philippe Meirieu, Bernard Stiegler, Julien Gautier and Guillaume Vergne, *L'École, le numérique et la société qui vient* (Paris: Mille et une nuits, 2012).

2 As if the true problem is debt, and not the major discredit through which the capitalist economy, which has systematically cultivated debt while privatizing everything, has established a generalized insolvency, beginning with the banks.

3 The expression 'addictogenic society' was used by Jean-Pierre Couteron, president of the Association nationale des intervenants en toxicomanie et addictologie (ANITEA).

4 Immanuel Kant, 'An Answer to the Question: "What is Enlightenment?"', *Political Writings* (Cambridge: Cambridge University Press, 1991), p. 54, translation modified.

5 There is great confusion about the meaning of this word, which, especially in the way it is understood in the United States, tends to paint Lyotard, Derrida and Deleuze, Baudrillard and Virilio, and even Barthes and Lacan, and others, all with the same brush. An example of this confusion can be found in Jeremy Rifkin, *The Age of Access* (New York: Tarcher/Putnam, 2000). Be that as it may, Jean-François Lyotard claimed that during this so-called 'postmodern' period, which he himself attempted to describe in detail – and I will return to this in chapter 4 – we must *stop telling stories*, namely, those speculative and emancipatory stories that would be the 'grand narratives' of Hegel and Marx. It should be remembered, however, that Plato too, condemned the 'storytellers' that in his eyes the Presocratics, and then the poets in general, were, in particular in the *Sophist* and the *Republic*.

6 On this point, see Bernard Stiegler, *For a New Critique of Political Economy* (Cambridge: Polity, 2010).

7 Karl Polanyi, *The Great Transformation: The Political and Economic Origins of Our Time* (Boston: Beacon, 2001).

8 François Hauter, 'L'école fabrique des élites, pas des équipes' ['French schools produce elites, not teams'], *Le Figaro*, 29 July 2011, as part of the series 'Le Bonheur d'être français'.

9 See the 'Manifesto' of Ars Industrialis, available at: http://arsindustrialis. org/node/1472. And see Bernard Stiegler, *The Re-Enchantment of the World* (London and New York: Bloomsbury Academic, 2014), p. 13.

10 Naomi Klein, *The Shock Doctrine: The Rise of Disaster Capitalism* (New York: Metropolitan Books, 2007).

11 I will return to the link between reason (or *logos*) and politics (or the *polis*). It is this link whose cultivation the French political class has to a large extent abandoned, and for quite some time. I do not, however, consider political representatives – politicians and the political class, 'politicals' – solely responsible. I attempt on the contrary to show that academics – so-called 'intellectuals' – share a large portion of the responsibility for this disastrous situation. And I will also try to show *why*: this is not a matter of pronouncing guilt (blaming people is always a dead end, even when there are people who are indeed guilty) but one of describing the processes through which responsibilities change or are displaced, and in relation to which it is a matter of inventing a new sense of responsibility.

12 Bernard Stiegler, *What Makes Life Worth Living: On Pharmacology* (Cambridge: Polity, 2013).

13 Joseph A. Schumpeter, *Capitalism, Socialism and Democracy* (London: Allen & Unwin, 1976).

14 I have developed this perspective in detail in *What Makes Life Worth Living*.

15 I have developed this question in greater detail in *Technics and Time, 1: The Fault of Epimetheus* (Stanford: Stanford University Press, 1998).

16 See Bernard Stiegler, *De la misère symbolique 2: La catastrophè du sensible* (Paris: Galilée, 2005), pp. 61ff.

17 *Translator's note*: '*formation*' in French also means 'training'.

18 See Alain Giffard, 'Des lectures industrielles', in Bernard Stiegler, Alain Giffard and Christian Fauré, *Pour en finir avec la mécroissance* (Paris: Flammarion, 2009), pp. 117ff.

19 See Jacques Derrida, *Of Grammatology* (Baltimore and London: Johns Hopkins University Press, 1998).

20 See pp. 127–8 and 170.

21 *Translator's note*: '*liberté conditionelle*' is the French term for conditional release, that is, parole.

22 More than fifty years after its appearance, deconstruction, the outlines of which were sketched in the 'Introduction' to Edmund Husserl's

'Origin of Geometry', has become a construction, less through Derrida than through his many epigones, brilliant or mediocre, and sometimes through the effect they have had on his own work, and on the reception of his work by himself, so to speak. The 'language' of deconstruction is thus made to function as the language of metaphysics, and by masquerading in the fascinating garb of *opposing* metaphysics – not, like the latter, through a play of oppositions (the necessity for deconstruction rests precisely on putting in question the oppositional pairs constitutive of 'metaphysics'), but through a dilution of differences and a general liquefaction of differ*a*nce.

The germ of this risk was contained in Speech and Phenomena (Evanston: Northwestern University Press, 1973). I have attempted to show why this is so in 'The Magic Skin; or, The Franco-European Accident of Philosophy after Jacques Derrida', *Qui Parle* 18 (2009), pp. 97–110. I will say here in advance, to the epigones, that these remarks are in no way a 'betrayal' of this man, whom I visited when, thanks to him, to Gérard Granel and to some others I cannot mention here, I was released on parole [*liberté conditionnelle*]. Continuing, therefore, a debate that began very early on (that I have tried to argue while being consistently astounded by the attention, thoughtfulness and kindness to which this wonderful man always testified, constantly worrying about saying something stupid) is precisely, for me, a matter of being faithful to my friend Jacques Derrida, that is: always taking deconstruction to its limits – which is limited just as everything is, that is, all that which, destined to become, is destined also to return, precisely in and through the experience of its limits.

23 See 'Attention, Rétention, Protention', in Victor Petit, *Vocabulaire d'Ars Industrialis*, in Bernard Stiegler, *Pharmacologie du Front national* (Paris: Flammarion, 2013), pp. 380–2.

24 See pp. 224–5, note 34, for why it is important to make this additional specification.

25 See Stiegler et al., *Pour en finir avec la mécroissance*, Stiegler, *For a New Critique of Political Economy*, Stiegler, *What Makes Life Worth Living*, and the updated 2010 'Manifesto' of Ars Industrialis. See also Paul Jorion, *Le Capitalisme à l'agonie* (Paris: Fayard, 2011).

26 It is for this reason that this book appeared simultaneously with *L'École, le numérique et la société qui vient*, which I co-authored with Kambouchner, Meirieu, Gautier and Vergne.

27 Paul Valéry, 'Freedom of the Mind', *The Outlook for Intelligence* (Princeton: Princeton University Press, 1989), p. 190, translation modified.

28 Bernard Stiegler, *Taking Care of Youth and the Generations* (Stanford: Stanford University Press, 2010), p. 112ff.

29 Ibid., p. 115.

30 This leads him in particular to ignore profoundly the question of marketing and the emergence of consumerism in the twentieth century. See ibid., pp. 128–35.

31 *Translator's note:* the reference here is to G. W. F. Hegel, *Phenomenology of Spirit* (Oxford: Oxford University Press, 1977), §87.
32 The transcript of the screenplay of *Inside Job* is available at http://www.sonyclassics.com/awards-information/insidejob_screenplay.pdf.
33 My emphasis.
34 Here are extracts from these interviews, conducted by filmmaker Charles Ferguson:

> *Charles Ferguson:* Over the last decade, the financial services industry has made about 5 billion dollars' worth of political contributions in the United States. Um; that's kind of a lot of money. That doesn't bother you?
> *Martin Feldstein:* No.
> *Narrator:* Martin Feldstein is a professor at Harvard, and one of the world's most prominent economists. As President Reagan's chief economic advisor, he was a major architect of deregulation. And from 1988 until 2009, he was on the board of directors of both AIG and AIG Financial Products, which paid him millions of dollars.
> *Charles Ferguson:* You have any regrets about having been on AIG's board?
> *Martin Feldstein:* I have no comments. No, I have no regrets about being on AIG's board.
> *Charles Ferguson:* None.
> *Martin Feldstein:* That I can s-, absolutely none. Absolutely none.
> *Charles Ferguson:* Okay. Um – you have any regrets about, uh, AIG's decisions?
> *Martin Feldstein:* I cannot say anything more about AIG.

> AIG is the insurance group that provided cover for a large proportion of the credit default swaps that lay behind the crisis of 2008, a mechanism for diluting responsibility that remains in force today, and in particular to enable the consequences of speculation to fall upon 'sovereign' countries, which are then downgraded by ratings agencies. Another interview, this time with Glenn Hubbard:

> *Glenn Hubbard:* I've taught at Northwestern and Chicago, Harvard and Columbia.
> *Narrator:* Glenn Hubbard is the dean of Columbia Business School, and was the chairman of the Council of Economic Advisers under George W. Bush.
> *Charles Ferguson:* Do you think the financial services industry has too much, uh, political power in the United States?
> *Glenn Hubbard:* I don't think so, no. You certainly, you certainly wouldn't get that impression by the drubbing that they regularly get, uh, in Washington.
> *Narrator:* Many prominent academics quietly make fortunes while helping the financial industry shape public debate and government policy. The Analysis Group, Charles River Associates, Compass Lexecon, and the Law and Economics Consulting Group manage a multi-billion-dollar industry that provides academic experts for hire. Two bankers who used these services were Ralph Cioffi and Matthew Tannin, Bear Stearns hedge fund managers prosecuted for securities fraud. After hiring The Analysis Group, both were

acquitted. Glenn Hubbard was paid 100,000 dollars to testify in their
defense.
Charles Ferguson: Do you think that the economics discipline has, uh, a con-
flict of interest problem?
Glenn Hubbard: I'm not sure I know what you mean.
Charles Ferguson: Do you think that a significant fraction of the economics
discipline, a number of economists, have financial conflicts of interests that
in some way might call into question or color –
Glenn Hubbard: Oh, I see what you're saying. I doubt it. You know, most
academic economists, uh, you know, aren't wealthy businesspeople.
Narrator: Hubbard makes 250,000 dollars a year as a board member of Met
Life, and was formerly on the board of Capmark, a major commercial
mortgage lender during the bubble, which went bankrupt in 2009. He has
also advised Nomura Securities, KKR Financial Corporation, and many
other financial firms.

35 As I have done elsewhere, for instance in Bernard Stiegler, 'Du temps-
carbone au temps-lumière', in Stiegler et al., *Pour en finir avec la
mécroissance*, pp. 13–43, and see the 2010 version of the Ars Industrialis manifesto.
36 See Karl Marx, *Grundrisse: Foundations of the Critique of Political
Economy (Rough Draft)* (London: Penguin, 1973).
37 This includes Jacques Derrida, who, in positing that the trace, the supplement, archi-writing, and so on constitute a 'quasi-transcendental'
question, would keep in extreme ambiguity the question of the technical constitutivity of différance acceding to the 'as such', or in other
words the question of the history of différance, or rather of what we
ought refer to as its genealogy: the trace, through the very fact of its
irreducible technical empiricity in becoming noetic différance, is the
foundation of its irreducibly pharmacological character. It should therefore not be thought under this category of the 'quasi-transcendental',
even if this 'quasi' seems to accord easily with this thought. I am not
ignoring the fact that Derrida wanted to show that there is in this materiality something that exceeds it, and that the play of différance that it
supports exceeds the empirical. But that this 'exceeding' is constituted
through this very technicity insofar as it engenders and conditions the
libidinal economy without which there is no *noēsis*, that is, no protention capable of promising – this is what I believe the pseudo-concept of
the 'quasi-transcendental' absolutely prevents us from thinking.
I have tried to show in 'The Magic Skin' that these problems begin
very early on – from the moment that Derrida, in contesting the opposition between primary and secondary retention in Husserl, ignores the
question of their difference, and at the same stroke ignores the
question of tertiary retention, and of how in differentiating itself it
nevertheless over-determines this difference between primary and secondary retention, and over-determines their play *as différance*, and as
différance *in its noetic stage*.

A similar difficulty (the repetition of the original repression of technicity) occurs in Gilles Deleuze, for instance in his analysis of Foucault's work via the concept of the diagram. See Gilles Deleuze, *Foucault* (Minneapolis: University of Minnesota Press, 1988), pp. 43–4, and my commentary on Deleuze in Bernard Stiegler, *The Decadence of Industrial Democracies: Disbelief and Discredit, 1* (Cambridge: Polity, 2011), p. 177, n. 60.

Finally, we shall see how Lyotard's position in 1986 is ultimately quite close to that of Heidegger (see p. 96), which, as I tried to show in *Technics and Time, 1*, again essentially consists in a repetition of this repression – to the point of inverting, however, the entire question of *Abbau* that I argue is concentrated on this question, that is, on the status of what I call tertiary retention.

38   This book derives on the one hand from a lecture on the university of the future that I delivered in June 2011 at the University of Cambridge, in closing a research programme of the CRASSH programme, and at the invitation of Martin Crowley, Mary Jacobus and Andrew Webber. I also presented a version of this lecture to the Collège international de philosophie in Paris, at the invitation of Martine Meskel and Jean-François Nordmann, and in the company of Marc Crépon. It derives on the other hand from work I began in collaboration with Julien Gauthier, Philippe Meirieu, Denis Kambouchner and Guillaume Vergne, in the framework of a partnership between Ars Industrialis and Skhole.fr, and that also led to the publication of *L'École, le numérique et la société qui vient.*

Chapter 1   Unreason

1   Theodor Adorno and Max Horkheimer, *Dialectic of Enlightenment* (Stanford: Stanford University Press, 2002), p. xiv.
2   Ibid., p. xvi.
3   Ibid., translation modified. The German text reads: '*Nimmt Aufklärung die Reflexion auf dieses rückläufige Moment nicht in sich auf, so besiegelt sie ihr eigenes Schicksal.*'
4   Louis Dumont, 'Préface' to the French edition of Karl Polanyi, *La Grande Transformation: Aux origines politiques et économiques de notre temps* (Paris: Gallimard, 1983), p. 1.
5   Polanyi, *The Great Transformation*, pp. 3–4.
6   See Stiegler, *What Makes Life Worth Living.*
7   Gilles Deleuze, *Nietzsche and Philosophy* (New York: Columbia University Press, 1983), p. 105.
8   Adorno and Horkheimer, *Dialectic of Enlightenment*, p. xvii.
9   On retention, see 'Attention, Rétention, Protention', pp. 380–2.
10 In particular in Bernard Stiegler, *Technics and Time, 3: Cinematic Time and the Question of Malaise* (Stanford: Stanford University Press, 2011), p. 140.

11   We shall see (on p. 53) that this 'retentional' perspective on the forma-
     tion of knowledge is a synthesis of two of Nietzsche's analyses, in *The
     Wanderer and His Shadow* and *The Genealogy of Morality*.

12   This hegemony, however, is no longer in a form that Gramsci would
     have recognized: it is no longer that of the bourgeoisie.

13   It is this decay of noetic inquietude that forms the horizon of the
     analyses of Dominique Lecourt in *Contre la peur* (Paris: PUF, 1990).
     That inquietude or restlessness is nevertheless the condition of think-
     ing, in the sense that Hegel makes it, precisely, the dialectical princi-
     ple of the reflexivity of reason as its negative, or as the experience of
     shame that, confronted in stupidity, requires thought, and that this
     inquietude or restlessness is also capable of generating that which
     paralyses the possibility of thinking, is undoubtedly what remains to
     be thought, faced with what I have tried to describe as the pharmaco-
     logical condition of thinking, where the *pharmakon* is the factor of
     primordial and irreducible inquietude, that is, *non-dialecticizable*
     inquietude.

14   *Hypomnēmata*: of which alphabetic writing is an instance at the heart
     of which the canons of reason themselves historically and socially form
     and actualize, during the period extending from Presocratic thought
     to the birth of philosophy properly speaking.

15   This is thus a matter of inverting the *autos*. And as we shall see (see
     pp. 189–90), it is a matter for Polanyi of positing in principle the
     necessity of heterogeneity – in this case, of a heterogeneity of
     causalities.

16   Polany, *The Great Transformation*, p. 3, translation modified.

17   In the sense given to this expression in Gilbert Simondon, *Imagination
     et invention* (Chatou: Transparence, 2008), for instance pp. 13–14.

18   See Adorno and Horkheimer, *Dialectic of Enlightenment*, p. 98, and
     my commentary in *Technics and Time, 3*, pp. 37–8.

19   *Translator's note*: on 1 August 2007, the new government of Nicolas
     Sarkozy enacted the 'Law on the Liberties and Responsibilities of
     Universities', known as the LRU law. While the law was promoted in
     terms of 'university autonomy', this was really a question of empower-
     ing university management to seek funding sources outside of govern-
     ment. Wide-ranging protests ensued, arguing that this so-called
     'financial autonomy' on the contrary tied universities and faculties to
     market mechanisms that would in fact threaten the independence of
     research and undermine courses deemed to be unprofitable.

20   See Immanuel Kant, *The Conflict of the Faculties* (Lincoln and London:
     University of Nebraska Press, 1979), and see p. 191.

21   Hauter, 'L'école fabrique des élites, pas des équipes'.

22   Ibid.: 'Germany and the United Kingdom face similar problems.
     The Americans and the British react with "charter schools" and
     "academies": governments grant to parents and teachers the means of
     collecting public funds on the same per-student basis as the public
     system.'

23 Ibid.: 'In underprivileged areas of large American cities, the charter schools, inventive and dynamic, obtain spectacular results.'

24 I refer to a society as 'hyper-industrial' when everything in it has become subject to modelling and industrial activity – distribution, health, leisure, education, and so on – a point of view that is obviously a complete break with the myth of 'post-industrial society'. See 'Industrie, industries culturelles et technologies de l'esprit', in Petit, *Vocabulaire d'Ars Industrialis*, in Stiegler, *Pharmacologie du Front national*, pp. 405–7.

25 Hauter, 'L'école fabrique des élites, pas des équipes', my emphasis.

26 François Hauter at this point denounces competition, yet he celebrates it when it consists in putting institutions or teachers into competition with one another. Hence his approval of the competition between schools that results from the abolition of school zoning: 'The state attempts to circumvent dogmas by taking small steps. It first abolishes school zoning. [...] It reinforces the power of school principals, granting them autonomy', and so on. If one defends putting institutions into competition and the logic of 'confrontation' to which it belongs, and a few lines later denounces this same logic on the grounds that it is 'pitting children against one another from childhood', then one must explain why this is bad when applied to individual children but good when applied to institutions. If it is not possible to do so, then this in turn requires explanation.

27 See *Lettre ouverte à cette génération qui refuse de vieillir* (available at http://www.editionsterrenoire.com/site%20FTP/p_lett.htm), and see p. 34ff.

28 See Immanuel Kant, 'Perpetual Peace: A Philosophical Sketch', *Political Writings*, p. 101: 'The form of government, in this case, will be either *republican* or *despotic*. *Republicanism* is that political principle whereby the executive power (the government) is separated from the legislative power. Despotism prevails in a state if the laws are made and arbitrarily executed by one and the same power, and it reflects the will of the people only in so far as the ruler treats the will of the people as his own private will.'

29 For example, the grandfather ridiculed in a Canal J advertising campaign. See Stiegler, *Taking Care of Youth and the Generations*, pp. 3–5.

30 Hauter, 'L'école fabrique des élites, pas des équipes', my emphasis.

31 *Translator's note*: the reference here is to the famous French song from 1935, 'Tout va très bien, madame la marquise', by Paul Misraki.

32 Michel Desmurget, *TV lobotomie: La vérité scientifique sur les effets de la télévision* (Paris: Max Milo, 2011).

33 That this malaise affects every social milieu is one of the key points of a study of secondary education by Dominique Pasquier, *Cultures lycéennes: La tyrannie de la majorité* (Paris: Autrement, 2005).

34 Hauter, 'L'école fabrique des élites, pas des équipes', my emphasis.
35 See Stiegler, *Taking Care of Youth and the Generations*, p. 12ff.
36 Bernard Stiegler, *Uncontrollable Societies of Disaffected Individuals: Disbelief and Discredit, 2* (Cambridge: Polity, 2013), p. 30.
37 Stiegler, *Taking Care of Youth and the Generations*, p. 8.
38 Stiegler, 'Du temps-carbone au temps-lumière', pp. 34–5.
39 See p. 37.
40 Hauter, 'L'école fabrique des élites, pas des équipes'.
41 See p. 207.
42 On this point, see p. 60.
43 Jacques Derrida, 'Mochlos, or The Conflict of the Faculties', *Eyes of the University: Right to Philosophy 2* (Stanford: Stanford University Press, 2004), p. 94, translation modified.
44 I shall return to this question in detail; see p. 86.
45 I use this word 'shadow' here with Nietzsche. See *Human, All Too Human* (Cambridge and New York: Cambridge University Press, 1986), Volume Two, 'Part Two: *The Wanderer and His Shadow*', §10: '*Feeling no new chains.* – So long as we do not *feel* that we are dependent on anything we regard ourselves as independent: a false conclusion that demonstrates how proud and lusting for power man is. For he here assumes that as soon as he experiences dependence he must under all circumstances notice and recognize it, under the presupposition that he is *accustomed* to living in independence and if, exceptionally, he lost it, he would at once perceive a sensation antithetical to the one he is accustomed to.'
46 See p. 67, and see '*Pharmakon*, pharmacologie', in Petit, *Vocabulaire d'Ars Industrialis*, in Stiegler, *Pharmacologie du Front national*, pp. 421–2.
47 On fire, see the lecture of 9 October 2010, session 2, that I gave at the philosophy school of Épineuil, available at http://pharmakon.fr/wordpress/39/.
48 It is due to the stupidity of Epimetheus that mortals, that is, prosthetic beings, arose with Prometheus, the clear-sighted one compensating for this stupidity with a theft. See Stiegler, *Technics and Time, 1*, and *What Makes Life Worth Living*.
49 See Gilles Deleuze, *Difference and Repetition* (New York: Columbia University Press, 1994), p. 150, and see p. 48.
50 See Jacques Derrida, *The Beast and the Sovereign: Volume 1* (Chicago and London: University of Chicago Press, 2009), p. 180, and see pp. 49–50. *Urgrund* and *Ungrund* are terms used by Heidegger in Martin Heidegger, *An Introduction to Metaphysics* (New Haven and London: Yale University Press, 2000), p. 3: 'To seek the ground: this means to get to the bottom [...] But because we are questioning, it remains an open question whether the ground is a truly grounding, [...] originary ground [*Ur-grund*]; whether the ground [...] is an abyss [*Ab-grund*]; or whether the ground is neither one nor the other, but merely offers

the [...] illusion of a foundation and is thus an un-ground [*Un-grund*].'

51   See Friedrich Nietzsche, *The Gay Science* (New York: Vintage, 1974), §328.

52   See Derrida, *The Beast and the Sovereign: Volume 1*, p. 183.

53   Avital Ronell, *Stupidity* (Urbana: University of Illinois Press, 2002), p. 3.

54   Ibid., p. 5.

55   On the question of the profession of the professor, see Derrida, 'The University Without Condition', *Without Alibi* (Stanford: Stanford University Press, 2002), p. 202, and see p. 43.

56   Ibid., p. 207.

57   Lelièvre, 'L'éducation, sujet majeur des présidentielles?'. Lelièvre is commenting on a BVA opinion poll conducted for France Info and *Les Échos*.

58   No Présent, *Lettre ouverte à cette génération qui refuse de vieillir* (Lyon: Terrenoire, 2009).

59   Ibid., p. 12.

60   Ibid., p. 5, taking up an expression used in the title of a book by François Ricard, *La Génération lyrique: Essai sur la vie et l'oeuvre des premiers nés du baby-boom* (Castelnau-le-Lez: Climats, 2001).

61   On this movement, see David Graeber, 'Occupy Wall Street rediscovers the radical imagination', *Guardian*, 26 September 2011, available at http://www.theguardian.com/commentisfree/cifamerica/2011/sep/25/occupy-wall-street-protest. On Occupy Frankfurt and the Young Pirates movement of Berlin, see Bernard Umbrecht, 'Occupy et pirates, des "je" à la recherche d'un "nous"', available at http://www.lesauterhin.eu/?p=771.

62   No Présent, *Lettre ouverte à cette génération qui refuse de vieillir*, pp. 3–4.

63   Ibid., p. 14: 'We want to get married, build a home, join the army, become bureaucrats, achieve the stability that you have always held in contempt; to you we are the *new reactionaries*.'

64   If it is true that the lyrical generation is *grosso modo* that of 1968, and that this protest movement and its 'artistic critique' contributed to putting in place a new capitalism, as argued by Luc Boltanski and Ève Chiapello in *The New Spirit of Capitalism* (London and New York: Verso, 2005), in relation to family structure, for example. I have myself explored this hypothesis in the second and third volumes of *Disbelief and Discredit*.

65   No Présent, *Lettre ouverte à cette génération qui refuse de vieillir*, pp. 15–16.

66   Ibid., p. 17.

67   See Stiegler, *Uncontrollable Societies of Disaffected Individuals*.

68   No Présent, *Lettre ouverte à cette génération qui refuse de vieillir*, p. 18.

69 Ibid., pp. 19–20.

70 Christopher Lasch, *The Culture of Narcissism: American Life in an Age of Diminishing Expectations* (New York: Norton 1979).

71 No Présent, *Lettre ouverte à cette génération qui refuse de vieillir*, pp. 22–3.

72 *Translator's note*: 'bobo' is a French abbreviation for '*bourgeois bohème*', that is, for those who like to maintain the appearance of a Bohemian 'lifestyle' even though they are economically middle-class.

73 No Présent, *Lettre ouverte à cette génération qui refuse de vieillir*, pp. 24–5.

74 Klein, *The Shock Doctrine*, p. 5.

75 Ibid.

76 Cited in ibid., p. 6.

77 Ibid.

78 See chs. 6–7.

79 Klein, *The Shock Doctrine*, p. 6.

80 Ibid., p. 10: 'In Latin America and Africa in the eighties, it was a debt crisis that forced countries to be "privatized or die", as one former IMF official put it.'

81 Milton Friedman, cited in ibid., p. 6.

82 Ibid., pp. 6–7.

83 Ibid., p. 8.

84 Ibid., p. 7. And see pp. 9–10: 'Seen through the lens of this doctrine, the past thirty-five years look very different. Some of the most infamous human rights violations of this era, which have tended to be viewed as sadistic acts carried out by antidemocratic regimes, were in fact either committed with the deliberate intent of terrorizing the public or actively harnessed to prepare the ground for the introduction of radical free-market "reforms."' The shock doctrine aims 'to bring the model of for-profit government [...] into the ordinary and day-to-day functioning of the state – in effect, to privatize the government' (p. 12).

85 To say that 'thought' has failed to do this or that is obviously questionable: what is this thing, 'thought'? There have been, over the years, a number of thinkers who have asked these questions, such as, for example, Andrew Feenberg or even Marshall McLuhan. Nevertheless, these thoughts have never managed to form any common horizon for thinkers, which they would (more or less) recognize as binding them to 'a' thought.

86 See 'Attention, Rétention, Protention', pp. 380–2.

87 See 'Économie de la contribution', in Petit, *Vocabulaire d'Ars Industrialis*, in Stiegler, *Pharmacologie du Front national*, pp. 393–5.

88 These proposals follow on from those I put forward in *L'École, le numérique et la société qui vient*.

Chapter 2 Doing and Saying Stupid Things in the Twentieth Century

1 Aeschylus, *Prometheus Bound*, 514.
2 Adorno and Horkheimer, *Dialectic of Enlightenment*, p. 214.
3 Jeanne-Marie Leprince de Beaumont, *Beauty and the Beast* (New York: Knopf, 1949), p. 32, translation modified.
4 Benedict de Spinoza, *Ethics*, Part II, §49, in *On the Improvement of the Understanding; The Ethics; Correspondence* (New York: Dover, 1955), p. 126.
5 Martin Heidegger, 'The Self-Assertion of the German University', in Günther Neske and Emil Kettering (eds.), *Martin Heidegger and National Socialism: Questions and Answers* (New York: Paragon House, 1990), p. 5.
6 See p. 257, n. 10.
7 Adorno and Horkheimer, *Dialectic of Enlightenment*, p. xiv.
8 Ibid.
9 Ibid., p. xiv.
10 Ibid., p. xv. This reference to Napoleon is found again in Pierre Macherey, 'Kant et le *conflit des facultés*', available at http://philolarge. hypotheses.org/47.
11 Éliane Kaufholz specifies in a note to the French translation that 'the authors here give [to the word *Aufklärung*] a very broad sense of "thought in progress", of "philosophy of progress", this progress being reason in its opposition to irrationality, source of obscurantism'. Kaufholz, in Theodor W. Adorno and Max Horkheimer, *La Dialectique de la Raison* (Paris: Gallimard, 1983), p. 16.
12 Adorno and Horkheimer, *Dialectic of Enlightenment*, p. xviii.
13 Ibid., p. xvi, my emphasis, translation modified.
14 This was the year of publication of *Dialectic of Enlightenment*, although it was written in 1944.
15 Karl Marx and Friedrich Engels, *The Communist Manifesto* (London: Penguin, 1967), p. 88, translation modified.
16 See Stiegler, *What Makes Life Worth Living*, pp. 22 and 131.
17 Ernest Jones, *Papers on Psychoanalysis* (London: Karnac, 1977).
18 Adorno and Horkheimer, *Dialectic of Enlightenment*, p. xvii.
19 See Gilbert Simondon, *Du mode d'existence des objets techniques* (Paris: Aubier 2001), p. 15, and 'Prolétarisation', in Petit, *Vocabulaire d'Ars Industrialis*, in Stiegler, *Pharmacologie du Front national*, pp. 424–5.
20 See 'Grammatisation (techniques de reproduction)', in Petit, *Vocabulaire d'Ars Industrialis*, in Stiegler, *Pharmacologie du Front national*, pp. 400–2. I return to this later, p. 93, and especially in ch. 6, pp. 132ff.
21 Immanuel Kant, *Groundwork of the Metaphysic of Morals* (New York: Harper, 1964).

22 The spread of this word, *malin*, particularly in marketing and advertising, which initially referred to the diabolical and which has come to designate cunning intelligence and a 'wise guy' ['*petit malin*'], is a symptom that typifies our misery.

23 Adorno and Horkheimer, *Dialectic of Enlightenment*, p. xvii.

24 See also Jürgen Habermas, 'The Public Sphere: An Encyclopedia Article (1964)', *New German Critique* 3 (1974), pp. 49–55.

25 See Adorno and Horkheimer, *Dialectic of Enlightenment*, p. 214, cited at the beginning of this chapter. The link made in this fragment by Adorno and Horkheimer between stupidity and frustrated desire, and which they inscribe here into a perspective that I call organological, must be analysed as a process of the regression from desire to the drives. The fragmentary and incomplete character of these notes and sketches, however, prevents going further here.

26 This is what became clear to Freud in 1920 (on this, see p. 139).

27 Ibid., p. xix, my emphasis.

28 Aristotle, *Metaphysics*, 982b.

29 Deleuze, *Nietzsche and Philosophy*, p. 105.

30 Dork Zabunyan, 'L'apprentissage de la bêtise', intervention in the seminar 'Deleuze', organized in 2004 by Patrice Maniglier in the École normale supérieure, Ulm. I have previously commented on this remark in Stiegler, *Uncontrollable Societies of Disaffected Individuals*, p. 24. Zabunyan has since published an article, entitled 'Pourquoi je suis si bête', on *Bréviaire de la bêtise* by Alain Roger, in *Critique* 738 (2008), pp. 867–77.

31 Deleuze, *Difference and Repetition*, p. 151.

32 Ibid., pp. 151–2, my emphasis.

33 Gilbert Simondon, *L'Individu et sa genèse physico-biologique* (Grenoble: Millon, 1995), p. 46.

34 See Hegel, *Phenomenology of Spirit*, §31, translation modified: 'Quite generally, the well-known, just because it is well-known, is not cognitively understood. The commonest way in which we deceive either ourselves or others about understanding is by assuming something as familiar, and accepting it on that account.' My citation of Hegel to support a proposition by Deleuze no doubt seems surprising. This is, however, precisely a question of the well-known belief, which is also to say, the stupid belief, that Deleuze – and Nietzsche – *oppose* Hegel.

35 Simondon, *Du mode d'existence des objets techniques*, p. 164.

36 Friedrich Nietzsche, *Thus Spoke Zarathustra* (London: Penguin, 1961).

37 In Simondon 'key points' are culminating points, highlights, those heights that mean there are base thoughts as the truths from which they are made. Cf. Deleuze, *Nietzsche and Philosophy*, p. 105: 'There are imbecile thoughts, imbecile discourses, that are made up entirely of truths; but these truths are base, they are those of a base, heavy and leaden soul. The state of mind dominated by reactive forces, *by right*,

expresses *stupidity and, more profoundly, that which it is a symptom of: a base way of thinking.*' In relation to the worst, and to the worst stupidity, see Sophocles, *Antigone*, and my commentary in *Uncontrollable Societies of Disaffected Individuals*, pp. 24ff.

38 See Stiegler, *Taking Care of Youth and the Generations*, pp. 180–1.
39 Albert Camus, *The Myth of Sisyphus* (London: Penguin, 1975), pp. 110–11.
40 Friedrich Nietzsche, *On the Genealogy of Morality* (Cambridge and New York: Cambridge University Press, 1994).
41 Deleuze, *Difference and Repetition*, p. 150.
42 *The Beast and the Sovereign* was the last in a series of seminars given by Derrida at EHESS entitled 'Questions of Responsibility'.
43 Derrida, *The Beast and the Sovereign: Volume 1*, p. 180.
44 Ibid., p. 1.
45 See Jacques Derrida, 'The Supplement of Copula: Philosophy Before Linguistics', *Margins of Philosophy* (Chicago and London: University of Chicago Press, 1982).
46 I have attempted to begin this analysis in *Technics and Time, 1*, pp. 222–5, and *Technics and Time, 2: Disorientation* (Stanford: Stanford University Press, 2009), pp. 32–5. I shall return to this question in the fourth volume of *Technics and Time*, and I also discuss it in a lecture on Plato's *Republic* available on pharmakon.fr.
47 Hegel, *Phenomenology of Spirit*, §58. I return to this question of ratiocination or quibbling later, see pp. 115–16.
48 If this is so, this is because Derrida plays the fool (*fait la bête*, which is not necessarily the same thing as making mistakes or doing stupid things, *faire des bêtises*), and not because he *is* stupid. Anyway, who could one say is stupid? Heidegger, for example? Surely not. Heidegger, who was not exactly stupid, who was not 'just stupid' [*juste pas bête*], as the younger generations say today, did – that is, said – stupid things. And in this case he was not content to 'play the fool'. However that may be, in relation to stupidity, being and not being perhaps do not agree, perhaps never agree, even when these copulas are determined or undetermined by the adverb 'exactly'. Between being (stupid), doing (stupid things) and saying (stupid things), the question of stupidity would be at the same time older, deeper and lower than the question of being and of spirit, including in *Of Spirit: Heidegger and the Question*, where Derrida approaches the question of the animal 'poor in world'. The default of spirit, that is, the feeling of not having any: such would be the commencement of spirit starting from that which is stupid, *ēpimethēia* (and this is also *la Bête de la Belle*).
49 Deleuze, *Difference and Repetition*, p. 152.
50 Ibid.
51 Derrida, *The Beast and the Sovereign: Volume 1*, p. 180, and see my citation of Heidegger, p. 229, n. 50.
52 Ibid.

53 This phrase comes from Jean de la Fontaine, and is cited and used repeatedly by Derrida in *The Beast and the Sovereign: Volume 1* (see in particular p. 2).

54 Simondon, *L'Individu et sa genèse physico-biologique*, pp. 157–8.

55 Sigmund Freud, *Civilization and Its Discontents*, in *The Standard Edition of the Complete Psychological Works*, Vol. 21 (London: Hogarth Press, 1964), p. 123.

56 Jacques Lacan, 'The Mirror Stage as Formative of the *I* Function as Revealed in Psychoanalytic Experience', in *Écrits* (New York and London: Norton, 2006).

57 I will return to this question of the indeterminate in Deleuze (see p. 53), which must be compared to the question of the indeterminate in Heidegger – in passing through the relation to death. On this point, see Stiegler, *Technics and Time, 1*, p. 212.

58 Deleuze, *Difference and Repetition*, p. 38.

59 Ibid.

60 Nietzsche, *The Gay Science*, §328.

61 To this must be added the process of technical individuation, which psychosocial individuation presupposes, even though Simondon is not very clear about this. See Bernard Stiegler, *Symbolic Misery. Volume One: The Hyperindustrial Epoch* (Cambridge: Polity, 2014).

62 Deleuze, *Difference and Repetition*, p. 150.

63 Gilbert Simondon, *L'Individuation psychique et collective* (Paris: Aubier, 2007).

64 It is this that enables Simondon to think industry. On this subject, see 'Industrie, industries culturelles et technologies de l'esprit', pp. 405–7. I have tried to analyse this inversion of relations between being and possibility in *Technics and Time, 3*, in Bernard Stiegler, *Économie de l'hypermatériel et psychopouvoir: Entretiens avec Philippe Petit et Vincent Bontems* (Paris: Mille et une nuits, 2008), and in *What Makes Life Worth Living*.

65 The crystal is the individuation of an amorphous milieu from which individuality emerges, that is, a physical individual. See Simondon, *L'Individu et sa genèse physico-biologique*, p. 83.

66 Simonon, *L'Individuation psychique et collective*, p. 15.

67 Ibid., p. 16.

68 Ibid., and Simondon, *L'Individu et sa genèse physico-biologique*, pp. 115ff. I shall return to these questions and to the question of animality in Bernard Stiegler, *Veux-tu devenir mon ami?*, forthcoming.

69 Deleuze, *Difference and Repetition*, p. 151.

70 Ibid., p. 152.

71 Nietzsche, *Human, All Too Human*, p. 306.

72 On adoption, insofar as it is not adaptation, see 'Adaptation/Adoption', in Petit, *Vocabulaire d'Ars Industrialis*, in Stiegler, *Pharmacologie du Front national*, pp. 371–3.

73 Nietzsche, *Human, All Too Human*, p. 306, translation modified.

74 I have tried to show that this is the logic at work in what Heidegger called '*das Man*' (the *they* or the *one*). See Bernard Stiegler, 'The Theatre of Individuation: Phase-Shift and Resolution in Simondon and Heidegger', *Parrhesia* 7 (2009), pp. 46–57, and Bernard Stiegler, 'To Love, To Love Me, To Love Us: From September 11 to April 21', in *Acting Out* (Stanford: Stanford University Press, 2009).

75 See Maurice Blanchot, *Friendship* (Stanford: Stanford University Press, 1997), and my commentary in *Veux-tu devenir mon ami?*

76 Simondon, *Du mode d'existence des objets techniques*, p. 248.

77 In the sense given to this in Simondon, *Imagination et invention*, p. 13.

78 Derrida, 'Différance', *Margins of Philosophy*, p. 3: 'I will speak, therefore, of the letter *a*, this initial letter which it apparently has been necessary to insinuate, here and there, into the writing of the word *difference*; and to do so in the course of a writing on writing, and also of a writing within writing whose different trajectories thereby find themselves, at certain very determined points, intersecting with a kind of gross spelling mistake.'

79 Ibid., p. 8.

80 Ibid.

81 Ibid.

82 See pp. 134 and 66ff. And this is a trait common to both Derrida and Deleuze.

83 Ibid.

84 In his interpretation of the theory of the three souls outlined by Aristotle in *On the Soul* – where vital individuation in the Simondonian sense includes both the vegetative and sensitive stages of the soul – Hegel shows that any noetic soul (any psychic individual) may regress to the stage of a sensitive soul. But this would not mean it returns to an animal state. It means that it is in a deferred and suspended relation to its own possibility, held within its 'in itself' without passing into the actuality of the 'for itself'. And this is not without relation to Deleuze's statement about stupidity as a form that does not take. See G. W. F. Hegel, *Lectures on the History of Philosophy. Volume 2: Plato and the Platonists* (Lincoln and London: University of Nebraska Press, 1995), pp. 180–202.

85 Simondon, *L'Individu et sa génèse physico-biologique*, p. 163.

86 Ibid., my emphasis.

87 Georges Bataille, *Lascaux, or The Birth of Art* (Lausanne: Skira, 1955) p. 121.

88 Simondon, *L'Individu et sa génèse physico-biologique*, p. 163.

89 Ibid.

90 Jacob von Uexküll, *A Foray into the Worlds of Animals and Humans, with A Theory of Meaning* (Minneapolis: University of Minnesota Press, 2010).

91   Simondon, *L'Individu et sa génèse physico-biologique*, p. 163, n. 6, my emphasis.

92   Ibid., p. 164.

93   It is true that Simondon's thesis, from which these lines are extracted, was defended seven years before André Leroi-Gourhan published *Gesture and Speech* (Cambridge, MA and London: MIT Press, 1993).

94   Simondon, *L'Individu et sa génèse physico-biologique*, p. 164.

95   Ibid.

96   Ibid., p. 165.

97   This sub-chapter is a response to a question posed to me by Ludovic Duhem in July 2011.

98   Ibid., p. 165, my emphasis.

99   Freud, *Civilization and Its Discontents*, p. 114.

100   Immanuel Kant, *Critique of Pure Reason* (London: Macmillan, 1929), pp. 328–83, and my commentary in Stiegler, *Technics and Time, 3*, pp. 57ff.

101   See p. 54.

102   That is, the interruption, suspension and trans-formation or individuation of an earlier individuation.

103   Simondon, *L'Individu et sa génèse physico-biologique*, p. 165.

104   On the doubly epokhal redoubling, see Stiegler, *What Makes Life Worth Living*, Stiegler, *Technics and Time, 1*, and Stiegler, *Technics and Time, 2*.

105   Deleuze, *Difference and Repetition*, p. 151, translation modified. *Translator's note: Moi* has been translated here as 'Ego' in order to retain the connection to the Freudian *das Ich*, rather than as 'Self', as Paul Patton does in his translation of *Difference and Repetition*, or as 'Me', as Geoffrey Bennington does in his translation of Derrida's *The Beast and the Sovereign*. The avoidance of 'Ego' by Patton and Bennington may well have been justified, but given the extent to which what follows (especially in the next chapter) is a commentary on Deleuze's relation to Freud (and Derrida's relation to Deleuze), we have preferred to retain the connection to psychoanalytic terminology. Nevertheless, we shall otherwise follow Strachey's practice of not capitalizing 'ego', unless it is a direct quotation from Deleuze, thereby allowing for some interpretative latitude in reading the relation between Deleuze and Freud.

106   Georges Canguilhem, *The Normal and the Pathological* (New York: Zone, 1991), p. 200, translation modified.

Chapter 3   Différance and Repetition

1   Jacques Derrida, 'Psyche: Invention of the Other', in *Psyche: Inventions of the Other, Volume I* (Stanford: Stanford University Press, 2007), p. 28.

2   The words 'act' and 'potential' are certainly not part of Simondon's
    vocabulary. A major reason for this is that the Aristotelian opposition
    between act and potential, or rather between *dunamis* and *energeia*
    (and *entelekheia*), is subject to the opposition between *hylē* and
    morphē, that is, between form and matter, an opposition Simondon
    explicitly rejects as metaphysical, constituting what he calls the hylo-
    morphic scheme. This rejection necessitates returning here to the ques-
    tion of the trace that Derrida, precisely, traced – which traces a circuit
    of transindividuation.
3   Deleuze, *Difference and Repetition*, p. 152, my emphasis.
4   This is so, even though Asia may well hold surprises in store in relation
    to collective 'intelligence'.
5   See Frédéric Kaplan's remarkable analysis of Google as the advent of
    a linguistic capitalism ('Quand les mots valent de l'or', *Le Monde
    Diplomatique*, November 2011), which constitutes according to my
    own analysis a new stage of control taken over processes of transin-
    dividuation – itself tied to a new stage of the grammatization process.
    The analysis of the possibilities of taking control of the transindividu-
    ation process in general through tertiary retention, and of struggling
    against this control, is the very goal of pharmacology being staked out
    here. It was also the theme of a seminar I conducted via videoconfer-
    ence and that is hosted on the pharmakon.fr website (available online
    only on request from contact@pharmakon.fr), and an August 2011
    seminar at the philosophy school of Épineuil, the archives of
    which are located at www.pharmakon.fr/wordpress/academie-dete-de
    -philosophie-depineuil-le-fleuriel/.
6   See Simondon, *L'Individuation psychique et collective*, pp. 9–11.
7   Derrida, 'The University Without Condition', p. 203, translation
    modified.
8   The title of the lecture was 'The Future of the Profession; or, The
    University Without Condition (Thanks to the "Humanities", What
    Could Take Place Tomorrow)'.
9   Deleuze, *Difference and Repetition*, p. 150, translation modified.
10 Derrida, *The Beast and the Sovereign: Volume 1*, p. 179, translation
    modified.
11 Deleuze, *Difference and Repetition*, p. 151.
12 Ibid., translation modified. *Translator's note:* see the translator's note
    on the translation of *Moi*, p. 237, n. 105.
13 Ibid., pp. 151–2, translation modified.
14 Ibid., p. 152.
15 Derrida, *The Beast and the Sovereign*, p. 181, translation modified.
16 Ibid., translation modified.
17 It may be that he would have preferred not to publish such a seminar.
    One can say things and advance hypotheses in a seminar, plant seeds,
    as any seminar ought to do, and then later pull out the weeds. Which
    means that one may choose not to publish them. Derrida was very

attentive to these issues and to these differences between the oral and the published regimes of the trace. The publication of these seminars, which is undoubtedly not only useful and valuable, but necessary, must nevertheless be done in full awareness of this undecidable limit for those who come after – deciding, in the place of the departed, what may or may not be published, a limit that threatens all posthumous publication.

18 See, for example, Deleuze, *Difference and Repetition*, pp. 16–19 and pp. 70–116.

19 Ibid., p. 6, my emphasis; translation modified.

20 Ibid., my emphasis; translation modified.

21 Ibid., p. 13.

22 Deleuze published *Nietzsche and Philosophy* in 1962, the year in which Husserl's 'Origin of Geometry' appeared, accompanied by Derrida's 'Introduction'.

23 See Simondon, *L'Individuation psychique et collective*, p. 30.

24 See, for example, Derrida, *Of Grammatology*, p. 65.

25 Deleuze, *Difference and Repetition*, p. 16.

26 Ibid.

27 Ibid., p. 17.

28 Sigmund Freud, 'The Ego and the Id', in *The Standard Edition of the Complete Psychological Works*, Vol. 19 (London: Hogarth Press, 1961), p. 23.

29 Ibid., p. 24. *Translator's note:* This discussion in 'The Ego and the Id' is part of Freud's attempt to set up his 'second topography' (composed of the id, ego and superego), in part motivated by the recognition that the division between conscious, preconscious and unconscious processes did not do justice to the role of the unconscious in all aspects of psychological life. Freud is here introducing this topography through a consideration of the relation between internal and external perception in terms of the systems that he refers to as consciousness (*Cs.*), the preconscious (*Pcs.*), the unconscious (*Ucs.*) and the perception system (*Pcpt.*). Freud explains (p. 23): 'After this clarifying of the relations between external and internal perception and the superficial system *Pcpt.-Cs.*, we can go on to work out our idea of the ego. It starts out, as we see, from the system *Pcpt.*, which is its nucleus, and begins by embracing the *Pcs.* [...] But, as we have learnt, the ego is also unconscious. [...] I propose [...] calling the entity which starts out from the system *Pcpt.* and begins by being *Pcs.* the "ego", and by following Groddeck in calling the other part of the mind, into which this entity extends and which behaves as though it were *Ucs.*, the "id".'

30 Ibid., p. 24.

31 Deleuze, *Difference and Repetition*, p. 111, translation modified.

32 Ibid., p. 18, my emphasis.

33 Ibid., p. 19.

34 Derrida, *The Beast and the Sovereign*, p. 181.

35 Ibid., translation modified.
36 Ibid.
37 Deleuze, *Difference and Repetition*, pp. 70–1, my emphasis.
38 Jacques Derrida, *The Problem of Genesis in Husserl's Philosophy* (Chicago and London: University of Chicago Press, 2003).
39 In Stiegler, *Technics and Time, 2*.
40 See pp. 135–9 and 145–6.
41 Adorno and Horkheimer, *Dialectic of Enlightenment*, p. xvi, translation modified.
42 Gilles Deleuze and Félix Guattari, *Anti-Oedipus* (Minneapolis: University of Minnesota Press, 1983), and Gilles Deleuze and Félix Guattari, *A Thousand Plateaus* (Minneapolis and London: University of Minnesota Press, 1987). Together, these works constitute *Capitalism and Schizophrenia*.
43 Jacques Derrida, in Michael Sprinker, 'Politics and Friendship: An Interview with Jacques Derrida', in E. Ann Kaplan and Michael Sprinker (eds.), *The Althusserian Legacy* (London and New York: Verso, 1993), p. 188. 'Althusser was conducting a struggle against a certain hegemony which was at the same time a terrifying dogmatism or philosophical stereotypism within the Party – a struggle that seemed to me (within the limits of that context) quite necessary. Yet, at the same time, I did not wish to nor could I formulate questions that would have resembled, from afar, those from the Marxism against which Althusser was fighting. Even though I thought it in another way, I could not say: "Yes, it's theoreticism and therefore leads to a certain political paralysis." I thus found myself walled in by a sort of tormented silence.'
44 Ibid., p. 193. 'And yet we lived in the same "house" where we were colleagues for twenty years and his students and friends were often, in another context, mine. Everything took place underground, in the said of the unsaid. It's part of the French scene and is not simply anecdotal.'
45 Ibid., p. 194.
46 Rainer Rochlitz, *Jacques Derrida: L'Écriture et la réification* (Limoges: Faculté des Lettres et des Sciences Humaines, 1986).
47 Deleuze and Guattari undoubtedly attempted to think capitalism, that is, the economy, otherwise. But this attempt, which from their side, too, took place in the isolation described by Derrida (see p. 240, n. 43, and n. 44), failed to open new prospects for the critique of political economy.
48 On the relation between financialization and psycho-power, see Stiegler, *For a New Critique of Political Economy*, pp. 96ff.
49 On this subject, see the very clear analysis given by Alexander Wilson during the summer school at Épineuil, available on video at http://pharmakon.fr/wordpress/academie-dete-de-lecole-de-philosophie-depineuil-le-fleuriel/academie-dete-2011/.

50 The theme of man and the ass as the most stupid of beasts, that is, the most stubbornly stuck in equilibrium, merits further analysis in relation to the question of will and stupidity, and by referring, for instance, to Spinoza: 'It may be objected, if man does not act from free will, what will happen if the incentives to action are equally balanced, as in the case of Buridan's ass? Will he perish of hunger and thirst? If I say that he would, I shall seem to have in my thoughts an ass or the statue of a man rather than an actual man. If I say that he would not, he would then determine his own action, and would consequently possess the faculty of going and doing whatever he liked. [...] I am quite ready to admit, that a man placed in the equilibrium described (namely, as perceiving nothing but hunger and thirst, a certain food and a certain drink, each equally distant from him) would die of hunger and thirst. If I am asked, whether such an one should not rather be considered an ass than a man; I answer, that I do not know, neither do I know how a man should be considered, who hangs himself, or how we should consider children, fools, madmen, &c.' Spinoza, *Ethics*, Part II, §49, pp. 123 and 126. This equilibrium is in general an illusion, including in relation to what concerns the universe, which is essentially movement. But this illusion is divided into very different fields of illusion, according to whether it is a matter of the mineral, the vegetable, the animal or the non-inhuman.

51 This is analysed in detail in Stiegler, *What Makes Life Worth Living*, pp. 37ff.

52 I am playing here on the animal, as Derrida enjoys doing in *The Beast and the Sovereign*: I am playing the fool [*fait la bête*]. *Translator's note*: aside from the reference to the ass in Spinoza, already discussed, first among the references being played upon here is Kant's dove, who appears so as to correct the mistake that would see the possibility of a priori knowledge as indicative of the possibility of pure concepts outside of intuition. 'The light dove, cleaving the air in her free flight, and feeling its resistance, might imagine that its flight would be still easier in empty space.' Kant, *Critique of Pure Reason*, p. 47. The second reference to doves is from Nietzsche: 'It is the stillest words which bring the storm. Thoughts that come on doves' feet guide the world.' Nietzsche, *Thus Spoke Zarathustra*, p. 168. The third avian reference is of course to the owl of Minerva, referred to by Hegel in the course of a discussion of philosophy's lateness that is worth quoting at length, because of its connections to many of the themes under discussion: 'A further word on the subject of *issuing instructions* on how the world ought to be: philosophy, at any rate, always comes too late to perform this function. As the *thought* of the world, it appears only at a time when actuality has gone through its formative process and attained its completed state. This lesson of the concept is necessarily also apparent from history, namely that it is only when actuality has reached maturity that the ideal appears

opposite the real and reconstructs this real world, which it has grasped in its substance, in the shape of an intellectual realm. When philosophy paints its grey in grey, a shape of life has grown old, and it cannot be rejuvenated, but only recognized, by the grey in grey of philosophy; the owl of Minerva begins its flight only with the onset of dusk.' G. W. F. Hegel, *Elements of the Philosophy of Right* (Cambridge and New York: Cambridge University Press, 1991), p. 23. The mention of philosophy's deafness may well contain an echo of the aphorism that Nietzsche entitled 'Better deaf than deafened' (and which comes only three aphorisms after that on harming stupidity), which ends as follows: 'This is surely an evil age for a thinker. He has to learn how to find his silence between two noises and to pretend to be deaf until he really becomes deaf. Until he has learned this, to be sure, he runs the risk of perishing of impatience and headaches.' Nietzsche, *The Gay Science*, §331. Finally, there may also be an echo of Derrida's commentary on Valéry's discussion of the Cartesian cogito, in which the issue is Valéry's assertion that the latter was possible only thanks to the timbre and style of the voice and text of Descartes himself, or in other words that it was dependent on Descartes 'risking the *I*' wherein the supplementarity of timbre and style endlessly complicates the question of the presentation of the *I* of 'I think': 'And this is why *I* loses itself here, or in any event exposes itself in the operation of mastery. The timbre of my voice, the style of my writing are that which for (a) me never will have been present. I neither hear nor recognize the timbre of my voice. If my style marks itself, it is only on a surface which remains invisible and illegible for me. *Point* of *speculum*: here I am blind to my style, deaf to what is most spontaneous in my voice. It is, to take up again the formulation from above, and to make it deviate toward a lexicographical monstrosity, the *sourdre* of the source.' Jacques Derrida, 'Qual Quelle: Valéry's Sources', *Margins of Philosophy*, p. 296. And here we should also read the note on this passage by Derrida's translator, Alan Bass: 'Derrida's "lexicographical monstrosity" involves a play on the word *sourdre* which means to well up, to surge up, as when a source emerges from underground. In this context, i.e. the discussion of being "*deaf* to what is most spontaneous in my voice," Derrida is playing on the *sourd*, deaf, in *sourdre*. He is forcing *sourdre* to mean "to make deaf" (which it does not), at the same time as it means to well up, and is playing on the consequences of this "monstrous" double meaning.'

53 See pp. 165–6.
54 This remark is intended in particular for David Wills – in response to a lecture and an interview he gave in Antwerp in December 1999, available at www.mariagederaison.be/topics/interviews/interview.htm.
55 See Bernard Stiegler, *The Lost Spirit of Capitalism: Disbelief and Discredit, 3* (Cambridge: Polity, 2014), ch. 2.

56 See Jacques Derrida, *Edmund Husserl's Origin of Geometry: An Intro-duction* (Lincoln and London: University of Nebraska Press, 1978), p. 88.
57 In that modality of incompletion that Derrida referred to with the term 'exappropriation'.
58 Derrida, *Of Grammatology*, pp. 4–5.
59 Ibid., p. 9.
60 With Peter Szendy, by reading his *Prophecies of Leviathan: Reading Past Melville* (New York: Fordham University Press, 2010), and then his *Kant chez les extraterrestres* (Paris: Minuit: 2011).
61 On this qualifier and the relativity of its validity, I have attempted an analysis in Stiegler, 'The Magic Skin', pp. 97–110.
62 See p. 221, n. 5.
63 In the sense of Ernest Jones, mentioned previously, on pp. 44.
64 Jean-François Lyotard, *The Postmodern Condition: A Report on Knowledge* (Minneapolis: University of Minnesota Press, 1984), p. 5.
65 Derrida, *The Beast and the Sovereign*, p. 183, translation modified.
66 In Bernard Stiegler, 'The Discrete Image', in Jacques Derrida and Bernard Stiegler, *Echographies of Television: Filmed Interviews* (Cambridge: Polity, 2002), pp. 145–63.
67 Simondon, *Imagination et invention*, p. 13.
68 Ibid.
69 Jacques Derrida, *Dissemination* (Chicago: University of Chicago Press, 1981). Dissemination is a trait characteristic of transindividuation processes.
70 Simondon, *Imagination et invention*, p. 13.
71 Ibid., p. 15.
72 Ibid., p. 16.
73 Ibid., pp. 18–19.
74 Ibid., p. 19.
75 Ibid., p. 20, my emphasis.
76 Ibid., p. 19, my emphasis.
77 Ibid., p. 139.
78 Ibid.
79 Derrida, 'Psyche: Invention of the Other', p. 1.
80 Ibid., p. 27.
81 Hence, 'the university without condition [...] should remain an ultimate place of critical resistance'. Derrida, 'The University Without Condition', p. 204.
82 Jean Laplanche and Jean-Bertrand Pontalis, *The Language of Psychoanalysis* (London: Karnac, 1988), p. 376: 'Thus defences, resistances arising during the treatment and reaction-formations are themselves subject to rationalisation.'
83 Georges Didi-Huberman, *Devant l'image* (Paris: Minuit, 1990), p. 193.
84 That is, blindly.

Notes to pp. 83–8

85 That is, deliberately. The combination of blind behaviour, in some way 'remotely controlled' by the 'logic of the supplement' in its techno-industrial stage, and deliberate behaviour, implemented by ideologues operating through 'think tanks' and other systems designed to produce and manipulate circuits of transindividuation, leads to great confusion and the worst naiveties. The best known of these naiveties is belief in conspiracy theories. But the most prevalent of these naiveties is the denial that anyone anywhere has anything to do with it, or the denial that there is any will lying behind these phenomena. The adversary, the enemy, thus becomes invisible, that is, invincible. The result of such naiveties is confusion between processes that are of systemic origin and procedures that are systematically pursued.

86 Derrida, 'Mochlos, or The Conflict of the Faculties', p. 87.

87 Ibid.

88 See pp. 72–3.

89 See the following chapter, p. 90ff.

90 See, for example, Jean-François Lyotard, *The Differend: Phrases in Dispute* (Minneapolis: University of Minnesota Press, 1988), p. 130.

91 Derrida, 'Mochlos, or The Conflict of the Faculties', p. 89.

92 On these questions, see p. 96.

Chapter 4   Après Coup, the Differend

1 Jean-François Lyotard, '*Logos* and *Techne*, or Telegraphy', *The Inhuman: Reflections on Time* (Cambridge: Polity, 1991), p. 57.

2 See 'Organologie', in Petit, *Vocabulaire d'Ars Industrialis*, in Stiegler, *Pharmacologie du Front national*, pp. 419–20. Organology attempts to describe the becoming of physiological organs, technical organs and social organizations as the co-deployment of three processes of psychic, technical and collective individuation insofar as they are inseparable.

3 See pp. 146, 169 and ch. 8, p. 173ff.

4 See Stiegler, *For a New Critique of Political Economy*, pp. 96ff.

5 See p. 175.

6 These lines are being written on 15 August 2011.

7 Jean-François Lyotard, 'Tomb of the Intellectual', *Political Writings* (London: UCL Press, 1993), p. 3.

8 Ibid.

9 Ibid., p. 4.

10 Lyotard, 'The Differend', in ibid., p. 9.

11 Lyotard, *The Differend*.

12 Lyotard, 'The Differend', p. 9.

13 Ibid., p. 10.

14 Lyotard, 'New Technologies', *Political Writings*, p. 18.

15 Lyotard, *The Differend*, p. xii: 'Phrases from heterogeneous regimens cannot be translated from one into the other.'

16 Lyotard explains: 'If we wish to discuss knowledge in the most highly developed contemporary society', which is the subject of this report on knowledge commissioned from Lyotard by the Conseil des universités du Québec, we must choose, he argues, between 'two basic representational models for society: either society forms a functional whole, or it is divided in two. An illustration of the first is suggested by Talcott Parsons [...], and of the second, by the Marxist current.' Lyotard, *The Postmodern Condition*, p. 11. In relation to the debate between Luhmann and Habermas, see ibid., pp. 12 and 60–1.

17 Ibid., pp. 11–12, translation modified.

18 Lyotard, 'New Technologies', p. 18.

19 Hence he writes that 'the history of the revolutionary movement has provided ample proof that this subject [the subject of history, the proletariat] has not arisen'. Lyotard, 'The Differend', p. 9.

20 Lyotard published *Dérive à partir de Marx et Freud* in 1973.

21 Lyotard, *The Postmodern Condition*, p. 37, my emphasis.

22 On this Freudian concept of *Durcharbeitung*, and on its use by Lyotard, see pp. 96–7.

23 See Lyotard, *The Differend*, pp. 130ff.

24 Lyotard was deeply involved with various Marxist movements and founded the anti-Leninist movement Conseil ouvrier.

25 This is for me a fundamental problem that I have addressed elsewhere, and to which I shall return in detail in the second part.

26 See Lyotard, *The Postmodern Condition*, p. 5.

27 Ibid., p. 38.

28 Ibid., p. 40.

29 And we shall see why Lyotard calls these passages anamneses. See p. 96.

30 Lyotard, *The Postmodern Condition*, p. 41.

31 Ibid., translation modified.

32 Ibid.

33 Ibid., translation modified.

34 In particular, those things I attempt to describe at the beginning of *What Makes Life Worth Living*.

35 See Habermas, 'The Public Sphere'.

36 This is what I attempt to show in *Technics and Time, 1*, pp. 10–13.

37 See 'Milieu (associé/dissocié)', in Petit, *Vocabulaire d'Ars Industrialis*, in Stiegler, *Pharmacologie du Front national*, pp. 414–16. This destruction is the worst effect of the global economic war because it destroys in advance the inventive capacities of those subjected to this war.

38 What Lyotard presents at the end of *The Postmodern Condition* as 'paralogy', in making language the essence of the 'pragmatics of knowledge' in dissensus, remains caught in this failure to question the economic limits (the economics of subsistence as well as of the libidinal economy) of the system that is here in question, namely, the exploitation of knowledge of all kinds in the context of capitalism.

39   This is what René Passet attempts in *L'Économique et le vivant* (Paris: Payot, 1979), published the same year as Lyotard's *The Postmodern Condition*.

40   Lyotard, 'Tomb of the Intellectual', pp. 3–4, translation modified.

41   Lyotard, *The Postmodern Condition*, p. 14. And see Lyotard, '*Logos* and *Techne*, or Telegraphy', p. 51: 'States are not the agencies in control of the general process of the new telegraphic breaching [which results from computerization and "new technologies"], which in principle goes well beyond them. Here we'd have to take up again the analysis – I'd say the metaphysical and ontological analysis – of capitalism. But these questions of apprenticeship and its control already come under a different memory-effect: not breaching but scanning.'

42   Lyotard, 'Tomb of the Intellectual', p. 4.

43   Ibid., translation modified.

44   Ibid.

45   Ibid.

46   Ibid., translation modified.

47   At the time Lyotard was responding to Gallo, the government of Laurent Fabius was launching a disastrous plan called 'Informatique pour tous'. It would undoubtedly have been worthwhile for the philosophical and scientific community to have mobilized itself at that point, in order to propose another approach than that the primary intention of which was to create a market for the Thomson TO7 computer. It was an approach that completely ignored what we know today to be true, and that *L'Informatisation de la société* already stated in 1978: the digital is the latest stage of writing and, as such, of the pharmacology of the spirit. It constitutes a new public thing in that it constitutes, as publication technology, a radically new public space and time. I will return to this throughout the second half of this work.

48   See pp. 147–8.

49   I refer here to my commentary, in *Taking Care of Youth and the Generations* (pp. 117–35), on what lies behind what Foucault called 'technologies of power'.

50   Martin Heidegger, 'Traditional Language and Technological Language', *Journal of Philosophical Research* 23 (1998), pp. 129–45.

51   See Stiegler, *Technics and Time*, 2, pp. 177ff.

52   Lyotard, '*Logos* and *Techne*, or Telegraphy', p. 48. *Translator's note:* the French term *frayage*, translated in Lyotard as 'breaching', is the term used in French to translate the Freudian term *die Bahnung*, translated in the *Standard Edition* as 'facilitation'. Freud uses this term mainly in the 'Project for a Scientific Psychology' but also in *Beyond the Pleasure Principle*, and it is used in relation to the neurological model of psychic functioning: it contains the sense of the breaking open of a pathway. See Laplanche and Pontalis, *The Language of Psychoanalysis*, pp. 157–8.

53 We should here discuss his analysis of the three Kantian syntheses of the imagination, and his silence in relation to the question of the schematism that lies at the heart of the analysis of Adorno and Hork-heimer's *Dialectic of Enlightenment*.

54 Lyotard, '*Logos* and *Techne*, or Telegraphy', p. 54.

55 Ibid.

56 Ibid., p. 56, translation modified.

57 The Platonic question of anamnesis was the subject of a course on Plato's *Symposium* that I conducted in the framework of the philosophy school of Épineuil, and in particular on 26 February 2011, available at http://pharmakon.fr/wordpress/cours-9-26-fevrier-2011/.

58 I have also attempted an interpretation of this question in a course on Plato's *Republic* at the philosophy school of Épineuil. See in particular the session conducted on 15 October 2011, available at http://pharmakon.fr/wordpress/cours-2011-2012-n°2-15-octobre-2011/.

59 Lyotard, '*Logos* and *Techne*, or Telegraphy', p. 56.

60 Ibid., p. 55, translation modified.

61 Jacques Lacan, *The Ethics of Psychoanalysis 1959–1960: The Seminar of Jacques Lacan, Book VII* (New York and London: Routledge, 1992), pp. 43–70.

62 This is obviously not my own view, but it is what makes it possible to think the history of onto-theology in its relationship to transcendence and therefore to the theologico-political history of the West, and as the common horizon of those monotheisms of which it is the unity, including on its eastern borders.

63 See Donald W. Winnicott, *Playing and Reality* (London: Routledge, 1971), and my commentary in *What Makes Life Worth Living*, pp. 1–4.

64 See 'Subsister, Exister, Consister', in Petit, *Vocabulaire d'Ars Industrialis*, in Stiegler, *Pharmacologie du Front national*, pp. 432–3.

65 Lyotard, '*Logos* and *Techne*, or Telegraphy', pp. 56–7.

66 Ibid., p. 57.

67 I should here inform the reader that I consider myself the specific addressee of these words, since this text is something like a response to a memo I wrote at the time as part of organizing a symposium – prepared in cooperation with Marcel Hénaff – at IRCAM. And I should also add that the posthumous debate I am here attempting to reopen with Lyotard, but which I had already begun while he was alive (firstly in my thesis, then in *Technics and Time, 2*), is a salute and a mark of recognition. After nearly thirty years, the idea that this differend, this dispute, requires clarification and deepening is perfectly normal and unsurprising. That Lyotard was always welcoming of this differend between us, and that he himself sought to clarify it in the most generous way imaginable, is what I also wish to bear witness to – in a differend.

68 Lyotard, 'Tomb of the Intellectual', p. 7, my emphasis.

69 Ibid.
70 On *catastrophē* and denouement, see *De la misère symbolique 2: La catastrophē.*
71 This is the subject of *Technics and Time, 3,* especially pp. 45–73.
72 Lyotard, 'Logos and *Techne,* or Telegraphy', p. 51: 'In Kant's terms, there are not only the syntheses of apprehension and reproduction, but the synthesis of recognition. [...] Which implies [...] the intervention of a meta-agency which inscribes on itself, conserves and makes available the action–reaction pair independently of the present place and time. So this is already a tele-graphy – the concept in Kant.'
73 Jacques Derrida, 'No Apocalypse, Not Now: Full Speed Ahead, Seven Missiles, Seven Missives', *Psyche: Inventions of the Other, Volume I,* p. 396.
74 Lyotard, 'The Differend', p. 8. This text is from 1982.
75 Such a response would be literally inconceivable in 2011, that is, it would be irresponsible. In writing this, I am not passing judgement on Lyotard's response at the time, but I believe that we must ask questions in full awareness of what came to pass and the immense question it still poses – not just in philosophy, but in politics – of knowing to what point he was responsible for responding this way, and to what extent the motives and content of this response were 'legitimate'. Measuring the abyss of this après-coup also means remembering that we can and even should suspect social democracy of being capable of making things worse, just as Althusser reproached the Communist Party twenty years earlier, in *For Marx,* in deploring the errors of the post-war period: 'We were at the age of enthusiasm and trust [...] So we spent the best part of our time in agitation when we would have been better employed in the defence of our right and duty to know [...]. In this way we came to realize [...] our "French misery": the stubborn, profound absence of any real *theoretical* culture in the history of the French workers' movement.' Louis Althusser, *For Marx* (London: Allen Lane, Penguin, 1969), pp. 22–3.
76 In relation to resistance, both in terms of the historical movement that was at the origin of the idea of public action in France after the Second World War, and in terms of the appeal signed by Raymond Aubrac, Walter Bassan, Marie-José Chombart de Lauwe, Daniel Cordier, Stéphane Hessel and Georges Seguy, see Sophie Wahnich, 'La résistance incantatoire', *Le Monde,* 15–16 May 2011; on the same register, *The Path to Hope* (New York: Other Press, 2012), co-signed by Stéphane Hessel and Edgar Morin, is literally pathetic.
77 On this subject, see Stiegler, *For a New Critique of Political Economy.*
78 Derrida, 'Mochlos, or The Conflict of the Faculties', p. 91. A reference to Deleuze's analysis of the 'I think' would here have been worthwhile.

79   This is what Lyotard reduces the role of school to, when it comes to the adoption of tertiary retention: he assigns it the task of 'teaching tele-graphy'. See Lyotard, '*Logos* and *Techne*, or Telegraphy', p. 51.

Chapter 5   Reading and Re-Reading Hegel
After Poststructuralism

1   Louis Althusser, 'From *Capital* to Marx's Philosophy', in Louis Althusser and Étienne Balibar, *Reading Capital* (London: NLB, 1970), p. 15.
2   Hegel, *Phenomenology of Spirit*, §11.
3   Ibid., §5.
4   *Translator's note*: a more conventional translation of *désamour* would be 'disenchantment' or 'falling out of love'.
5   This is what I try to do in the course on Plato at the philosophy school of Épineuil, where I try to distinguish the dialogism of Socrates – and on this question, we can also refer to a presentation on Bakhtin's dialogism that Axel Andersen gave during the Épineuil summer school (available at http://pharmakon.fr/wordpress/academie-dete-de-lecole-de-philosophie-depineuil-le-fleuriel/academie-dete-2011/) – from the Platonic dialectic that prepares the way for the ontology of essences and its methods of slicing into being.
6   See Kostas Axelos, *Alienation, Praxis, and Techne in the Thought of Karl Marx* (Austin and London: University of Texas Press, 1976).
7   This must obviously be seen in relation to Michel Foucault's analyses in 'Self Writing', in *Ethics: Subjectivity and Truth: The Essential Works of Michel Foucault 1954–1984* (London: Penguin, 1997). I continue here the analysis I began in *Taking Care of Youth and the Generations*, pp. 135–43.
8   Through such and such a subject who thinks through such and such an epoch of the history that is this phenomenology.
9   See pp. 151ff.
10   I will return to reading as process of individuation via Wolfgang Iser and Henry James in Bernard Stiegler, *Mystagogies: De l'art et de la littérature*, forthcoming.
11   In this process, the interior does not come first – it is only the individuation of exteriority with a view to its re-exteriorization, that is, its re-expropriation: it forms a spiral.
12   Hegel, *Phenomenology of Spirit*, §4.
13   Ibid., §10. *Translator's note*: a few words of Hegel's German and Hyppolite's French translation have on a couple of occasions been added for the sake of clarity.
14   Ibid., §11.
15   Ibid., §12.
16   Ibid.
17   Ibid., §13.

18   See p. 49ff.
19   See p. 79ff.
20   This is visible and legible in Immanuel Kant, 'On the Common Saying: "This May Be True in Theory, but It Does Not Apply in Practice"', *Political Writings*, p. 62; cf. my commentary in *Technics and Time, 3*, pp. 193ff.
21   *Translator's note:* on Stiegler's use of 'accidental' and 'accidentality', see Bernard Stiegler, *Philosopher par accident* (Paris: Galilée, 2004), pp. 18–19, in which he explains that, contrary to Aristotle and metaphysics, he believes that between the origins and the ends of the questions pursued by philosophy lies a process that is accidental and not essential, or in other words, where the end is not contained in the origin, and hence that what philosophy must know how to think is precisely this 'accidentality', which for Stiegler is intimately tied to what he calls 'prostheticity'.
22   Hegel, *Phenomenology of Spirit*, §17–18.
23   Ibid., §23.
24   This is what in *Mystagogies: De l'art et de la littérature* I call the passage to the act of reading by entelechy.
25   On memory as associated milieu, see Simondon, *L'Individuation psychique et collective*, p. 164.
26   Hegel, *Phenomenology of Spirit*, §63.
27   Catherine Malabou, in whom I re-read that the reading of Hegel is the future of Hegel, draws the conclusion that the 'reader is at the same time projected in advance: required to give form. [...] [T]he reader is brought to formulate new propositions [...]. The return of the concept into itself would amount to nothing if it didn't involve its own enunciation, the new era of its saying, the grammaticality of its appearance. [...] Because this understanding was not derived from itself [...], the reader must have produced it, which means that the reader must also be a *philosopher*.' Catherine Malabou, *The Future of Hegel: Plasticity, Temporality and Dialectic* (London and New York: Routledge, 2005), pp. 179–80. This is the conclusion she reaches, but I am not convinced that she draws all the consequences that follow from it, in particular that if philosophical works are essentially read, that is, re-read, and thus repeatable, writing is the element of understanding that determines by supplementing, being its elementary supplementarity, which is also the work of the concept that is the phenomenology of the spirit. But Hegel does not thematize writing: it is for him just a stage in the life of the spirit on its way towards absolute knowledge. The future of Hegel, and many others, passes through Marx, but it doesn't stop there. It doesn't stop there any more than the future of any philosophical work – which always calls its readers, as Malabou shows so well, to 'formulate new propositions' – stops with one of its readers.

As for Malabou's proposition, it consists in making plasticity Hegel's cardinal concept. But this plasticity is possible only on the condition of passing through its sterilizing exteriorization, that is, its solidifying and fixing exteriorization – namely, through this fixing that is writing, without which there can be no reading, and that is a specific moment of technics become process of grammatization. This pharmacology of the fluid and the solid is also what conditions the plasticity of the noetic brain, which too is one of Malabou's primary interests. Hegelian, or post-Hegelian, plasticity is constituted (and destituted) by its 'inorganic moment', as Hegel says.

28 See Hegel, *Phenomenology of Spirit*, §31. It forms an agglomeration that I refer to, in *The Decadence of Industrial Democracies*, as stereotypical psychic secondary retentions and collective secondary retentions (p. 111).
29 Ibid., §28.
30 Ibid., §33.
31 That is, between Fichte and Schelling.
32 Ibid., §33.
33 Ibid., §51.
34 Ibid., §53.
35 On this question, see *Technics and Time, 3*, pp. 47–78 and 138f.
36 See G. W. F. Hegel, *The Philosophy of History* (New York: Dover, 1956), pp. 61 and 162–3.
37 Jean-Pierre Vernant, *Myth and Thought Among the Greeks* (New York: Zone Books, 2006).
38 Derrida certainly highlighted the logocentrism of Hegel's perspective when, for example, the latter wrote that 'alphabetic script is in itself and for itself the most intelligent' (Hegel, cited in Jacques Derrida, *Of Grammatology*, p. 3). But this perspective is logocentric only because writing is conceived as dissolving its technical accidentality into an absolute knowledge of *logos* of which it would therefore be merely an accidental moment. That logocentrism *implies* an ethnocentrism is also what Derrida shows. But we must reflect above all on that which, in the reference to writing as the condition of the world-historial destiny of the West, also turns out to *contradict* this logocentrism.
39 André Leroi-Gourhan, *L'Homme et la matière* (Paris: Albin Michel, 1943).
40 Hegel, *Phenomenology of Spirit*, §5.
41 See p. 20ff.
42 See especially Stiegler, 'Pharmacology of Capital and Economy of Contribution', in *For a New Critique of Political Economy*.
43 On this question, see Stiegler, *Économie de l'hypermatériel et psychopouvoir*, and 'Hypermatière', in Petit, *Vocabulaire d'Ars Industrialis*, in Stiegler, *Pharmacologie du Front national*, pp. 402–3.
44 See pp. 98 and 199.
45 Hegel, *Phenomenology of Spirit*, §95.

46 Kant, 'An Answer to the Question: "What is Enlightenment?"', p. 54.
47 Malabou, *The Future of Hegel*, p. 179. The quotation is from Hegel, *Phenomenology of Spirit*, §60, translation modified.
48 On this question, see Bernard Stiegler, 'Le nouveau système des objets', available at http://amateur.iri.centrepompidou.fr/nouveaumonde/enmi/conf/program/2009_2.
49 I have elaborated on this point in *What Makes Life Worth Living*, pp. 1–5.

Chapter 6 Re-Reading the *Grundrisse*

1   Marx, *Grundrisse*, p. 702.
2   Alfred Jarry, 'King Ubu', in Philip G. Hill (ed.), *Our Dramatic Heritage. Volume 6: Expressing the Inexpressible* (Cranbury, NJ: Associated University Presses, 1992), p. 53.
3   Althusser, 'From *Capital* to Marx's Philosophy', in Althusser and Balibar, *Reading Capital*, pp. 17–18.
4   G. W. F. Hegel, *Science of Logic* (London: George Allen & Unwin, 1969).
5   Lyotard, '*Logos* and *Techne*, or Telegraphy', p. 56, and see p. 97.
6   *Technics and Time* attempts to draw the consequences of this primordial *fatum*.
7   I have developed this point in 'Une insensible incertitude: Technique et facticité du temps', *Les Cahiers de Fontenay* 51/52 (1988), pp. 143–64, and in *Technics and Time, 2*, pp. 37–64.
8   See p. 113.
9   I repeat here what I developed in *What Makes Life Worth Living*, pp. 81–7. On these questions, see also 'Attention, Rétention, Protention', pp. 380–2.
10 See pp. 147–8.
11 It would no doubt have been easier to say this nearly twenty years later, when Lyotard, friend of Sylviane Agacinski, also became the friend of Lionel Jospin.
12 Hegel, *Phenomenology of Spirit*, §195, translation modified.
13 Ibid., §196, translation modified.
14 See also Stiegler, *The Re-Enchantment of the World*, pp. 34–7.
15 Marx and Engels, *The Communist Manifesto*, p. 88, translation modified.
16 Jean-François Lyotard, *The Postmodern Explained to Children: Correspondence 1982–1985* (Sydney: Power Publications, 1992).
17 Lyotard, *The Postmodern Condition*, p. 4.
18 See Stiegler, *For a New Critique of Political Economy*.
19 See Althusser, 'Foreword to the Italian Edition', in Althusser and Balibar, *Reading Capital*, p. 7.

20 See Lyotard, *The Postmodern Condition*, p. 86, n. 17. *Translator's note:* the reference to '*mise en exteriorité*' occurs on page 4 of the English translation, and is translated as 'exteriorization'.
21 As Andy Warhol said. See pp. 215–16.
22 And here the discourse of Lyotard must confront the analyses of Pierre Legendre.
23 See p. 94ff.
24 I have commented on these questions in *What Makes Life Worth Living*.
25 Gregory Bateson, *Steps to an Ecology of Mind* (Frogmore: Granada, 1973), p. 281.
26 On this subject and its relation to the question of habit in Hegel, see the discussion by Julien Gautier, available at http://arsindustrialis.org/atelier-des-techniques-de-soi.
27 On this subject, see 'Milieu (associé/dissocié)', pp. 414–16, and Stiegler, *The Re-Enchantment of the World*, pp. 34–5.
28 Karl Marx and Friedrich Engels, *The German Ideology* (Moscow: Progress Press, 1976), p. 37.
29 Ibid.
30 Marx, *Grundrisse*, p. 692.
31 Ibid., pp. 692–3.
32 Simondon, *Du mode d'existence des objets techniques*, p. 15.
33 Marx, *Grundrisse*, p. 693.
34 Ibid.
35 Ibid., p. 694.
36 Simondon, *Du mode d'existence des objets techniques*, p. 12. This suggests functioning matter (see Stiegler, *Technics and Time, 1*), and this functioning of organized inorganic matter leads to hyper-matter (see Stiegler, *Économie de l'hypermatériel et psychopouvoir*).
37 Marx, *Grundrisse*, pp. 694–5.
38 Ibid., p. 699.
39 In the sense indicated in the preceding chapters.
40 Marx, *Grundrisse*, p. 700, my emphasis.
41 See Karl Marx, *Capital: A Critique of Political Economy, Volume 3* (London: Penguin, 1981), p. 132f. I have commented on this theory and its critique in Stiegler, *For a New Critique of Political Economy*, p. 75f.
42 Marx, *Grundrisse*, p. 704.
43 Ibid.
44 Althusser, 'From *Capital* to Marx's Philosophy', in Althusser and Balibar, *Reading Capital*, p. 17.
45 I should note here that I owe this concept to Sylvain Auroux, and that I have extended it to all spheres of the discretizable, that is, beyond the linguistic field, and in a sense that is not Auroux's.
46 In 1990, during a ten-day conference at Cerisy-la-Salle dedicated to Jacques Derrida, later published under the title *Le Passages des*

frontières, Étienne Balibar said to me, after a speech in which I referred frequently to Leroi-Gourhan, that, for himself and for the group led by Althusser, the true structural anthropology was that of *L'Homme et la matière*, *Milieu et technique* and *Le Geste et la parole*.

47   Cited in Étienne Balibar, 'The Basic Concepts of Historical Material-ism', in Althusser and Balibar, *Reading Capital*, p. 212. The quotation is from Karl Marx, *Capital: A Critique of Political Economy, Volume 2* (London: Penguin, 1978), p. 120.

48   Marx, *Grundrisse*, p. 706.

49   On the difference between these two types of judgements, see Kant, *Critique of Pure Reason*, p. 48f.

50   On this point, see Stiegler, 'Du temps-carbone au temps-lumière', p. 50.

51   On this subject, see Robert Linhart, *Lénine, les paysans, Taylor* (Paris: Le Seuil, 1976), pp. 84–116.

52   On this point, see pp. 188–90.

53   Simondon, *Du mode d'existence des objets techniques*, p. 12.

54   See p. 130.

55   The logic of the supplement, which is the true fate of materialism, but which cannot be understood independently of a material history of the supplement, radically changes the relations between the four causes – material, formal, efficient and final – which, having become transductive, require going beyond both substantialism and hylomorphism.

56   On this point, see Stiegler, *For a New Critique of Political Economy*, pp. 81–3.

57   Sigmund Freud, *Beyond the Pleasure Principle*, in *The Standard Edition of the Complete Psychological Works*, Vol. 18 (London: Hogarth Press, 1955), p. 18.

58   This will be the main subject of *La Technique et le temps 5: La guerre des esprits*, to appear.

59   Jean-François Lyotard, *Libidinal Economy* (London: Athlone, 1993).

60   Jean-François Lyotard, *Dérive à partir de Marx et Freud* (Paris: Union Générale d'Éditions, 1973).

61   The question of desire is certainly always posed *through* that of the drives, so long as the latter is correctly posed: the drive is the trans-formation of the dynamic that in animals is called instinct, but it is *not* instinct precisely because its goals can be diverted, both into poly-morphous perversion and into sublimation. The drive-based regression of desire is therefore a privative mode of the libido, an unbinding of the drives resulting from a failure of the socialization of the drives in which desire consists.

62   I have tried to show, in *The Lost Spirit of Capitalism*, why and how Marcuse himself plays out this confusion.

63   It is interesting to read from this angle the remarks made by Aquilino Morelle, published in *Le Monde* on 8 September 2011 under the title

'La démondisalisation inquiète les partisans d'un libéralisme aux abois' [De-globalization worries the advocates of a beleaguered liberalism] (available at http://www.lemonde.fr/idees/article/2011/09/07/la-demondisalisation-inquiete-les-partisans-d-un-liberalisme-aux-abois_1568675_3232.html). In the next part I will show why it seems to me the question should not be posed in terms of 'de-globalization' but rather of 're-globalization', and of a re-territorialization of 'world-making' and of the 'whole world'. Except on this point, I adhere quite closely to Morelle's analysis of social democracy as the management of contradictions that it poses as being a priori without possible alternatives.

64 Passet, *L'Économique et le vivant.*

65 On these questions see especially Christian Fauré, 'Dataware et infrastructures du cloud computing', in Stiegler et al., *Pour en finir avec la mécroissance*, and see 'Dataware', in Petit, *Vocabulaire d'Ars Industrialis*, in Stiegler, *Pharmacologie du Front national*, pp. 387–8.

66 Richard Stallman developed his ideas about free software at MIT during the 1970s, where he also developed the GNU operating system in 1983.

67 Marx and Engels, *The Communist Manifesto*, p. 82: 'The bourgeoisie, historically, has played a most revolutionary part.'

68 I owe to Gorz the discovery of the role of Edward Bernays in the consumerist evolution of American capitalism. Gorz was also the first to understand the importance of free software and to rethink the question of work in its relation to knowledge. But he overlooks the material questions and gets stuck in the 'immaterial' economy. I will return to his analyses in *Veux-tu devenir mon ami?*, forthcoming.

69 *Translator's note*: the more literal 'popular classes' is preferred here to 'working class', because the precariousness and proletarianization of work are precisely what is at issue here.

70 On the proletarianization of decision, see Stiegler, *What Makes Life Worth Living*, pp. 37–54.

71 The Institut de recherche et d'innovation (IRI) is essentially dedicated to the conception and design of these technologies. And these questions constitute the central theme of the working group on 'relational technologies' led by Christian Fauré within Ars Industrialis (see www.arsindustrialis.org/groupe-de-travail-technologies-relationnelles).

72 René Descartes, *Meditations on First Philosophy* (Cambridge: Cambridge University Press, 1986), p. 12, translation modified.

73 *Translator's note*: 'créance' today has the meaning of claim or debt, or of credibility, but, as the author states, in Descartes's more archaic French it means the set of beliefs to which one gives credence. All these resonances are played upon in the paragraphs that follow.

74 Lyotard, *The Postmodern Condition*, p. xxiv.

75 Lyotard, 'Time Today', *The Inhuman*, p. 66.

76 See Stiegler, *For a New Critique of Political Economy*, p. 66.

77 See Bernard Stiegler, 'Pharmacologie des métadonnées', in Stiegler et al., *Pour en finir avec la mécroissance*, p. 87.

78 I argue in the second part that this requires the setting up of an economy of contribution, founded on contributory research, on the constitution of an internation where universities throughout the world together assume (and network) their responsibilities, and on a new intergenerational social contract or arrangement of technological (that is, pharmacological) nativities from which the generations are derived – which is the condition of contemporary contributory research.

79 See Jorion, *Le Capitalisme à l'agonie*, p. 180.

80 In this regard, European academics have been especially blind or resigned. They have not ceased, most of them, to extol the virtues of a united Europe, without paying attention to the characteristics of its political economy, which has been, from a monetary perspective, the most neoliberal on the planet. On this point in particular, the naivety, and at times the foolishness, not to say the stupidity or beastliness, of the debates in France about the stakes of the Maastricht treaty, which are staggering, all derive from the effects of the successive shocks under the pressure of which the European Union has been 'constructed' – while the ideological machine that exploits these effects continues to operate at all levels of society, whether via the mass media, think tanks, consulting firms, lobby groups, or whatever.

81 Donella H. Meadows, Dennis L. Meadows, Jørgen Randers and William W. Behrens III, *Limits to Growth* (New York: Signet, 1972), a report commissioned by the Club of Rome in 1970 and made public in 1972.

82 'The notion of *fab lab* (a contraction from the English *fabrication laboratory*) refers to any kind of workshop consisting in machine-tools controlled by computers and new information technologies [...], which can produce various sorts of items rapidly and on demand [...]. This includes products that might not be able to be produced on a large scale (possibly unique pieces). These *cooperatives of the future* bring together computer scientists, designers, and artists in *hacklabs*.' 'Fab lab', article in the French *Wikipédia*.

83 Bernard Stiegler, *Pour une économie de la contribution*, forthcoming.

84 Lyotard, *The Postmodern Condition*, p. 67.

85 Ibid.

Chapter 7 The New Responsibilities of the University

1 A graduate school is a school of researchers.

2 This presupposes what with Amartya Sen might be called a *capacitation*.

3 See Stiegler, *Taking Care of Youth and the Generations*, p. 140f.

4   See 'Transindividuation', in Petit, *Vocabulaire d'Ars Industrialis*, in Stiegler, *Pharmacologie du Front national*, pp. 439–41.

5   See 'Attention, Rétention, Protention', pp. 380–2.

6   See '*Pharmakon*, pharmacologie', pp. 421–2.

7   Edmund Husserl, *The Crisis of European Sciences and Transcendental Phenomenology* (Evanston: Northwestern University Press, 1970), p. 17, translation modified.

8   Jacques Derrida, 'The University Without Condition', p. 202.

9   It should be recalled here that Derrida submits the question of truth to the question of its performativity, and to the question of overcoming the opposition between 'constative' and 'performative' that for centuries has been the starting point – probably since Plato's definition of *alētheia* as *orthotēs* – for distinguishing that which is true from that which has not been proven.

10 I believe that daring to assert and to argue for such an assertion (*sapere aude!*) *may* create a new situation in the noetic, diseased body of the university, through the various corporations and incorporated scholars, as Kant calls them, that constitute universities.

11 Interpreting *will* after *performativity* is a subject that has remained unresolved since the death of Derrida, despite the fact that, in a general situation of carelessness and neglect, it is urgent that the question of will be revisited, especially since it is in part tied to the question of truth beyond the opposition of the performative and the constative.

12 Polanyi, *The Great Transformation*, p. 4.

13 In Katherine Hayles's sense. See Hayles, 'Hyper and Deep Attention: The Generational Divide in Cognitive Modes', *Profession 2007* (2007), pp. 187–99.

14 On this question, and Canguilhem's way of engaging with this question, see Stiegler, *What Makes Life Worth Living*, p. 28; on the questioning being that we ourselves are to the immeasurable extent [*dans cette la mesure et la démesure*] that we are technical and pharmacological, see ibid., pp. 101–18.

15 I have proposed a commentary on these passages in ibid., pp. 9–15.

16 Paul Valéry, 'The Crisis of the Mind', *The Outlook for Intelligence*, p. 23.

17 Ibid., p. 24, translation modified.

18 This question lies at the heart of the first *Ars Industrialis* manifesto (2005), in Stiegler, *The Re-Enchantment of the World*, pp. 11–15.

19 To what extent is this question posed in an original way in North America? This would require detailed examination.

20 *Manifesto for the Digital Humanities*, available at http://tcp.hypotheses.org/411.

21 On this question, see Bernard Stiegler, 'The Formation of New Reason: Seven Proposals for the Renewal of Education', in Darin Barney, Gabriella Coleman, Christine Ross, Jonathan Sterne and Tamar

Tembeck (eds.), *The Participatory Condition* (Minneapolis: University of Minnesota Press, forthcoming). *Translator's note:* In ancient Greece, *kanon* referred to a reed or cane used for measurement (as a ruler) by a builder or mason, and by extension it came to refer to a 'rule' or 'model'.

22 Plato, *Symposium*, 207e–208a.

23 Edmund Husserl, *Logical Investigations, Volume 2* (London and New York: Routledge, 1970), pp. 87–9.

24 Edmund Husserl, *On the Phenomenology of the Consciousness of Internal Time (1893–1917)* (Dordrecht: Kluwer, 1991).

25 Edmund Husserl, 'The Origin of Geometry', in Derrida, *Edmund Husserl's Origin of Geometry: An Introduction*, pp. 178–9.

26 Ibid., pp. 162–5.

27 Ibid., pp. 179–80.

28 The condition of experience that is not experienced as such by experience – which constitutes the possibility of experience, but that is still not transcendental because it itself has its provenance in experience.

29 See 'Grammatisation (techniques de reproduction)', pp. 400–2.

30 On this subject, see the seminar organized at the IRI by Xavier Guchet and Sacha Loève, and the thesis by Sacha Loève, 'Le concept de technologie à l'échelle des molécules-machines', available at https://sites.google.com/site/sachaloeve/these.

31 I argued this point in *Taking Care of Youth and the Generations*, ch. 7.

32 I have developed this point in *Technics and Time, 1*.

33 See Pierre Hadot, *What Is Ancient Philosophy?* (Cambridge, MA: Harvard University Press, 2004).

34 Everything that must be learned is technical. Hence walking or swimming for Marcel Mauss, and hence also language: this is why it is always necessary to train or form attention.

35 Stiegler, *For a New Critique of Political Economy*, p. 29.

36 Plato, *Phaedrus*, 246d.

37 Mortality is here synonymous with forgetting, according to the mythology of the river Lethe, which we must obviously also relate to Heidegger's discourse on the meaning of *alētheia* ('truth'/'reality').

38 This is what I have tried to argue in a commentary on the 'transcendental deduction' by positing that, more profoundly, it is constitutive of what Kant called the transcendental imagination and the schematism.

39 This is explained in *Technics and Time, 3*.

40 '*Sachant*', in the sense Lyotard uses this term.

41 It would be necessary here to return to the statement by Jean Jaurès: 'Humanity does not exist at all yet or it barely exists.' Derrida discussed this statement during a speech to the 'Fête de l'Humanité', and for the association of the friends of *L'Humanité* – a sentence to which I also returned at the 'Fête de l'Humanité', and in *What Makes Life Worth Living*, p. 112. See Jacques Derrida, 'My Sunday

"Humanities"', *Paper Machine* (Stanford: Stanford University Press, 2005), p. 100.

42 This disintoxication presumes that the necessity of intoxication has been recognized; see pp. 129–30.

43 See 'Transindividuation', pp. 439–41.

44 There is a commentary on the dialogue between Socrates and Meno in the second part of the twelfth course of the philosophy school of Épineuil, available at http://pharmakon.fr/wordpress/cours-du-7-mai-2011-seance-12/.

45 On this 'more or less', see Stiegler, 'The Formation of New Reason: Seven Proposals for the Renewal of Education'.

46 See p. 97ff.

47 These re-functionalizations, the features of which I have tried to think in *De la misère symbolique 2* by drawing on Freud, are the result of the fact that psychic individuation can become collective only because the two poles of this psychosocial individuation are formed at the core of a third process of individuation: technical individuation. By individuating themselves, psychic individuals participate in collective individuation, and in so doing they also participate – mostly without knowing it – in technical individuation. The latter (and in fact all three forms of individuation) occurs through quantum leaps, via which the technical landscape that forms technical objects is transformed, changing the condition of psychosocial individuation itself. This process was thought by Freud himself on the basis of an initial de-functionalization of the sense of smell that accompanied the achievement of the upright stance. This technical becoming compensates for these de-functionalizations, producing tertiary retention in all its forms (which fall within what I call epiphylogenesis; see Stiegler, *Technics and Time, 1*, p. 175), and this tertiary retention constitutes the hypomnesic funds from which writing emerges. Leroi-Gourhan called this becoming the process of exteriorization. Cerebral plasticity forms a system with this becoming – as modification of the vital layer that, trans-formed by the technical layer, becomes the psychic layer in Simondon's sense. Here, the technical plasticity of clay, for the one who shapes it and who at the same time shapes themselves by producing knowledge, is not just a metaphor for neuronal plasticity, but its condition.

48 See the preceding note.

49 This is argued in greater detail in the final chapter of Stiegler, *The Decadence of Industrial Democracies*, ch. 4, 'Wanting to Believe: In the Hands of the Intellect'.

50 Husserl, *Logical Investigations*.

51 Edmund Husserl, *Ideas Pertaining to a Pure Phenomenology and to a Phenomenological Philosophy* (The Hague: Martinus Nijhoff, 1983).

52 This phrase was Marcel Detienne's.

53 On the figure of the salmon, see the courses on the *Symposium* and the *Republic* at the philosophy school of Épineuil, available at

www.pharmakon.fr/wordpress/cours-du-4-decembre-2010 and www.pharmakon.fr/wordpress/cours-2011-2012-n°2-15-octobre-2011.

54 Derrida, 'No Apocalypse, Not Now: Full Speed Ahead, Seven Missiles, Seven Missives', p. 396.

55 Elizabeth L. Eisenstein, *The Printing Revolution in Early Modern Europe*, second edition (New York: Cambridge University Press, 2005).

56 Gaston Bachelard, 'Noumena and Microphysics', *Angelaki* 10:2 (2005), pp. 73–8.

57 'In physics, a phase transition is a transformation of the system under study, caused by the variation of a particular external parameter (temperature, magnetic field, etc.). This transition occurs when the parameter reaches a threshold value (floor or ceiling, depending on the direction of variation). The transformation is a change in the properties of the system.' 'Transition de phase', article in the French *Wikipédia*.

58 Derrida, 'The University Without Condition', p. 204.

59 See 'Otium/Negotium', in Petit, *Vocabulaire d'Ars Industrialis*, in Stiegler, *Pharmacologie du Front national*, pp. 420–1.

60 On the proletarianization of knowledge and of teachers, see Guy Dreux and Francis Vergne, 'La prolétarisation des enseignants, au-delà du salaire', *Libération* (16 September 2011), available at http://www.liberation.fr/societe/2011/09/16/la-proletarisation-des-enseignants-au-dela-du-salaire_761521. And see Guy Dreux, Francis Vergne, Christian Laval and Pierre Clément, *La Nouvelle école capitaliste* (Paris: La Découverte, 2011).

61 See Barbara Cassin and Philippe Büttgen, 'L'excellence, ce faux ami de la science', *Libération* (2 December 2010), available at http://www.liberation.fr/politiques/2010/12/02/l-excellence-ce-faux-ami-de-la-science_697720.

62 This is the context for what is called 'slow science'. See http://slowscience.fr/?page_id=43.

63 Lyotard, 'Time Today', p. 74.

64 This commentary would build on the work of Pierre Macherey cited earlier, 'Kant et le *conflit des facultés*'.

65 I repeat and develop here the seven proposals for the school that I put forward in *The Participatory Condition*.

66 Founded on a libidinal economy as the power to sublimate or to make sublime.

67 See Patrick Chamoiseau, *Écrire en pays dominé* (Paris: Gallimard, 2002).

68 See p. 203ff.

Chapter 8 Internation and Interscience

1 See Stiegler, *Pour une économie de la contribution*, forthcoming.

2 See pp. 60–1, 112 and 141.

3 See Stiegler, *What Makes Life Worth Living*, pp. 104–8.
4 This increase in the power to infinitize is a question of libidinal economy and we must in this regard articulate Frédéric Lordon's Spinozian-based reflections with the Freudian theory of desire – without which desire will again tend to be confused with drive (see ch. 6, especially p. 139ff). For example, when Lordon writes in *Willing Slaves of Capital: Spinoza and Marx on Desire* (London and New York: Verso, 2014) that 'capital's power [*pouvoir*] to draw the powers of acting [*puissance*] of employees to its own enterprise [...] represents the liberation of a master-desire that no longer feels restrained by anything and is ready to avail itself of every opportunity to impose its will unilaterally. This kind of tyranny [...] has [...] its paradigm [in] the particular master-desire of *financial* capital in the form of *liquidity*' (p. 43), he is talking about a drive-based system that is precisely not desire, but rather its decomposition into drives. And this is also true when Lordon describes 'perfect flexibility – the unilateral affirmation of a desire that engages knowing that it can disengage, that invests with the guarantee of being able to disinvest, and that hires in the knowledge that it can fire (*at whim*)' (p. 44). It is indeed a question of disinvestment. But if the object of desire is precisely that in which one invests, this 'unilateral affirmation' is precisely not that of desire. Reading Spinoza today can be quite fruitful, provided that his work is not taken as an all-inclusive Bible – as a Revelation. Much work has been done since the seventeenth century on the question of desire, especially at the end of the nineteenth century and the beginning of the twentieth. Adhering to an uncritical Spinozism leads back to the difficulties – and amnesias – of poststructuralism.
5 Carl von Clausewitz, *On War* (Harmondsworth: Penguin, 1968), p. 101, translation modified.
6 See Stiegler, *Taking Care of Youth and the Generations*, p. 58.
7 See Stiegler, 'Du temps-carbone au temps-lumière', p. 68.
8 'Homer uses the expression *laon ageirein*, meaning to assemble the army. The warriors assembled in military formation, that is, in a circle. This circle formed a definite space used for public debate, involving what the Greeks called *isegoria*, the right to free speech. Thus, at the beginning of Book Two of the *Odyssey*, Telemachos convenes the agora in this way, assembling the military aristocracy of Ithaca. Once the circle is formed, Telemachos enters it and stands *en mesōi*, at the center. He takes the sceptre in his hand and speaks freely. [...] Following a series of economic and social transformations, this military assembly became the agora of the city.' Vernant, *Myth and Thought Among the Greeks*, p. 206. Vernant shows in this book that the condition of these transformations is the widespread socialization of writing.
9 Only this performative affirmation will allow the materialization of the proposition that Derrida believed could be described as the

university without condition, and which is in fact a university under pharmacological conditions capable of elaborating, with its *pharmaka*, therapeutic propositions.

10   This is what I argue in *For a New Critique of Political Economy*, p. 96f.

11   Bertrand Gille, 'Prolegomena', *History of Techniques, Volume 1* (New York: Gordon and Breach, 1986).

12   In the global economic war, 'mobilisation is a matter of co-linearity. The desire of the enlistees must be *aligned* with the master-desire. In other words, if the conatus to be enlisted is a force acting with a certain intensity, it must be given a "correct" orientation, namely a direction that conforms to the direction of the boss's desire (whether the latter is an individual or an organisation).' Lordon, *Willing Slaves of Capital*, pp. 33–4.

13   This becoming is the horizon of Derrida's analyses in *Right to Philosophy* – even though the absorption of *otium* into *negotium* was not problematized as such: 'A whole field is largely open to the analysis of this university "outside" that Kant calls "academic". In Kant's day, this "outside" could be confined to a margin of the university. This is no longer so certain or simple. Today, in any case, the university is what has become its margin. Certain departments of the university at least have been reduced to that condition. The State no longer entrusts certain research to the university.' Derrida, 'Mochlos, or The Conflict of the Faculties', p. 94.

14   We must interpret, from this perspective, the hypotheses of Gabriel Tarde and René Girard. Both must be interpreted in terms of what they say about imitation, and Girard in terms of what he says about envy. And at the same time we should revisit the Hegelian theses on recognition.

15   On this subject, see Stiegler, *The Decadence of Industrial Democracies*.

16   Such discourses of 'resistance', which can still be heard so often today, have in fact functioned more as a *confirmation* that 'there is no alternative': they have said, and they always say, in some way, that 'yes, in fact, there is no alternative, it is not possible to invent a way of opposing this disastrous situation, there is "nothing left to invent" except to resist as long as we can' – as everyone winds up cultivating their little corner of the philosophical garden, the artistic garden, and so on and so forth. In the same vein, Sophie Wahnich rightly criticizes the call by former resistance fighters and militants, including Stéphane Hessel and Raymond Aubrac, to claim for the twenty-first century the programme of the Conseil national de la Résistance (see p. 298, n. 76). What 'downgraded', angry youth need today is new thinking, and not the inevitable fantasy that results from a repetition of historical slogans from which all content immediately vanishes – that is, all credit. The world constantly changes: this is a fact that we must transform into

law, but this law cannot be founded on the denial of this fact. To this denial Hegel gave the name 'edifying thought', and he showed why this is precisely *not thinking*, but that in the name of which one avoids having to think, which is also to say, to suffer, the avoidance of the duty to learn something new every day.

17 This is, however, in the process of changing, for example in Portugal. Four economists from the universities of Coimbra and Lisbon have indeed filed a complaint against three ratings agencies: 'For one of them, José Reis, "these three agencies have committed three wrongs: they represent a ninety per cent concentration of credit ratings, which is a barrier to free competition; they possess investment funds, so there is a conflict of interest; and they enjoy privileged access to information. Nobody disputes that the Portuguese economy has structural problems, but we do not wish to have our fate dictated by private interests." Manuel Brandão Alves, professor of economics at Lisbon, has a similar analysis: "Through these agencies, we want to point a finger at their customers, who are the main culprits: financial institutions, pension funds, and even certain governments"' (*Libération*, 14 June 2011). The president of the European Commission, José Barroso, himself took up this initiative a few days later, followed by vice president Viviane Reding (see *Libération*, 15 July 2011).

18 See 'Adaptation/Adoption', pp. 371–3.

19 Marcel Mauss, *Oeuvres* (Paris: Minuit 1969), p. 630. The *Revue du Mauss* drew the academic consequences of this internation project in its second issue for 1997, entitled 'War and peace between the sciences': 'Is it not time to bring forward, in a way that is complementary to what Marcel Mauss called the internation, forms of interscience?'

20 On these questions, see Philippe Aigrin, *Cause commune: L'Information entre bien commun et propriété* (Paris: Fayard, 2005).

21 Bernard Stiegler, *La Télécratie contre la démocratie: Lettre ouverte aux représentants politiques* (Paris: Flammarion, 2006).

22 The so-called World Trade Organization is in reality the global organization of the market – against trade. Trade or commerce is an exchange not just of commodities but of savoir-vivre, founded on savoir-faire and on theorizing knowledge (as the free trade of minds). Economic war passes here through a war of vocabulary that consists in emptying words of their meaning by making them say the opposite of what the processes of transindividuation have elaborated as common knowledge conveyed by language. Here, the role of the media is crucial, and the grotesque development of English newspapers under the spiritual banditry of Rupert Murdoch is only one particularly crude case.

I have tried to explain why trade is not simply the market in a lecture at Saint-Émilion that can be found on the Ars Industrialis website (available at www.arsindustrialis.org/du-marche-au-commerce). On this point, see also Stiegler, *For a New Critique of Political Economy*, p. 14.

23 See Stiegler, *Taking Care of Youth and the Generations*, p. 13.
24 To be 'anchored' is not the same thing as identity-based membership.
25 'Université de Bologne', article in the French *Wikipédia*.
26 See Habermas, 'The Public Sphere'.
27 *Translator's note: 'retourner comme un gant'* ('to turn back like a glove') is an idiomatic expression that means 'to change someone's mind'.
28 It is this need that is on the horizon of the '*Appel de Fukushima*' ('Fukushima: putting the catastrophe under citizen control') of the journal *Multitudes* (12 April 2011), available at http://www .multitudes.net/L-appel-de-Fukushima-Fukushima/.
29 On this subject, see the lecture I gave on 7 May 2011 on the question of idealization in geometry, available at pharmakon.fr/wordpress/ cours-du-7-mai-2011-seance-12/.
30 On this subject, see Stiegler, *The Decadence of Industrial Democracies*, pp. 119–30.
31 See p. 206. See also 'Organologie', pp. 419–20.
32 Part of this text is included in Derrida, *Eyes of the University* (see 'Titles' and 'Sendoffs', pp. 195–249). In addition to everything in the works of Jacques Derrida that has nourished me, and in the works of Jean-François Lyotard, in addition to the remarkable hospitality shown to me by Derrida after my release from prison, I must say here something about the Collège international de philosophie and its founders, and about Lyotard's time as its second president, when he always supported everything I was attempting to do. The Collège and its founders made possible, through the audacity that they put to work – and as a collective work – all that which allows me to continue my efforts today, at this dreadfully toxic time, that perhaps neither Derrida nor Lyotard, despite their extraordinary lucidity and often striking prescience, were able to see coming in its doubly pharmacological way. But there is, no doubt, some law of the *pharmakon* or of the pharmacological condition that protects us against anticipating the worst, and does so in order that we may continue anticipating, and to open the improbability of a better unknown, a better unheard-of or unexpected. I have the chance today to continue an ongoing dialogue with Dominique Lecourt; however, I always find it painful to continue publicly, later on, a dispute of which these wonderful friends Derrida and Lyotard were not unaware, friends who are now gone and whom I miss terribly – and who were not just mistaken. It is painful to me like the *penia* of Eros, which, however, also sets things in motion. Certain minor heirs of these great masters are unable to understand this. Yet this is the very thing that makes a masterpiece: it is work that goes beyond itself, that bears within it that which does not resemble it, but which it alone has made possible.

33 On the question of light-time, see p. 175. The link between the accel-
    eration of innovation and the dissemination of systems of publication
    is clear from the very origin of modernity – in the birth of the modern
    age, then as modern society, that is, industrial society, wherein mass
    publication, newspapers, then the analogue media, have played a
    decisive role in the becoming and the destruction of industrial
    democracy.

34 See the 2010 Ars Industrialis 'Manifesto'.

35 This does not mean that it is impossible to turn this new writing of
    the social into a new process of collective individuation. But doing so
    requires an epokhal redoubling to occur.

36 This involves what Franck Cormerais calls 'societal innovation', pro-
    ducing 'societal value'. See Franck Cormerais, 'Innovation, valeur de
    la production et économie', in Bernard Stiegler (ed.), *Le design de nos
    existences: Á l'époque de l'innovation ascendante* (Paris: Mille et une
    nuits, 2008), and Cormerais, *Innovation et usages du numérique*,
    doctoral thesis, Université de Nantes.

37 In Amartya Sen's sense. On this question, see 'Industrie, industries
    culturelles et technologies de l'esprit', pp. 405–7.

38 Long circuits of transindividuation assume that each individual par-
    ticipating in the circulation of a circuit – that is, in its facilitation
    [*frayage*], its trans-formation, its expression – is a point of origin of
    this circuit, capable in principle (if not in fact) of re-initializing it, of
    re-individuating and of re-appropriating it each time as their own, that
    is, as an irreversible moment of *their* individuation. This is what
    geometry teaches us: we cannot learn it if we do not ourselves, each
    time, go back over the apodictic path. We must have the impression
    of being Pythagoras, demonstrating his theorem to himself and encoun-
    tering the evidence of his demonstration, in order to be able to do
    geometry. This point of view no longer seems obvious to scholars
    today: this is something I have observed in numerous discussions. And
    one reason for this is that the intellectual division of labour has led to
    specialization occurring at a very early stage, which is a disaster – so
    that today one finds, for example, philosophers who willingly admit
    to not being very 'mathsy' [*matheux*], to 'not liking' mathematics very
    much (or even to being 'allergic to numbers'). Conversely, one finds
    people who *are* 'mathsy' but who say they aren't 'writerly' [*lettreux*],
    which is just as bad. That predispositions exist, and therefore different
    tastes, is obvious and legitimate, and even fortunate, but to philoso-
    phize and more generally to theorize are activities that become impos-
    sible for someone who is not able to overcome such inclinations
    insofar as they may be detrimental to the life of the mind or spirit.

39 See p. 124.

40 The four causes are the material cause, the formal cause, the efficient
    cause and the final cause. See Aristotle, *Physics*, II, 3–9, and *Metaphys-
    ics*, A, 3. This criteriology of *negotium* totally submitted to efficient

causality fails to include the material cause inasmuch as it is true, for example, that it destroys configurations of hardware [*configurations matérielles*] and reserves of raw materials, and ignores, by its irresponsible practice of 'dis-economics' (taking as a first principle that waste is a potential source of profit), that a fundamental element of modern physics is the finitude of the universe.

41 Karl Polanyi, *Essais* (Paris: Le Seuil, 2002), p. 563.

42 A deficit of *established* knowledge, which is the only knowledge they are qualified to teach in colleges and schools.

43 A question is always in some way, for this questioning being that we are, that which results from a challenge or a placing in question inscribed in a process of epokhal redoubling, then in a technological state of shock. See also Stiegler, *What Makes Life Worth Living*, pp. 101–18.

44 Kant, *The Conflict of the Faculties*, p. 25.

45 *Translator's note*: Kant's phrase was '*Societäten der Wissenschaften*', translated into French as '*Sociétés savantes*' and into English, in the translation by Mary J. Gregor cited here, as 'scientific societies'. As here, this phrase will therefore often be translated as 'scholarly or scientific societies'.

46 Sylvain Auroux, *La Révolution technologique de la grammatisation: Introduction à l'histoire des sciences du langage* (Liège: Mardaga, 1994), pp. 71–149.

47 Johann Sleidan, *An Address to the Estates of the Empire* (1542), cited in Eisenstein, *The Printing Revolution in Early Modern Europe*, p. 167.

48 Gabriel Plattes, 'A Description of the Famous Kingdome of Macaria', cited in ibid.

49 John Foxe, *Foxe's Book of Martyrs*, cited in ibid., pp. 167–8.

50 One may translate νους (transcribed into the Latin alphabet as *nous* or *noos*) as either *intellectus* or *spiritus*.

51 Eisenstein, *The Printing Revolution in Early Modern Europe*, p. 179.

52 See the letter from Frederick William II of Prussia, in Kant, *The Conflict of the Faculties*, pp. 11–13.

53 Eisenstein, *The Printing Revolution in Early Modern Europe*, p. 179.

54 Ibid., p. 181.

55 Auroux, *La Révolution technologique de la grammatisation*, pp. 73, 82 and 95.

56 Giffard, 'Des lectures industrielles', pp. 117f.

57 I have attempted to demonstrate this, in relation to Foucault, in *Taking Care of Youth and the Generations*.

58 See the IRI session of 18 October 2011 devoted to Wikipedia, available at http://www.iri.centrepompidou.fr/evenement/museologie-museographie-et-nouvelles-formes-dadresse-au-public/.

59 See the session on these questions held by Ars Industrialis at the Théâtre de la Colline on 6 March 2010, available at http://

arsindustrialis.org/logiciel-libre-et-économie-de-la-contribution
-le-temps-de-la-déprolétarisation-0.

60 Kant, *The Conflict of the Faculties*, p. 25.

61 Ibid., p. 33. 'Writings' here certainly refers firstly to the Bible as sacred text, but what Kant clarifies in his text is the relationship between profane writings and sacred writings in general insofar as they constitute a milieu of the spirit based on the book.

62 'But by the public use of one's own reason I mean that use which anyone may make of it *as a man of* learning addressing the entire *reading public.*' Kant, 'An Answer to the Question: "What is Enlightenment?"', p. 55.

63 See Stiegler, *Technics and Time, 2*, pp. 57–64.

64 *Translator's note*: see the translator's note on 'accidentality', p. 250, n. 21.

65 As Derrida points out, this is Husserl's problem in the *Logical Investigations*, and then – and especially – in 'The Origin of Geometry'. Language, insofar as it is received, is always a heteronomic vector that nevertheless constitutes the condition of thought, understood as 'autonomy'. To examine this problem fruitfully today, it is necessary to think with Simondon – and, on this basis, beyond him: tertiary retention, with its effects each time specific, that is, characterizing the history of the supplement each time otherwise, which is in fact what specifies it as a 'supplement', conditions in its turn this conditioning of thought by language – and which rebounds, not just on language, but on individuation in general.

66 *Translator's note*: see the translator's note on the LRU law, p. 227, n. 19.

67 Kant, *The Conflict of the Faculties*, p. 25.

68 Ibid.

69 I refer here to the speech act theory outlined in J. L. Austin's *How To Do Things With Words* (Oxford: Oxford University Press, 1975). This theory forms the background to everything Derrida says about the university, distinguishing between constative utterances, which simply state, and performative utterances, which don't just say but do – usually as statements by an authority who creates a situation by the fact of stating it. Austin's example is when a chairman declares a meeting open. The question of performativity in Derrida is highly complex, since he tends to blur the distinction between the constative and the performative. Nevertheless, it is on the basis of a performative understanding of professed truth, that is, stated by the academic [*universitaire*] (and therefore of a universal itself performative), that he can posit that 'the university *professes* the truth' (Derrida, 'The University Without Condition', p. 202).

70 In 1954, only 1 per cent of French homes were equipped with a television; in 1961, 13.1 per cent; in 1970 it was 70.9 per cent, and by 1990 it was 94.5 per cent.

71   See Stiegler, *Taking Care of Youth and the Generations*, p. 13.
72   See Stiegler, *What Makes Life Worth Living*, pp. 1–5 and 129–33.
73   Derrida, 'Psyche: Invention of the Other', p. 27.
74   Ibid.
75   Ibid., p. 39.
76   Ibid, pp. 29–30.
77   Ibid., p. 41, translation modified.
78   Gottfried Wilhelm Leibniz, cited in ibid., p. 41.
79   Ibid., p. 39.

Chapter 9   Interscience, Intergeneration
and University Autonomy

1   See p. 98.
2   On this subject, see the thesis defended by Victor Petit at the University Paris-VII, on the concept of the 'milieu'.
3   The Institut national de recherche en informatique et en automatique (INRIA) has made the development of digital technologies for science amateurs one of the objectives of its 2008–2012 programme.
4   See www.treteauxdefrance.com/projets/2011.
5   This means the programme of action research understood in its broadest sense: on this point, see Michel Liu, *Fondements et pratiques de la recherche-action* (Paris: L'Harmattan, 1997). But the advent of the digital considerably enriches the stakes of this approach. This is illustrated by the Tavistock Institute of Human Relations and by the Norwegian industrial democracy movement. The Centre d'études, de recherches et de formation institutionnelles (CERFI), created and run by Félix Guattari, borrowed from this thinking and these experiments. Digital studies should ask how the issues investigated by Kurt Lewin and his successors can be reactivated in the epoch of collaborative technologies and of the contributory economy, and prioritize an international research programme to examine the internation in these terms.
6   In relation to performativity, Derrida wrote that 'the concept of invention distributes its two essential values between these two poles: the constative – discovering or unveiling, pointing out or saying what is – and the performative – producing, instituting, transforming.' Derrida, 'Psyche: Invention of the Other', p. 12.
7   See Jean-Pierre Dupuy and Françoise Roure, *Les Nanotechnologies: Éthique et prospective industrielle* (Paris: La Documentation française, 2004).
8   Bachelard, 'Noumena and Microphysics', pp. 75–6.
9   Gaston Bachelard, *L'Activité rationaliste de la physique contemporaine* (Paris: PUF, 1951), pp. 9–10, my emphasis.

10 See 'Techniques de soi', in Petit, *Vocabulaire d'Ars Industrialis*, in Stiegler, *Pharmacologie du Front national*, pp. 433–5.

11 This new maieutic presupposes a new field of academic inquiry, the study of digital tertiary retention, or what in the Anglo-Saxon style and language is referred to as 'digital studies' – where we rediscover Leibniz, but in the second moment of the epokhal redoubling. That the Characteristic conceptualized an element of the first moment was still a subject of philosophical astonishment to Lyotard three centuries later.

What are referred to as 'digital humanities' in a sense correspond, in the epoch of digital technologies, to what previously, in the humanities and philology, were referred to as the auxiliary sciences (epigraphy, archival science, library science, documentary science, and so on). The stakes of the digital humanities, however, for the sciences in general, for their epistemology and for the conditions of scientific research as of artistic creation, or of invention and social innovation, are far greater.

Besides the fact that the digital humanities already allow the practice of new forms of research that relate to the contributory research previously mentioned, what is at stake is something it is tempting to understand as an 'anthropological rupture' induced by digitalization – provided, however, that it is recognized that hominization is a process constituted through the constant possibility of ruptures, and where this capacity for rupture proper to the technical form of life is also called freedom. We can refer to anthropological rupture in the sense that digitalization profoundly changes the process of psychic and collective individuation that Leroi-Gourhan described as a process of exteriorization. It is for this reason that the digital humanities must be understood as a branch of what we propose calling digital studies: the digital humanities are neither practicable nor theorizable without the prior conceptualization of the organology of knowledge that unfolds with the digital – which concerns all forms of knowledge: savoir-faire, savoir-vivre and theoretical knowledge.

Of the forms of academic theoretical knowledge, digital organology profoundly affects both the human sciences and contemporary physics, and more generally the experimental sciences. Nanotechnology, for example, as applied quantum mechanics, would not be possible without the digital *organon* that is the scanning tunnelling microscope. This is also the case for genomics and biotechnology, which require tools [*organes*] to process digitally the information into which the nucleotides of the living thing are turned. Furthermore, the development of web science and web philosophy (or philosophical engineering) constitutes the properly instrumental layer of this new age of grammatization. These issues are clearly even more important than those that arose in the age of missions with the grammatization of vernacular language.

12 This point was the subject of a seminar at the philosophy school of Épineuil in 2011, and it was in part reactivated by Francesca dell'Orto

during the summer academy there in August, on the basis of a presentation on the concept of motivation in Husserl. This theme will be taken up again in the 2012 seminar.

13 We have seen what Lyotard has to say about the technicity of performativity in *The Postmodern Condition*. This analysis must be compared with what Derrida writes, no doubt thinking of Lyotard: 'Is it not, today, for reasons involving the structure of learning, especially impossible to distinguish rigorously between scholars and technicians of learning, just as it is to trace, between knowledge and power, the limit within whose shelter Kant sought to preserve the university edifice?' (Derrida, 'Mochlos, or The Conflict of the Faculties', p. 96). This obviously does not invalidate Lyotard's statement, which itself raises this question, and it in no way legitimates having the universities run by the technicians of management. It does raise once again the question of the *pharmakon* as that which ties all these actors together by placing them mutually under the pharmacological condition.

14 I will return to the technical and thus pharmacological dimension of nativity in *Veux-tu devenir mon ami?* A discussion on this subject took place with Simon Lincelles in August 2011 at the philosophy school of Épineuil.

15 See Immanuel Kant, 'Perpetual Peace: A Philosophical Sketch', p. 104: 'This federation does not aim to acquire any power like that of a state, but merely to preserve and secure the *freedom* of each state in itself.'

16 On this subject, see the course given at the philosophy school of Épineuil on 2 April 2011, available at http://pharmakon.fr/wordpress/cours-du-2-avril-2011-seance-11/.

17 I have tried to show why in *Pour en finir avec la mécroissance*, pp. 91 and 113.

18 Edmund Husserl, *Logical Investigations, Volume 1* (London and New York: Routledge, 1970), Investigation I. On this subject, see the *intercours* of 7 November 2010 at the philosophy school of Épineuil, available at http://pharmakon.fr/wordpress/intercours-7-novembre-2010.

19 Husserl, *Logical Investigations, Volume 2*, Investigation IV.

20 On this point, see Pierre Aubenque, *Le Problème de l'être chez Aristote* (Paris: PUF, 1962).

21 See E. R. Dodds, *The Greeks and the Irrational* (Berkeley and London: University of California Press, 1951). This question was examined at the philosophy school of Épineuil during the course of 5 February 2011, available at http://pharmakon.fr/wordpress/cours-du-5-fevrier-2011-seance-8/.

22 Derrida, *Eyes of the University*, pp. 195–6.

23 This is clearly the first lesson of *Of Grammatology*. And yet, when Derrida posits the necessity of affirming in law, if not in fact, as a promise, but not as a possible reality, the autonomy *without condition* of the university, he seriously neglects what, in the interior, from within

the inside of the university, is already an external heteronomous factor. This needs to be thought in terms of a positive pharmacology such that it constitutes a powerful invention – which in the era of the Republic of Letters occurred, precisely, outside the academic sphere.

24 Husserl, 'The Origin of Geometry', p. 164.

25 I have attempted to outline some reflections on this point in 'Teleologics of the Snail, or the Errancies of the Equipped Self in a WiMax Network' and 'The Indexing of Things', both in Ulrik Ekman (ed.), *Throughout: Art and Culture Emerging with Ubiquitous Computing* (Cambridge: MIT Press, 2013), pp. 479–502.

26 *Translator's note: 'pensée unique'* is a French term developed as part of a critique of certain political tendencies in France and elsewhere. It refers to the convergence of mainstream political discourse around what is broadly referred to as neoliberalism and to the feeling that there is in fact less and less difference to be found between ostensibly 'opposed' political parties.

27 I propose a detailed analysis of the stakes of these social engineering technologies in *Veux-tu devenir mon ami?*

28 Hopefully the recent electoral success (almost 9 per cent of the vote) of the youthful Pirate Party in the Berlin elections will lead the European political gerontocracy to concern themselves with questions such as these.

29 The Lignes de temps software is a platform for producing such audiobooks and videobooks, currently being developed at the IRI.

30 This was foreshadowed by new modalities of production that were created at the hypermedia production studio of the Institut national de l'audiovisuel (INA). This initiative was met with a 'conspiracy of fools': it was understood neither by the heads of the INA (who wanted innovation in relation to production to be eliminated from the INA), nor by the 'professionals', who thus legitimated the governmental efforts to get rid of this mission of the INA.

31 And it is the goal behind the use of the Ligne de temps software by Ars Industrialis. We intend this platform to become a contributory system of indexation.

32 See Gérard Leblanc, Frank Beau and Philippe Dubois, *Cinéma et dernières technologies* (Paris and Brussels: INA and de Boeck, 1998).

33 So declared Pierre Corvol, head of the Collège de France and occupant of the chair in experimental medicine, when he announced during a symposium held at the Collège de France on 16 June 2011 that 9.5 million hours of recordings from Collège courses have been uploaded to the internet since 2010, declaring as a first principle that we are all bearers of the scientific spirit.

34 Auroux, *La Révolution technologique de la grammatisation*, p. 113.

35 Including in the very broad sense given to it by Kant in 'Perpetual Peace: A Philosophical Sketch', p. 101: '*Republicanism* is that political

principle whereby the executive power (the government) is separated from the legislative power.'

36 *Translator's note:* the French law of 1905, on the separation of church and state.

37 See Philippe Meirieu, 'L'école transformée en machine à désintégrer', *Libération*, 9 December 2011.

38 *Translator's note:* on the 'cosmopolitical', see also Jacques Derrida, 'The Right to Philosophy from the Cosmopolitical Point of View (the Example of an International Institution)', *Ethics, Institutions, and the Right to Philosophy* (Lanham: Rowman and Littlefield, 2002).

39 Andy Warhol, *The Philosophy of Andy Warhol (From A to B and Back Again)* (New York: Harcourt Brace Jovanovich, 1975), pp. 100–1.

40 On 17 November 1883, in a letter addressed to French schoolteachers, Jules Ferry wrote that 'the legislature [...] has as its first goal to separate the school from the church, to ensure freedom of conscience for teachers and students, to finally distinguish two domains that have for too long been confused: that of beliefs, which are personal, free and variable, and that of knowledge, which is common and indispensable to all'. This separation is also at stake in the entire Platonic enterprise.

41 Maurice Blanchot, *The Infinite Conversation* (Minneapolis and London: University of Minnesota Press, 1993), p. 75.

42 Patrick Le Lay, *Les Dirigeants face au changement, baromètre 2004* (Paris: Éditions du Huitième jour, 2004). *Translator's note:* Le Lay was in 2004 the head of the French television network TF1. He infamously stated that what television networks sell to Coca-Cola is available human brain time. This notion is discussed by Stiegler in *The Decadence of Industrial Democracies*.

43 On 16 February 2009 Glissant and Chamoiseau wrote, along with Ernest Breleur, Serge Domi, Gérard Delver, Guillaume Pigeard de Gurbert, Olivier Portecop, Olivier Pulvar and Jean-Claude William, in the context of the social conflict then ongoing in Guadeloupe and Martinique, that 'behind the prosaic concern over "purchasing power" or "the housewife's shopping basket" looms the essential need for what gives meaning to our life, namely, poetry. All human life that is fairly evenly balanced will satisfy both the immediate, vital needs of food and drink (to put it plainly: the prosaic) and the aspiration to self-fulfillment nourished by dignity, honour, music, songs, sports, dancing, reading, philosophy, spirituality, love – leisure time for the satisfaction of one's great innermost desire (to put it plainly: the poetic).' Breleur et al., 'A Plea for "Products of High Necessity"', *L'Humanité*, 5 March 2009, available at http://www.humaniteinenglish.com/spip.php?article1163.

44 On this subject, see Stiegler, *La Télécratie contre la démocratie*, p. 171.

45 See p. 182.

46   See Bernard Stiegler, *Constituer l'Europe. 1: Dans un monde sans vergogne* (Paris: Galilée, 2005), pp. 14–16.

47   And on its relation to the culture industries – on these questions, see Stiegler, *The Decadence of Industrial Democracies*, pp. 4–26.

48   See Isabelle Bruno, Pierre Clément and Christian Laval, *La Grande mutation: Néolibéralisme et éducation en Europe* (Paris: Syllepse, 2010).

49   See Paul, Epistle to the Corinthians, Epistle to the Romans.

50   Today, it is no longer a matter of struggling against believers – but against those who destroy all credence and all credit. This question lies at the heart of an interview with Jean-Luc Nancy, published in Alain Jugnon (ed.), *Pourquoi nous ne sommes pas chrétiens* (Paris: Max Milo, 2009).

51   See Friedrich Nietzsche, *The Birth of Tragedy*, in *The Birth of Tragedy and The Genealogy of Morals* (New York: Doubleday, 1956).

52   Plato, *Symposium*, 207d.

Index